Mentorship in the Primary School

Edited by

Robin Yeomans and John Sampson

 The Falmer Press

(A member of the Taylor & Francis Group)
London • Washington, D.C.

UK	The Falmer Press, 4 John St, London WC1N 2ET
USA	The Falmer Press, Taylor & Francis Inc., 1900 Frost Road, Suite 101, Bristol, PA 19007

First published 1994

A catalogue record of this publication is available from the British Library

ISBN 0 7507 0262 1 cased
ISBN 0 7507 0263 X paper

Library of Congress Cataloging-in-Publication Data are available on request

Jacket design by Caroline Archer

Typeset in 10/12pt Caledonia by
Graphicraft Typesetters Ltd., Hong Kong

Printed in Great Britain by Burgess Science Press, Basingstoke on paper which has a specified pH value on final paper manufacture of not less than 7.5 and is therefore 'acid free'.

Mentorship in the Primary School

For those close to us who will be as pleased as we are to see this book completed.

Contents

Contents

Acknowledgments

We would like to thank Denise Honour and Vivien Holt for their patience, persistence and fortitude in transcribing many hours of audiotape interviews, and Martin Fletcher for performing many sleights of hand with his Apple Mac.

We are indebted to the Paul Hamlyn Foundation for their generosity in funding the research from which much of this book is derived, and to Bedford College of Higher Education for providing additional research time and resources for the TEAM project.

Finally we would like to thank all our colleagues at Bedford College and in the twelve schools, together with the students who were mentored, for their willingness to give generously of their time. Their perspectives of the mentoring process have contributed significantly to our understanding.

Introduction

The growing interest in work of mentors within school-based initial teacher training courses in England and Wales is a phenomenon of the recent past. The development of innovative schemes within secondary education, such as the Oxford Internship scheme (Benton, 1990) generated a national debate about the nature of partnership between schools and higher education institutions, which the government joined when it introduced experimental forms of initial teacher education in the Licensed and Articled Teacher schemes (DES, 1988 and 1989). These were extensively school-based, and included both secondary and primary schools. They were built around mentors who were teachers in the schools, and accepted major responsibility for the training, education and assessment of students. By 1992 school-based initial teacher education became government policy for secondary teaching (Circular 9/92), and has now been followed by a development for primary teaching which is similar in form though different in detail (Circular 14/93).

In parallel with these developments there has been a growing concern with the contribution mentors make to school-based education. Inevitably, discussion and research has largely focused on development within secondary initial teacher education, given that mentoring in primary schools was confined to a few higher education institutions (for example, Bedford and Sussex) until Licensed and Articled Teacher schemes were established. For example, only two chapters in the two books on mentoring recently published (Wilkin, 1992; McIntyre, Hagger and Wilkin, 1993) related specifically to primary contexts, and are largely concerned with mentor training. Yet government policy 'accepts the issues involved in extending school-based training to primary schools are in some ways more complex than those for secondary schools' (Circular 14/93, p. 12) — an indication that assumptions about mentoring derived from secondary school experiences may not apply to the primary context. Further, current strategies for training primary school mentors are largely based on hypotheses about what mentors ought to be doing, derived from secondary school models or extrapolation from current practices of higher education student supervisors. Thus, even within the developed American context it could be suggested that 'We know little about what thoughtful mentors teach novice teachers and how they make their knowledge available' (Feiman-Neimser, 1991, p. 3).

There exists only a limited empirical research base from which to make assertions about what primary school mentors in England and Wales should do or from which to build forms of mentor support, including training courses.

'Mentoring' is traceable to Mentor, a trusted friend of Odysseus in Homer's *Odyssey*, who acted as a guide and counsellor to Odysseus' son Telemachas. Thus 'mentoring' generally refers to a supportive relationship between a novice and a more experienced guide. But meanings vary, partly due to the range of mentoring contexts within and across professions. For example, in noting the confusion over the term within nurse mentoring within the Health Service, Armitage and Burnard (1991) have suggested separation into two roles of mentor and preceptor. Within teacher education, McIntyre Hagger and Wilkin (1993) have acknowledged the lack of clarity about 'what the role is and should be', and what 'mentoring' means (p. 11). Mentor-like behaviour may come from many sources within a school, and the appointed mentor may engage in such unmentor-like activities as making formal summative assessments of students with career-shaping implications of 'passing' and 'failing'.

This volume is an attempt to provide some illumination and indicate some of the central issues to be addressed. Its authors take an interactionist view that it is the actors in a social situation who give meaning to the roles they occupy. With guidance on the broad structure and responsibilities of the role, and little by way of a 'role-model' to guide, mentoring in action is a process of defining the role by constructing its detail. The contention that mentors' behaviour determines what mentoring is underpins the decisions to conduct twelve case studies of primary mentors in action within three forms of initial teacher education schemes within Bedford College courses (BEd, Articled Teacher and PGCE). The research was generously supported by a grant from the Paul Hamlyn Foundation and by resources provided by Bedford College. We are very grateful to both sources of support. The majority of chapters are derived from this research, and their authors were members of the Teacher Education And Mentorship research project team (TEAM). The key questions the team sought to address and details of the methodology used are to be found in chapter 3.

To contextualize the research Furlong charts the rise of mentorship in initial teacher training. This is part historic account part analysis of the pressures that have produced the current situation. He describes three different but interacting influences on the policy process. The influence of the political new right through the writings of the Hillgate Group, O'Hear, Lawlor and others is seen as a key factor in the move to considering teacher education and training as an essentially practical activity best learnt by doing. Furlong argues that the influence of the centre is also clear. This has tended to provide ammunition and support for new right ideas by the provision of evidence, through various agencies, of inadequacies in aspects of initial teacher training. This has particularly focused on the practical, school-based aspects. In Furlong's opinion the third contribution to the rise of school focused school-based work, and hence mentorship, has come from the profession itself.

The schemes of Oxford, Cambridge University Department and Sussex have been well publicised. The way that mentorship has developed at Bedford in the primary phase is recounted by Stephenson. Many of the national factors that Furlong has drawn attention to were significant here as was the role of the professionals. Stephenson suggests that some of this professional pressure has arisen as a result of a significant number of new staff from primary schools being appointed to the college combined with the writing of new courses and the impetus and encouragement of other colleagues.

In chapter 3 Wooldridge describes the research methodology used to gather and interpret evidence. The variety of course structures in which mentorship was occurring are described so that later chapters can be seen in context. The choice of multi-site qualitative case study is explored and the stance of the researcher in their relationship with the schools is explained.

Mentorship naturally evolved in different ways in different schools with students following different courses. The procedures adopted by schools were influenced by many factors and in chapter 4 Frecknall explores the procedures developed by the schools from the initial selection of the mentor. The chapter attempts to describe aspects of mentorship within the various course schemes, pointing out the similarities and differences between these. Frecknall also begins to raise issues such as the status of the mentor, the pressure of time and the possible conflict between supportive and assessing elements of the role of mentor which are explored in later chapters.

Although the research carried out by TEAM was across a number of mentorship schemes, Sampson and Yeomans suggest that it is possible to formulate a theoretical framework to describe what mentors do. In chapters which examine the role of the mentor and the different strategies and skills they employ, a complex activity is described as a series of interrelated dimensions and elements. These chapters attempt to make sense of what the TEAM researchers saw happening in schools, and build an analytical structure within which to frame discussion and description of mentoring. The role of the mentor is split into three broad dimensions and several different elements of the role are attributed to each dimension. Specific strategies and skills are linked to these different dimensions so that the framework is simplified. The authors recognize that this simplicity does not exist in practice as elements may have implications for more than one dimension and similar strategies or skills may be of relevance to more than one element. Nevertheless the framework is offered as a tool for understanding what mentors do.

Central to mentorship is the relationships between the people involved. In chapters 7 and 8 Yeomans draws on the evidence from the case studies to examine the complex web of relationships that exist between mentor and student and between mentor, student and all the other participants including other teachers and college tutors. These chapters are concerned with the personal qualities of mentors and students and the nature of the relationship between the various participants. Issues explored in the light of data include the friend/colleague relationship, the tensions produced through the role elements of assessment and support, and the possible role conflicts that arise as a result of the complexity of the web of relationship within the school as a whole.

In those settings where a close relationship develops between student and mentor, or where students spend significant amounts of their time in a single school setting, the greater the pressure for the student to 'fit into' the dominant culture of the school. In their chapter on Induction, Acculturation and Education Wooldridge and Yeomans explore the ways in which mentors and other members of the school staff contribute to the development of the individual student's understanding of classroom processes. The issue highlighted is one of the degree to which students need to be inducted to the individual school as opposed to the danger of students become narrowly acculturated into one specific model of teaching and learning.

Chapter 10 then uses previous chapters to build a set of hypotheses about the nature of effective mentoring, its central concept is that of 'optimum fit' between a mentor's preferred strategies, and contingent factors such as course phase, context, the student's personal qualities and stage of development, the mentor's own skills, and available time for development. Consideration of all of these factors determines strategies and skills applied.

Circular 14/93 places an obligation on higher education institutions to have clear criteria for the inclusion or exclusion of schools from partnership schemes. It has been suggested in other chapters that mentors need particular qualities and skills. Stephenson and Sampson look beyond these to consider the factors that appear to have led to effective mentoring practices. They concentrate more on the school and its staff. The importance of the mentor's standing within the school is drawn out. The chapter looks beyond the mentors themselves and so considers the role of the headteacher and the whole staff. It may well be that particular schools will provide better conditions for effective mentoring than others. If so the key factors may be the importance given to the scheme by the headteacher, the collaborative nature of the staff, the size of school and the availability of time, as well as factors concerned with the mentor such as their credibility within the school, their status, and their own professional development.

The central assumption of Circular 14/93 is that placing more of initial training for primary students into schools will enhance the quality of that training. The implications for the maintenance of quality in school-based schemes needs to be examined. In chapter 12 Sampson uses data gathered from the research project to suggest a number of ways in which schemes that rely heavily on mentorship can sustain the quality of the student experience.

The final chapter considers the implications of the TEAM Project's findings for the practice of school-based education. It draws together earlier chapters in this book to highlight both the potential strengths and weaknesses of school-based teacher training and to consider appropriate ways of organizing the mentoring process. Evidence from the project is also used to consider the nature of future partnerships between schools and higher education institutions, and the form of their individual contributions.

We have used the case studies to generate hypotheses about the nature of primary school mentoring in initial teacher education. It is for others engaged in primary mentoring and mentoring research to decide how widely our hypotheses are generalisable. We do not imply that the skills these mentors demonstrated necessarily represent effective and skilled mentoring. But we do suggest that, given that the mentors were committed volunteers working within innovative contexts, having the confidence of their headteachers, they tended to be competent experienced teachers. In general, positive student reactions to this group suggest that they do represent a level of skill which provides a model from which we can learn. However, we do not suggest that mentoring is easy, nor that the skills of these mentors necessarily mean that any teacher can be an effective mentor. We recognize the importance of the mentor's role, value the active contribution mentors make to student teacher development, and seek to understand more clearly the qualities, behaviour and skills through which mentors give meaning to the role.

There are many questions about mentors that this volume does not seek to address. Two of particular importance are the primary mentor's role in development of student teachers' subject expertise, and systematic analysis of the nuances of mentor-student dialogue which may reveal the fine detail of mentor skill. Both have been beyond the scope of our data collection. However, we hope that the following chapters will provide an informative base from which to launch research into these and other aspects of primary school student teacher mentoring, as well as being of value for those engaged in mentoring and mentor training.

Chapter 1

The Rise and Rise of the Mentor in British Initial Teacher Training

John Furlong

Introduction

As the Modes of Teacher Education (MOTE) project has recently reminded us (Barrett *et al.*, 1992a; Whitty *et al.*, 1992), initial teacher education in England and Wales is a sizeable industry. Currently 24,000 students wishing to become teachers are recruited to higher education institutions (HEIs) each year and overall there are some 45,000 students on 370 different initial teacher training (ITT) courses at any one time. During the last few years this major sector of higher education has changed a great deal. There have been changes in the courses offered: in addition to conventional BEd and PGCE courses, prospective students can now choose shortened courses, conversion courses, part-time courses and the Articled Teacher and Licensed Teacher schemes (Barrett *et al.*, 1992b). The population entering these courses has also changed; currently 60 per cent of students on ITT courses are over 24 years of age while 29 per cent are over 31 (Barrett *et al.*, 1992a).

But by far the most significant change to initial teacher education in the last ten years has been the growing insistence by the government that schools take on a greater and more consistent involvement in the training process. And it is this growth of school-based teacher education that has led to the development of the role of the 'mentor'.

The most recent government reforms in the area of secondary initial teacher education (DFE, 1992), are specifically intended to encourage a school-based approach. As well as increasing the amount of time students must spend in school, the new Circular envisages that schools and teachers will have a far more important role, taking 'a leading responsibility' in a number of areas, including 'the training of students to teach their specialist subjects, to assess pupils and to manage classes' (DFE Circular 9/92, para 14). These reforms within the secondary PGCE build on two earlier government-led experiments in school-based training — the Articled and Licensed Teacher schemes. At the time of writing, similar initiatives are being introduced in the area of primary initial teacher education (DFE, 1993).

A new model of initial training is therefore progressively being introduced in England and Wales. That model is intended to alter the relationship between HEIs and their local schools, lead to changes in the roles and responsibilities of college-based tutors and school-based teachers and alter the way in which the 'partnership' between them is managed. In this new vision of ITT, the role of the mentor is central.

However, even before the new government regulations began to be felt, many courses had taken preliminary steps to institutionalize the role of the mentor. By 1990/91 the MOTE national survey revealed that course leaders on slightly under half of all ITT courses in England and Wales reported that teachers involved in the supervision of students were being given a special title such as mentor or teacher tutor; on half of all courses surveyed, teachers were offered some form of in-service training to support their work with students; on one-quarter of all courses mentors or their schools received some form of payment for their work. More detailed case study evidence from the MOTE research confirms Wilkin's (1991) suggestion that rhetoric does not always meet reality in this field; nevertheless the MOTE data indicates a growing recognition throughout ITT that practising teachers in schools must play a central role in the training process and that that role must be recognized.

McNair and After

This growing recognition of the importance of the contribution of schools to the preparation of new teachers represents a considerable change of perspective on the part of teacher educators. The SPITE survey of university-based teacher education undertaken in 1981 (Patrick *et al.*, 1982) revealed a very different picture, showing little collaboration between schools and universities in the support of students. At that stage, neither the concept nor the title of the mentor was widely used. Yet it is important to recognize that the idea that teachers, acting as mentors, should be involved in the training process is not a new one. As Gardner (1993) has documented, training in the nineteenth century was largely school-based, though in the early part of this century it was progressively replaced by a predominantly college-based system. However, as long ago as 1944, the McNair Committee, (McNair, 1944), appointed by the then Board of Education to look into the 'supply, recruitment and training of teachers', concluded that the key to more effective teacher training was to give the practical side of preparation greater weight. Specifically, McNair proposed that the staff in schools (i.e. mentors) in which students were placed on teaching practice, 'should be primarily responsible for directing and supervising (them)' (para 261). It was also suggested that in order to achieve more effective training, training institutions would have to 're-linquish a measure of responsibility in the training of their students' (para 270).

But the McNair proposals fell on deaf ears and it has taken a further fifty years for such ideas to come to the forefront of educational policy. The reason for McNair's failure, as I have argued elsewhere (Furlong, 1992), was because its highly pragmatic vision of initial training was out of sympathy with the models of professionalism that dominated educational debate before and after the last war. As Gardner (1993) demonstrates, the development of college-based courses at the beginning of the century had already indicated a move away from a practically based notion of professional training. Such a movement reached its height during the 1950s, 1960s and 1970s when the discourses of liberal and progressive education came to dominate professional debate and policy making.

For example, the liberal educationist view of the professional teacher is someone who themselves has a fully rounded liberal education. They must themselves be 'rationally autonomous' adults if they are to develop this characteristic in their pupils and this is therefore the most important aim of teacher education. It is *education* rather than training that is needed. Teacher education must also address the pedagogic and curriculum planning skills necessary to foster rational autonomy in pupils. An unanalyzed notion of 'teaching skills' is insufficient. Liberal educationists therefore argued that students needed to spend substantial periods of time in the academic study of education through the disciplines of sociology, psychology, philosophy and history. These disciplines, it was suggested, would 'equip students for intelligent and informed discourse about educational issues, sharply distinguished from practical expertise'. Studying the disciplines was 'part of the education of the scholar who happened to be a teacher' (Bell, 1981, p. 13).

Progressive education, which was also highly influential at the time, also emphasized the contribution of higher education over that of the school. From the progressivist perspective, the ideal teacher is someone who has a deep understanding of the individuality of children and the way they develop and can adapt his/her teaching strategies to the children's needs and stages of development. Initial teacher education must therefore develop such understandings in students and cultivate appropriate forms of pedagogy and curriculum planning. Initial training, from this perspective, therefore emphasized the study of developmental psychology, certain aspects of sociology that related to 'educability' and the application of specialised, child centred teaching strategies. Such teaching strategies, it was believed, were not always present within the schools to which students were sent on teaching practice. In helping students learn how to 'apply' the progressivist approaches they had learned in college, it was therefore college tutors who had the most important role. Far from being mentors, classroom teachers were often represented as a reality from which student teachers had to be protected.

Given the dominance of these views of teaching and teacher education, it is hardly surprising that McNair's proposals to increase the role of the school fell on deaf ears.

The Growth of Central Control

In explaining the change of perspective that has encouraged the widespread development of the role of the mentor, it is essential to acknowledge the part played by the government, for during the last ten years the government has been highly interventionist in initial teacher education, pursuing policies that have led to the development of school-based training. But why is it that the government itself has taken the lead in this field; why have they increasingly come to insist that mentors in schools should take on more responsibility for initial training? Before answering that question it is necessary to pose a prior question, for one must ask how is it that the government itself has come to take such a detailed interest in what was previously an autonomous sector of higher education? Governments do not presume to specify in any detail the character of professional training offered to solicitors, accountants or doctors. Why therefore, during the last ten years, should they have developed such a close interest in the training of teachers?

The history of increased government involvement in the field of initial teacher education is familiar enough to those in HEIs. Intervention first began in 1984 with the issuing of DES Circular 3/84 (DES 1984). It was with this Circular that the then Secretary of State for Education and Science, Sir Keith Joseph, established the Council for the Accreditation of Teacher Education (CATE) which was charged with the responsibility of overseeing initial teacher education in England and Wales on his behalf. In retrospect, the substantive changes introduced by Circular 3/84 do not seem particularly radical: college and university lecturers responsible for 'pedagogy' in ITT courses had to return periodically to schools to undertake 'recent and relevant' school experience; teachers had to be involved in the process of interviewing students; the time that students must spend in schools during their training was defined for the first time. In retrospect such proposals seem relatively modest though the government's interest in establishing a closer involvement with schools was clearly signalled. However, constitutionally, the Circular was revolutionary (Wilkin, 1991). For the first time it established the right of the Secretary of State to have a say in the detailed content and structure of initial teacher education in this country. In establishing the mechanism of increased central control the Circular was of fundamental significance.

Since 1984 there have been three further Circulars that have extended and elaborated central control and in each case the role of schools in the training process has been significantly enhanced. Circular 24/89 (DES, 1989a) reformed the organization and powers of CATE while at the same time introducing far more detailed specification of the content and form of ITT courses. The time that students must spend in school was more carefully specified as were the requirements of 'recent and relevant' experience for teacher trainers. The amount of time students had to spend on 'subject study' in their first degree or in the BEd was also specified and a list of topics to be covered in the ITT curriculum was set out. As has already been noted, 1992 and 1993 saw the introduction of yet further changes. With Circular 9/92, CATE was reformed yet again and further detailed proposals for secondary courses of ITT were introduced (DFE, 1992). Circular 14/93 introduced similar changes to primary courses (DFE, 1993).

Two further government initiatives of the late 1980s — the Articled and Licensed Teacher schemes — have also been highly influential in the establishment of school-based training and particularly the role of the mentor. The Articled

Teacher scheme is a school-based PGCE. Students, who must be graduates, spend two years, rather than one year, in training, 80 per cent of the time being spent in school. The Licensed Teacher scheme is somewhat different. Here, trainees, who do not necessarily have to be graduates, are recruited to specific vacancies in schools. They are granted a 'licence' to teach and provided training in and out of school appropriate to their particular needs. In both schemes, the role of school-based mentors has been seen as central. In the majority of schemes, designated mentors have been appointed, paid and provided with training for their role (Barrett and Galvin, 1993).

As the MOTE study has demonstrated, the size of the Licensed and Articled Teacher schemes is very small. In 1990/91, 1.6 per cent of all new entrants to ITT were recruited to Articled Teacher schemes (Barrett *et al.*, 1992) and about 2.4 per cent of new entrants were recruited to Licensed Teacher schemes (Barrett and Galvin, 1993). Yet despite their size, the two schemes have been highly influential for they have been given a high profile by the government. Each has been generously financed and widely publicised. As a consequence, these school-based schemes have been seen as a test bed for the development of new government policy in this field. It certainly seems that much of the philosophy behind the most recent government directives on ITT, Circulars 9/92 and 14/93, is drawn from experience within the Articled Teacher scheme.

But why has the state made such determined efforts to intervene in what was in the past a relatively quiet backwater of higher education? Why has it felt it so important to take control of the structure and content of initial teacher education? The answer to this question must be sought in the changing relationship between the state and the teaching profession as a whole. As Grace (1987) has demonstrated, that relationship has gone through a number of distinctly different stages throughout this century. In the first part of the century, between 1900 and 1920, Grace suggests that relations between the state and the profession could be characterized as ones of 'cultural and professional condescension'. It was not until the 1920s, with the threat of significant teacher and trade union radicalism, that the state adopted a more conciliatory attitude towards the profession. It was during this period that the Conservative President of the Board of Education, Eustace Percy, recognized that the best guard against the politicization of education was to give teachers a reasonable sense of independence. It was the beginnings of what Grace characterized as 'legitimized professionalism': reasonable pay, reasonable conditions, an end to the Revised Code which gave central control over the curriculum, in return for a non-political professionalism. This 'legitimized professionalism' reached its height in the social democratic consensus of the post-war period. Between the 1940s and the early 1970s teachers achieved significant control over the curriculum. They did not achieve the major economic rewards, nor the professional autonomy of other professions but in that most central aspect of their professionalism, the curriculum, they were granted substantial freedom by the state. Indeed their control over the curriculum became the most significant aspect of their claim to be a true profession.

The late 1970s, Grace argues, saw a return to the 'politics of confrontation'. A long-running dispute in the mid-1980s resulted in the removal of pay bargaining rights, the imposition of new contracts with defined hours of work and the introduction of appraisal. The curriculum also saw a range of measures which progressively challenged teacher autonomy culminating in 1988 with the establishment of the National Curriculum. With the coming of the National Curriculum, Grace foresaw that teachers would lose the central and most important aspect of their claim to professional autonomy.

It is against this background of the changing relations between the state and the teaching profession that the government's progressive intervention in ITT needs to be understood. On a wide range of issues, the government has, since the late 1970s, sought to 'reign in' the autonomy of the teaching profession. State intervention in initial teacher education, as Wilkin (1992) argues, is the last, and certainly the most ambitious, attempt to challenge the autonomy of the profession. Through their growing intervention in ITT, the government are claiming a right to control more than the hours teachers work; they are claiming the right to control more than what teachers teach. Through their progressive intervention in this sphere, the government are claiming the right to have a say in the very construction of the professionality of the next generation of teachers, to determine what they learn, to determine how they learn it and to determine the professional values to which they are exposed. As such, state intervention in ITT represents an even greater challenge to professional autonomy than that foreseen by Grace in 1987; it goes to the very heart of professionalism itself.

But to recognize that state intervention in initial teacher education is part of a broader project on the part of the government does not explain why that intervention has taken the form that it has. It does not explain why it is that the government has progressively insisted that practical work in schools, under the supervision of mentors, should have greater prominence in the training process. In order to explain the direction of central government policy it is necessary to examine three very different influences on the policy process. These are the influence of the New Right critique of initial teacher training; the influence of HMI and DES reports and research on initial teacher education; and debates within the teacher education profession itself. These groups have all, in their different ways, increasingly argued for a growing role for schools in initial teacher education; where they differ is their vision of what the role of the mentor might be.

The View from the New Right

From the late 1960s onwards in Britain, a small group of New Right pamphleteers, loosely aligned around 'neo-liberal' free market philosophies, have mounted a sustained attack on many aspects of contemporary educational policy including initial teacher education (Hillgate, 1989; Lawlor, 1990; O'Hear, 1988a and 1988b).

Their views on current provision are trenchant. For example, the Hillgate Group (1989) accuse most courses of being intellectually 'feeble and biased' and being overly concerned with topics such as race, sex, class and even 'anti-imperialist' education. According to the Hillgate Group, these 'preoccupations' appear 'designed to stir up disaffection, to preach a spurious gospel of "equality" and to subvert the entire traditional curriculum' (Hillgate Group, 1989, p. 5).

Such views stem from a vision of education that stands in marked contrast to liberal and progressivist philosophies outlined earlier. From the New Right perspective, the central aim of education is the preservation of a refined cultural heritage. In the words of the Hillgate Group (1989), education 'depends on . . . the preservation of knowledge, skills, culture and moral values and their transmission to the young' (p. 1). If our cultural heritage is to be passed on to our children then teachers must themselves be thoroughly educated in the disciplines they teach. The primary task for initial teacher education, from this perspective, is therefore to develop professionals who are themselves experts in their own subject area. Such preparation should take precedence over training in pedagogy; indeed according to Lawlor (1990) the chief weakness of current approaches to initial training is that they are dominated with preparing students in *how* to teach rather than *what* to teach.

On the development of practical teaching competence, New Right commentators have argued for a school-based, apprenticeship model. For example O'Hear argues that teaching is an essentially practical skill which cannot be learned from the kind of theoretical study of teaching which he suggests dominates current courses. In similar vein, the Hillgate Group argue that there is a long tradition going back to Aristotle that some skills, including many that are difficult, complex and of high moral and cultural value, are learned best by the emulation of experienced practitioners and by supervised practice under guidance. 'In the case of such skills, apprenticeship should take precedence over instruction and even when formal instruction is necessary it can never substitute for real practical training' (Hillgate Group, 1989, p. 9).

For those of the New Right then, college-based training is at best of secondary importance; at worst it is pernicious. As teaching is an essentially practical activity, the most important 'trainer' is experience itself. Students need to actually do the job of teaching; there is no other way of learning. Lawlor (1990) makes the point most forcibly by arguing for the entire abolition of formal training. Instead, 'Graduates (should) be sent to school to train on the job, designated to an experienced mentor — a senior teacher in the subject' (p. 38). As Lawlor implies, the notion of apprenticeship suggests that students will benefit from occasional support and direction from designated mentors. But from this point of view, being a mentor is relatively unproblematic. Students learn through 'emulation' and 'supervision of practice'. Even mentors are therefore not trainers; rather they are experienced 'master teachers' to whom the student can turn for practical advice and guidance. For the New Right then, the role of the mentor is important, but essentially non-specialist. Mentors need to be no more than good teachers themselves.

The View from the Centre

It is hard to underestimate the influence of the New Right critique of initial teacher education in recent years. Their views have progressively had more and more influence on the shape of government policy in this area and that influence currently seems to be on the increase. However, their radical critique of current provision would have been easier to resist if, throughout the 1980s, there had not been repeated evidence from the DES and HMI which questioned the quality of existing approaches to initial teacher education. During the last ten years these two bodies have issued a vast array of research findings (HMI, 1988a and 1992), inspection reports and documents (DES, 1983 and 1988; HMI, 1983, 1987 and 1988b) and directives (DES, 1984 and 1989b; DFE, 1992 and 1993), many of them implicitly and explicitly critical of existing approaches to teacher education. And in almost every case, the focus of those criticisms has been on the development of students' practical teaching competence.

Two stand out as of particular political importance — they are the two national surveys of newly-qualified teachers in schools conducted by HMI in 1981 and 1987 (HMI, 1982 and 1988a). (At the time of writing, the results of a third national survey are awaited). These surveys, each of which looked at approximately 300 new teachers working in England and Wales, were highly influential in the growing demands for reform, not least because their findings readily led to alarmist headlines in the press. The first survey found that while the majority of newly-qualified teachers were well trained, appointed to appropriate posts and given appropriate support in their new schools, a significant minority were not. In the judgment of HMI, nearly one in four were in some respects poorly equipped with the skills needed for teaching. And this view was corroborated by the new teachers themselves. On a range of key practical teaching skills, between one-fifth and three-fifths of teachers rated themselves as having been inadequately prepared. The 1987 survey revealed that things had improved somewhat, though there was still considerable cause for concern. In the view of HMI, 20 per cent of primary and 11 per cent of secondary teachers lacked some or many basic skills. Two-thirds of new teachers themselves were well or reasonably well satisfied with their training they had received; one-third were not.

Despite the improvement by 1987, newly-qualified teachers in both surveys complained that in their courses too much emphasis had been placed on academic study in general and on education studies in particular and that there was too little emphasis on teaching method and teaching practice. Clearly something had to be done to increase the quality of training and particularly the quality of practical training in schools. Both of these surveys were quickly followed by government initiated reforms outlined earlier — that is Circular 3/84 and Circular 24/89 (DES, 1984 and 1989b).

In understanding the development of HMI thinking on the role of the mentor it is interesting to compare these two studies. In the 1982 report, school experience, although vitally important, was still being constructed as a testing ground for students; training took place elsewhere. For example the report was particularly concerned with the fact that some students who were 'temperamentally ill fitted for the task of teaching' were still finding their way into the classroom. 'There is little doubt that, while the great majority of the students who are passed at the end of their course are fitted for teaching, some are not' (HMI, 1982, p. 81). The report went on, 'It may well be that teaching practice, which should expose the strengths and weaknesses of the students in the classrooms, is less rigorous than it should be'. At this stage then, school experience was seen as vital and in need of being strengthened, however, the role assigned to teachers in the training process was still relatively minor.

By 1988 the vision was different. By this stage, HMI were arguing that more attention needed to be given to defining the level of competence in different professional skills which might reasonably be expected of teachers at the conclusion of their training. Moreover, the development of 'teaching competence' was seen as clearly involving systematic preparation in the training institution as well as supervised 'training' in school. There was no explicit mention of the role of teachers in this process. Nevertheless an important shift had occurred in that the school was by this stage constructed as a site for training rather than practising and testing teaching competence. By 1988, HMI were therefore assigning teachers a role in the training process even though that role was largely undefined.

Both of these documents contrast markedly with the most recent HMI report on school-based training (HMI, 1991). By this stage the vision of the role of the teacher in the training process was much more fully developed:

> 'the success of school-based training depends on the quality of the relationship between the training institution and the school, the significant involvement of teachers in the planning, supervision and assessment of the students' training and the active involvement of tutors in supporting the students' work in schools. (*ibid*., p. 3)

In this latest HMI vision of ITT, the fully developed mentor has arrived.

The View from the Profession

But what of the professional justifications for the development of the role of the mentor in ITT? In the teaching professions' own debate on the future of initial training there have been a number of players: the training institutions that have been developing new courses; the academic debate on the character of professional knowledge conducted mainly by the philosophers of education; the CNAA and their influence on courses; and the teacher unions (Wilkin, 1991). In each case, they have all, in their different ways, been arguing for a greater role for teachers. Of these different voices however, the most influential, perhaps unsurprisingly, has been that of the training institutions themselves. Throughout the 1970s and 1980s, a few well publicised training institutions began to redesign their courses to place greater emphasis on practical training; with the advent of the Articled Teacher scheme a great many other courses did the same. The initial reason for redesigning courses was to respond to continued demands from students and from teachers that the 'theory' taught in training institutions should be more directly relevant to schools than it had in the past. From these redesigned courses, as well as from the Articled Teacher scheme, has developed a body of research and writing (Wilkin, 1992; McIntyre *et al.*, 1993) that has provided clearer professional and intellectual justification for school-based teacher education in general and the role of the mentor in particular. Some of the best known work in this field has come from research and development conducted at Cambridge and Oxford universities; indeed it was through the publication of innovative work undertaken at Oxford that the term 'mentor' gained general currency.

The Cambridge research, undertaken by Furlong *et al.* (1988), was funded by the DES. It involved an evaluation of two primary and two secondary school-based PGCE courses. The research began by making a series of cases studies of the four courses and from those case studies the research team developed an analytical model in which four different levels or dimensions of training were distinguished. Those different levels of professional training were as follows:

Levels of Professional Training

Level (a) Direct Practice
Practical training through direct experience in schools and classrooms.

Level (b) Indirect practice
'Detached' training in practical matters usually conducted in classes or workshops within training institutions.

Level (c) Practical principles
Critical study of the principles of practice and their use.

Level (d) Disciplinary theory
Critical study of practice and its principles in the light of fundamental theory and research. (Furlong *et al.*, 1988, p. 132)

The research team's argument was that professional training demands that trainees in their courses must be exposed to all of these different dimensions of professional knowledge. Moreover they suggested that courses need to establish ways of working that help trainees integrate these different forms of professional knowledge. Trainees, they argued, need to be systematically prepared in practical classroom knowledge — they need to be prepared at Level (a) — it is a distinctive form of professional knowledge and training can not be left to chance. But, Furlong *et al.*, suggested, it is only teachers who have access to that level of knowledge — it is only they who know about these children, working on this curriculum in this classroom. No matter how much 'recent and relevant' university and college lecturers have, Furlong *et al.*, suggested they will always remain outsiders. Teachers, acting as mentors, are therefore essential to the training process.

Furlong *et al.*, also argued that although individual teachers might be in a position to prepare trainees at Levels (b), (c) and (d), the nature of their job meant that their greatest strength was at Level (a). This was the level of professional knowledge utilized in their day to day work as teachers. However, lecturers, because of their involvement in a variety of different schools, because of their familiarity with the professional literature and because of their involvement with research, had access to other forms of professional knowledge. Training, Furlong *et al.*, therefore suggested, must be a partnership between higher education institutions and schools where teachers, acting as mentors, have a consistent and structured involvement in the training process.

The Cambridge study was based on an evaluation of four existing school-based courses. One of these courses, at the University of Sussex, was long established and in the early to mid-1980s a number of other experimental courses were begun. However it was a different course — that developed at the University of Oxford — that in 1987 succeeded in drawing public and professional attention to the value of school-based training and in particular, to the importance of developing the role of the mentor (Benton *et al.*, 1990). Although they were developed separately, and although there are important differences between them (McIntyre, 1991), the Oxford and Cambridge visions of training and the role they assign to mentors are very similar. Indeed, in many respects, the Oxford scheme can be seen as operationalizing the principles of school-based training identified by the Cambridge research.

As in the Cambridge model, within the Oxford scheme, there is a shared belief that no satisfactory initial teacher education course is possible without much closer and more effective integration of school-based and university-based elements of the course than has been common. As McIntyre (*ibid.*) notes, 'leaving the task of integrating "theory" and "practice" to student teachers has demonstrably and not surprisingly been quite inadequate' (p. 141).

Both schemes also recognize the importance of the different contributions which practising school teachers and university lecturers can make. The conditions of university lecturers' work, McIntyre (*ibid.*) suggests, 'enable and oblige them, much more than is generally possible for practising teachers, to know about alternative teaching approaches being used elsewhere, to study relevant research and theoretical literature and to explicate and critically examine the principles which should or could inform the practice of teaching' (p. 114). However, it is only practising school teachers, who can directly introduce students to the practice of teaching and 'especially to the use of the contexualised knowledge (of individual pupils, of established relationships with classes, of resources and their availability and of schools customs and procedures) which is such a crucial element of professional teaching' (*ibid.*, p. 141). As a result, students on the Oxford scheme spend much of their time in school working in pairs under the supervision of experienced teachers who act as mentors.

There are some important differences between the Oxford and Cambridge schemes and each has subjected the other to critical review (Hirst, 1990; McIntyre, 1991; Wilkin, 1993). McIntyre (1991), for example, criticizes the Cambridge model for its notion of levels and certainly given that the term does carry overtones of a hierarchy then it would seem inappropriate — different 'domains' of professional knowledge might have been a more appropriate term. However McIntyre argues that there is an implicit hierarchy in more than the language — he suggests that the model prioritizes academic knowledge at Level (d), implying that that is the only route to professional rigour. In the Oxford scheme, McIntyre asserts that 'The partnership between university and schools is secure only because teachers appreciate that the aspects of professional education for which they are best placed to help (students) are recognized by university staff as of equal status to those aspects which are best provided by the university' (McIntyre, 1991, p. 121).

In the Oxford scheme then, no one form of knowledge is seen as inherently superior to another — they are simply different. While on the surface such an argument seems reasonable, one still has to ask, as does Hirst (1990), by what criteria one can judge the superiority of one approach to practice over another? The difficulty with the Oxford approach is that in the end it leaves it to the student to make up his or her own mind about what are appropriate forms of practice. They are left, according to Wilkin (1993), with a kind of post-modernist relativism!

The professional debate continues but where most teacher trainers now agree is that teachers, acting as mentors, must have a full and equal role to play in the training process. Their knowledge is vital and training without their contribution is fundamentally flawed. However, it is important to note that the model of the mentor is somewhat different from that put forward by the New Right, or even by HMI. The mentor from this point of view must be highly skilled. They have a distinctive body of professional knowledge into which they must somehow induct the student teacher. This demands skills over and above that of being a successful teacher for they are indeed a trainer, not merely a 'master teacher'. If they are to be effective therefore, mentors need to develop observation skills, the skills of 'needs analysis', collaborative teaching skills, a repertoire of supervisory strategies, and counselling skills. Above all they need to develop a 'language of teaching' so that they can articulate to others the basis of their own professional knowledge.

The view from the profession then is that the mentor will emerge as a new sort of professional; a teacher grounded in his/her particular teaching context but with highly sophisticated training skills equal to those of the college or university lecturer.

Conclusion

The development of the role of the mentor in initial teacher education in Britain therefore has an interesting, if unnatural, parentage; pressure from the New Right, critical research from HMI, research and development within the profession itself. All of these groups have had a different vision of what the mentor must be, yet they have had enough in common to allow them all to find ways of supporting government policy in this area. The role of the mentor in initial teacher education in this country is now here to stay.

Yet if there is one fundamental weakness in all that has been written so far, it is that the debate has been almost exclusively dominated by those concerned with secondary initial training. This is most clearly true of the New Right, with its didactic, subject-based model of teaching and apprenticeship. However, it is equally true in the professional sphere where the 'Oxford model' has achieved almost total dominance. This model too is distinctively secondary. Moreover, as the MOTE national survey has revealed (Barrett *et al.*, 1992), apart from the Articled Teacher scheme, most school-based courses are indeed secondary PGCEs. As yet, it seems, there has been little systematic exploration of what the distinctive role of the mentor might be within the primary context.

Much remains to be done in both the primary and secondary area in clarifying the skills, knowledge and understandings mentors need if they are to be effective. As McIntyre *et al.* (1993) have recently commented:

> mentors in schools do not know how to do the job because it is not only a demanding one but also quite different from anything they have done before, while people based in universities (and colleges) do not know how to do the job because it is quite different from anything they have done or studied. There are no experts on how to do the job of mentoring in initial teacher education. (p. 19)

The research reported in this volume focuses exclusively on the role of the mentor in the primary context. It is therefore a timely and important contribution to the professional debate that will be welcomed both by those in higher education and mentors themselves.

The Anatomy of a Development

Joan Stephenson

In *Mentoring in Schools* (Wilkin, 1992) the introductory chapter closes with a series of questions thrown up by the process of mentoring in its various forms:

> To what extent is mentoring a reversion to an earlier form of apprenticeship training . . . ? Will there be problems for teachers concerning the articulation of their craft knowledge? What are the intrinsic dangers and difficulties of the mentoring role? Can we in teacher education learn from the mentoring traditions in other occupations? (p. 26)

These certainly ring true for the practice of mentoring as we have seen it develop at Bedford College of Higher Education. These and other queries will be considered later in this book. In this present chapter I seek to explore how the circumstances in which all these questions raise themselves came about.

The history at Bedford of what we are presently calling 'mentoring' is really the development of several individual careers within higher education interacting with change in governmental and public expectations, detailed by Furlong in chapter 1, which themselves stimulated change. It is largely the story of staff who have joined the college since 1986 and how their personal experiences in education, shaped by influences in the present-day wider educational and commercial world, have led to innovation and change of emphases. I propose to look at these developments in chronological order.

It would be insulting to our colleagues who have worked for many years in teacher education to pretend that the context which we joined was not fertile, open and recognizing the need to follow changes in the world of schools. They were in many ways our greatest supporters, not least in their healthy scepticism of 'new broom' over-simplifications!

The Beginnings

In 1986 the first of a wave of primary practitioners, all with recent further study, were employed to meet an expansion of initial teacher training numbers. This group, which expanded rapidly over the next two years, had spent substantial time in the classroom, in many cases they had wide management experience and a particular curriculum interest. Many also had cross-curriculum interests and all had been involved in the inservice training of their colleagues in schools. The James Report of 1971 with its impetus towards 'professional tutors' and the accompanying professional centres to support this move, had gradually influenced and added valuable experience in peer support in the school setting. These expereriences were to have an influence on the various forms of practice that led to mentoring processes that are now a feature of our courses. These people have been the core of the TEAM researchers.

Towards a Partnership

In September 1986 Bedford had two primary BEd degrees. One course was running out and a newly-validated degree was taking its first cohort of students. A full HMI inspection had taken place in 1984. This had led to a decision to write the new course with an increase in the amount of student time spent in school. Circular 3/84 (DES, 1984) brought further changes and before the rewrite was even underway the need for closer cooperation with teachers in schools had been recognized and acted upon. However, the fruits of these decisions were first seen in a major and systematic way, not in the BEd, which only had first year students, but in a Primary PGCE the first course of this kind at Bedford.

My new job in the Education Department was not only to add recent and relevant experience to the BEd teams in maths and education, but also to begin writing the new PGCE that was to start the following September. Having worked and studied with Pat Ashton at the Centre for the Evaluation and Development of Teacher Education at the University of Leicester, my experience of Partnership and IT-INSET (see Ashton *et al.*, 1989) was brought to bear on the shape of our new course.

The Primary PGCE

The course was written to comply with Circular 3/84, which strengthened the move towards greater cooperation between institutions and schools. The course was designed around a series of experiences in school, each having distinct aims which build on previous experiences. I had visited the Department of Educational Studies, University of Oxford, to explore their system of internship (Benton *et al.*, 1990), but the writing team as a whole felt this secondary model was not appropriate to the primary school. We were worried about a possible lack of breadth of types of children, schools, organization and teaching approaches to which primary students might be exposed. We opted for what was for then a highly school-focused course, but with a variety of schools and modes of practice. At the beginning of the course the students spent two weeks in a school near their homes, where observational tasks provided experiences for them to use when they first come into college. Students were to be in school for some part of thirty-two of the thirty-six weeks of the course. This included two blocks of four and six weeks respectively, the first of which was planned to be diagnostic. For twelve weeks during the first two terms, students were to spend two days a week, two per class, in a 'partnership' school in their chosen age range. When the course began this included an IT-INSET project, where class teacher, students and college tutor, work as a team to investigate an aspect of classroom or school practice chosen by the teacher. In keeping with IT-INSET principles this was followed by immediate evaluation and discussion. Various information gathering or planning visits were to take place in the remaining weeks, including a serial three-week 'placement' in the language unit of a multicultural school for those opting for the early years age phase. A policy of exposing students to a variety of schools and approaches was followed. Practical teaching was to be assessed on a pass/fail basis at the end of the final block experience which was placed at the end of the summer term. There were also courses in language, mathematics, science and movement education whilst the remaining subjects in the primary curriculum were covered through the arts/humanities led 'topics' throughout the year.

The large amount of time spent in schools allowed a continuous interplay of ideas and skills from college workshop to classroom activity and back to college. We saw as crucial a close working partnership between college, classroom teachers and heads in host schools. It was this need, caused by the deliberate design of the course, which led us into setting up ways to establish closer working relationships and shared responsibilities with our colleagues in schools. Ultimately this led to the development of, and continued interest in, mentoring and its effectiveness.

Monaghan and Lunt (1992), in their recent article, give a detailed overview of different approaches to mentoring activity over a long period. Our experience of mentoring over five years, in both the PGCE and BEd course confirms the concerns they posed. We too have been concerned about the interpretation of the term 'mentor' and the accompanying role. We had debated and researched the relationship between apprenticeship and role modelling.

At Bedford we have moved from a position of class teachers as supervisors within school placements to the more wide-ranging role of mentors in our PGCE affiliated schools, which is described in detail in chapter 4. A guiding practice throughout has been:

> Clearly there is an urgent need to establish the complementary roles of school teachers and college lecturers. Whilst such roles can be developed, college lecturers and school teachers should not spend inordinate time doing what the other can do better. (Hill, 1991, p. 29)

The Primary PGCE Partnership

A key feature of the PGCE structure is the placement of pairs of students in one teacher's classroom from the beginning of the course — the 'Partnership' phase.

The idea of having two students to a classroom was based on a variety of aims. One was the belief that by having another colleague in the same situation, there would be a natural forum for mutual help, and most importantly, a culture of discussion leading to analysis. In this we were influenced by our knowledge and experience of the work and writing of Stephen Rowland (1984) and Michael Armstrong (1980). The decision to include a period of IT-INSET in the partnership experience was based on the conviction that the process of observation, questioning and analysis that characterized this form of working, laid the best possible foundations for making reflection an integral part of any teacher's way of thinking and working. It also enabled students, teachers and college tutors to work together as equal members of a team. This fitted in well with our views on and hopes for partnership.

I had been a member of several IT-INSET teams during my time at the University of Leicester. During 1986/87 a number of my Bedford colleagues had joined training sessions, conferences and IT-INSET team practices in a variety of local education areas throughout the country. This had been made possible through our membership of the Midlands branch of the Centre for the Evaluation and Development of Teacher Education (CEDTE). Dr Pat Ashton held a very successful workshop at Bedford that was attended by a wide variety of staff. This climate of growing school-college partnership became fertile ground for the later work towards mentoring in the primary BEd.

In short, by the summer of 1987, we had a nucleus of staff within the proposed PGCE course team who had experience of, and were committed to, partnership and IT-INSET. There remained the task of identifying and wooing partnership schools.

Partnership Schools

During the writing of the course local headteachers, teachers and advisors had contributed to its philosophy and content. Through their good offices we were able to approach individual schools. Extensive knowledge of individual schools was also to be found within college, where the placing of students on school practice had involved local heads and LEA officials for some years. The local education authority, who had attended some of the preparations for IT-INSET, also lent their considerable support, by agreeing to fund supply cover for each school taking part. IT-INSET was seen as a valuable form of staff development and whole school development, at a time when schools were involved in formulating whole school plans and training staff development tutors. Some of us had served in this role before coming into college. The nature of the teams taking part allowed each member to have an equal but different role. Each person had something of value to bring to the planning, execution and analysis of the focus of the investigation. We now had to act upon our convictions and make the objectives of achieving a closer partnership with schools into a reality.

The Ground Work

First of all we telephoned all the schools in the county which the LEA had recommended. An appointment was made to speak to the head. Following this meeting, at which the course philosophy and aims and the outline of partnership were explored, a booklet about partnership was sent to the school and arrangements were made to attend a staff meeting. On the cover of the four-page booklet was a photograph of children working at a science activity in the school of one of our writing team heads. It opened with a short introduction to the format and philosophy of the course and went on to make certain statements about the teachers' and the schools' roles in ITT. In essence these were:

- supervision and oversight of planning, preparation, and delivery of areas of the curriculum in the classroom;
- guidance and practical help on the organization of the classroom, the curriculum and the children;
- an overview and detailed introduction to the workings of the school and educational system in practice;
- cooperation in blending work studied in college with its realisation in school;
- the analysis and evaluation with the teacher of their own and the student's classroom practice.

In this initiative can be found the roots of what ultimately became our mentorship programmes.

Attendance at a full staff meeting in interested schools involved the course leader and the tutor in charge of school placements. The local advisor for the areas involved also participated where the schools so wished. We had decided from experience gained from more conventional practices, that most mutual benefit seemed to occur where whole schools were at least aware of what was happening with students and hopefully participated to some degree in their programme. The course writing team decided that all the staff should agree to take part. The evidence from the evaluation of the projects subsequently undertaken as part of academic standards quality control and by one of the participating headteachers (Jones, 1989) suggests whole staff participation in such decisions is an effective determinant of success. At this meeting an outline of the course was presented, examples of standards of work and targets to be achieved were discussed along with the roles of teacher, school, tutor and college. These discussions led to the writing of an annually reviewed course manual setting out the roles and responsibilities of each of the partners in a partnership. They also led to the formation of a forum for all partnership teachers and self-help groups.

Following these meetings and after further correspondence where more information was requested, schools were invited to say whether and when they wanted to participate. The majority opted to join at once, two asked to be considered for subsequent years and one declined because of imminent staff changes.

Beginnings

The first year then began with four partnership schools all in Bedfordshire, two in the south and two in the north of the county. Six students were allocated to each of these schools on a geographical and degree subject basis. We also tried to match pairs within a classroom to achieve the widest possible spread of subject expertise. The teachers involved with the pairs of students had been self-chosen, they reflected a cross section of age, experience and curriculum leadership within the schools. 'Link tutors' were allocated to each school to act as support to the teacher and to take the tutor role within IT-INSET. Draft documentation was sent to the schools and as soon as the students arrived in college an evening meeting for teachers, heads, students and tutors was held in college. This was both a social and a working occasion to discuss the term's work and to induct the teams into the processes of partnership and IT-INSET. The observational schedules were outlined and some discussion took place about the nature of the 'tasks' the pairs of students were to try out in schools. In an attempt to make the tasks adaptable they dealt with concepts rather than specific content. In most instances these subsequently worked reasonably well. Once the ground plan had been laid the respective link tutors and teachers formulated which activities fulfilled the needs of the children in the classroom and the curriculum studied in college. In some of our later mentorship schemes this pattern was extended so that teachers took some of the responsibility for curriculum delivery.

Teachers found the course manual most helpful, with its agreed criteria for development and illustrations of poor, acceptable and good practice. They praised its clarity, but still relied very heavily on the perceived objectivity of the link tutor in decision-making. Given the newness of this function for them and the fact that emphasis was placed on analysis and diagnosis, the arrangement worked satisfactorily whilst numbers were small. But with the second intake of students and doubling of the number of partnership schools to eight (including four from a new authority) the *ad hoc* nature of guidance and support for teachers began to show strains. Separate meetings for tutors and teachers as well as the joint meeting with students resulted, along with consultation as to the timing of curriculum topics to fit in to the pattern within schools. The question of reward for those involved was also addressed. Both counties agreed to fund supply cover for the IT-INSET projects, pay for transport to meetings and support staff who wished to complete an account of their IT-INSET experience for a college certificate linked to a regional diploma. By this time news of the original Bedfordshire scheme had spread to neighbouring counties and we were invited to address the combined heads meeting of Buckinghamshire at Milton Keynes to outline our proposals for developing partnership. This meeting was to have many valuable outcomes for both the PGCE and BEd courses. A wider network of teachers was established, a greater range of practice became available and consequently students had a greater wealth of experience to bring back to college sessions. Advisors in Buckinghamshire gave the same support as had their colleagues in Bedfordshire.

Whilst partnership was developing other changes in and outside the teaching profession influenced our thinking and stimulated further moves towards school-based training. The political spotlight was moving onto higher education. The National Curriculum was making INSET a very necessary part of every classroom teacher's life. CATE note 4 (CATE, 1986) stressed that initial training schemes should have equal benefit for student teachers; teacher trainers; and teachers in schools. Teacher supply shortages, growing awareness of market forces and prevailing educational philosophies were bringing into question the current types of training. Articled Teacher and Licensed Teacher schemes were being discussed and developed. Training in other professions and jobs was also changing or being reassessed. Probation and induction were beginning to be debated and training as a lifelong concept was being reiterated.

The effects of some of these changes were being felt in the college. For a number of years Bedford had run a part-time BEd degree for non-graduate serving teachers. This had been well supported and popular. It was, however, interesting to note that at about this time the proportions of nurse tutors who made up the membership of this course increased dramatically. With them they brought experience and analysis of their own practice and of the growth of mentoring within nursing. This led to some interesting and stimulating debate on the nature of education and/or training. (For a continuing debate see Armitage and Burnard, 1991.)

About the same time, teachers' need for support in the evaluation of students' performance within partnership schools, began to outstrip the availability of link-tutors. The demands from schools to take part in IT-INSET for their school self-development, meant an added pressure on tutor time that we could not sustain. The ideas of skills and competencies, negotiated and agreed between teachers, tutors and students seemed an alternative strategy, and so experiences from nursing, industry and the United States began to be actively explored. This was ultimately to lead to a 'Profile', piloted in the Articled Teacher scheme and in the modular 1992 primary BEd degree course. This pre-dated the focus on 'certain competencies' stressed by the Secretary of State for Education and Science at Southport in January 1992 (Clarke, 1992).

Mentorship within the BEd

Concurrently the 1986 Bedford BEd degree was in its second year. Many staff members taught on both courses and they adopted some of the principles rising from the IT-INSET training and experience within micro-teaching which took place in the spring term. Schools were very enthusiastic about their added role in the analysis of what happened within the science-based group teaching sessions in their classrooms. The schools selected had to be near to college, since sessions were held during an afternoon for five consecutive weeks. This was not a partnership exercise, since teachers did no more than observe and comment, but it illustrated their willingness to give of their time, without supply cover, to analyze why good practice was successful. Many commented on how their participation had made them review their own practice.

A further influx of college staff straight from schools had taken place in September 1987 and again during 1988. These were people who had been committed to their own development as staff whilst in schools and many had INSET training experience in a variety of LEAs. Their arrival was an impetus to the planning and implementation of the first Bedford programme to have class teachers called 'mentors'. The desire to improve the quality of the support students received from schools led to the development of a school-based mentorship scheme. This was placed in the third year of the 1986 BEd degree. Students had already had experience of schools prior to the third year experience. In the first year there had been two periods of experience each for two weeks and in the second year there had been a five-week experience. These gave students experience of both primary age phases and enabled them to choose an age phase for their third year experience.

By this time the accredited course offered to partnership teachers had been raised to a module within a CNAA validated diploma. Another module in this course was the unit on mentor training. This was now deemed essential if teachers were to be successful in running the supervision and support for students in school-based parts of courses, especially where the teacher has responsibility for assessment of practice. Annexe b of Circular 24/89 (DES, 1989a) had laid down the increased involvement of serving teachers in the supervision and assessment of practical work, the addition of the words 'is understood by all' in relation to their role, seemed to us to point to ministerial pressure for training for mentorship, which experience and conviction led us to applaud. The clear definition and understanding of the role was also highlighted particularly in the production of joint handbooks. The responsibilities of senior management in the schools in this preparation brought INSET and professional development very much into the frame also.

Once again the support and encouragement of the LEA staff and headteachers was evident in the setting up of a pilot project that began in March 1990. This pilot was based in the south of the county in Luton and at Milton Keynes in Buckinghamshire under the auspices of the same advisors who had taken part in launching the Partnership Scheme. One of these was indeed acting as tutor in one of the IT-INSET projects in Milton Keynes on that year's Partnership Scheme.

Similar letters were sent out to schools in both authorities and a series of meetings was held in local schools. Cambridgeshire schools also took part later. The necessity of offering a formally instigated and obligatory training programme as well as a network of support for mentors, as we shall now call them (although those involved with the PGCE still preferred to be known as teacher-tutors) had become apparent.

The original proposal was a culmination of what had gone before and was to greatly influence the mentorship schemes that were to be established later. This proposal was spelt out as follows:

BEDFORD COLLEGE OF HIGHER EDUCATION AND BEDS/BUCKS LEA

PROPOSALS FOR THIRD YEAR STUDENT SCHOOL EXPERIENCE IN THE LUTON/MILTON KEYNES AREA

Teacher educators are being encouraged by the Council for the Accreditation of Teacher Education to involve schools more closely in the training and assessment of student teachers at a time when the college's resources are becoming increasingly stretched. Our response to these needs is to try and find new ways of being more effective in how we use our time. At the same time we recognize the important role school staff already play in supporting our students on school experience. Bedford College of Higher Education (1989)

For these reasons schools were invited to participate in a pilot project for our third year students, starting in Spring 1990. The chief elements of the scheme were described as follows:

1 That we place three or four students in classes in one school for the month of their third year school experience (5–29 March 1990, with day visits on 1 January, 5 and 21 February). By grouping students in this way, we are able to ensure that the school is 'paid' for its efforts by being able to free at least two staff for most of that month, so that staff time can be used for school-based in-service, assessment or other whole-school development needs the school identifies. At a time of shortage of supply cover, the time generated is in the order of £2000 cash equivalent.

2 The day-to-day supervision of the students would be dealt with by one of the school staff as mentor, thus releasing the other two or three at times when the students were teaching and for discussion of students progress (the guideline for third year students is two-thirds teaching commitment).

3 The tutor would visit the school before the experience started and twice during the month, but their chief role would be to support the school staff in supporting the students.

4 In the event of a student starting to have difficulties, early feedback from school to college would lead to a member of a central 'flying squad' of tutors making additional visits to support the student directly.

5 The college would not expect the school to take sole responsibility for the final pass/fail assessment, so the final report would be jointly compiled by school and tutor though clearly relying heavily on the teacher's judgment.

6 The college will undertake to run a training programme for mentors, which will include work on observation and assessment, and the place of school experience within the BEd degree. Such a course would attract

CFPS certification as a general mentor training course, and become a module within the planned college INSET modular structure.

7   The details of the programme will be negotiated with the participating school. It is envisaged that in the first year we would want to place about thirty students (sixty in all) with you, but we hope to interest a sizeable pool of schools to take a growing student body in later years.

8   The project will be monitored and the college will present a report on its progress after the first year.

9   Second and final year students would continue to be supervised according to the existing pattern. Bedford College of Higher Education (1989)

It was suggested to schools that there would be a number of benefits to teachers, schools, and the college. These were:

TEACHERS in providing training and experience in observation and assessment, and time to meet their curriculum coordination obligations, without significantly increasing the load of the valued contribution they already make to student supervision.

SCHOOLS in creating further predictable time for school development needs without having to call on their supply budget under LMS; in introducing potential staff to the advantages of working in the area.

COLLEGE in ensuring students receive the support they need, enhancing the relevance of courses by the increased teacher involvement, whilst making the most effective use of available course staffing. Bedford College of Higher Education (1989)

In all twenty-four schools in Luton and Milton Keynes agreed to join the pilot scheme for 1990. Training sessions for these mentors took place locally to their schools. At this stage training included sessions on the national structure of teacher education, the course itself, constructing a model of an effective student, the role of the mentor and the classteacher, the school experience file, and the development of observational, diagnostic, counselling and assessment skills.

Meanwhile a school experience booklet similar in format to the PGCE manual was written for the use of mentors, tutors and students. In this the role of the mentor as seen at this point was set out:

THE ROLE OF THE MENTOR

1   The mentor is the key person in school-led school experience. She/he is the link between students and tutor and is the person who will oversee and monitor the progress of the students, whilst the tutor chiefly works with the mentor rather than the students. The mentor will normally have undergone a programme of mentor training.

2   The mentor ensures that students' planning and preparation are such as will adequately safeguard the interests of the school and its pupils throughout the school experience.

3   The mentor acts as the student's 'sponsor' in relationships with other colleagues, so as to help students participate as fully as possible in the benefits and obligations of staff membership.

4   The mentor liaises with the college tutor on matters of college supervision policy and to discuss the progress of the students with difficulties.

5   The mentor liaises with class teachers on matters concerning the students, carries out direct observation of the students equivalent to a half-hour per day per student, and feeds back appropriate support and advice. Mentors on a formal training course will be keeping an observational journal as the basis of their feedback.

6   The mentor will make a formal interim assessment of each student during week 2. Mentor and tutor will jointly make the final assessment of students during week four. This final written report will be discussed with the students.

7   The judgment and observations of class teachers will be a valued additional source of informal support and assessment of student performance, but there will be no formal requirement for the class teachers to assess students, unless a particular school wishes each teacher to perform a mentor function. Bedford College of Education (1990)

This proposal differed in two important ways from earlier PGCE partnership work. The students were to be placed one to a class and it can be seen from point 7 above, that the function of a class teacher and that of a mentor were being separated in the matter of assessment. Up until this point in the PGCE, the assessment of the students and their support and direction, including classroom observation had been performed by the teacher of the class in which the pair of students had been placed. One teacher had acted as 'lead teacher' during IT-INSET sessions in some schools where students had combined to take a whole school focus for their investigation, but apart from this they had fulfilled the 'mentoring' function within their own classroom. The mentor was also to have an identified function in the pass/fail marking of an essential part of the course although college still retained the decisive voice.

This led us to think about the relationship between the mentor and the class teacher and possible effects on the mentoring process. Would there be an appreciable difference between classes in which the class teacher and mentor were the same person and those where the roles were taken by two people? If so what, with what effect and for whom? This is one issue illuminated by our current research.

Just as the development of mentoring within the BEd had partly been a response to growing student numbers so the dramatic increase in student numbers stimulated change in PGCE Partnership experience. We were no longer able to supply college staff to tutor students in all our schools. However, some of our teachers were now having their fourth experience of partnership and an IT-INSET programme. Since we wished to increase the level of involvement and responsibility for initial training for those teachers who were willing, we suggested that those teachers experienced in supporting students take on the tutor role. The teachers had two main concerns. First, that any new role needed precise definition. Second, that they might not give their students appropriate learning opportunities because they lacked the 'overview' of a college tutor. The answer seemed to be a link tutor role redefined to emphasize the provision of support and information for the mentor. Early evaluations were positive and the idea of having a larger role for this pivotal person was incorporated into the Articled Teacher scheme, which was by this time being written.

The Articled Teacher Scheme

All the experiences gained on partnership and in third year BEd block experience in encouraging successful school-based training, were pooled in writing the Articled Teacher course and in refining the roles of the mentor, class teacher, student and link tutor within the school-based and college-based parts of the course. *The Invitation to Bid for Funding* (DES, 1989b) had included the phrase that training should, 'be delivered by both the institutions' academic and professional tutors and by selected members of staff at the school'. In the Articled Teacher scheme we called these colleagues 'mentors' as in the BEd third year experience.

From the start of partnership, curriculum matters had flowed from college sessions into practice through the tasks done by the pairs of students in their partnership classes. After the initial uncertainties the match of task had become more satisfactory and with the increase in hours given to the three core subjects in 1988/89, some content had its directed time fulfilled in school. This was extended in the Articled Teacher Scheme so that the mentors were responsible for the delivery of a proportion of the three core subjects. Mentors had curriculum responsibility for each of the core curriculum areas within each of the clusters of schools. They, with the support of the link tutor and the relevant college-based subject tutor, were to teach the students within the cluster.

This has proved to be not without tensions. Firstly, mentors have not been confident of their ability to deliver this part of the course. Secondly, tutors have needed considerable time to support the mentors. Concern has been alleviated by a clear definition of content matter and lines of demarcation together with an increase in non-contact time and additional training for the mentors. Thirdly, mentor and class teacher relationships have been brought into focus, see chapter 8. Fourthly, the conflict between supporting and assessing has, at times, been problematic. Finally, much of the potential tension between class teacher and mentor may have centred on the possible conceived assessment by colleagues of each other.

Affiliated Schools

The start of the Articled Teachers Scheme coincided with the development of the mentoring function in the one year PGCE into areas other than partnership. In 1991 schools who had already taken part in partnership projects were invited to increase their commitment to initial teacher education by becoming 'affiliated schools'. A detailed description of what this entails will be found in chapter 4. It is sufficient for our purposes here to say that this involves a contractual arrangement between schools and institution with clearly defined rights and responsibilities for each of the partners. The school agrees to take responsibility for students through a mentor. The mentor receives an accredited training programme and funds are transferred from the College to the school for that part of the course for which the school assumes responsibility. The mentor works with students during both serial and block experiences. The role, which is explored further in chapter 5, includes work in their own and others classrooms and some responsibility for the application of core and increasingly, foundation curriculum subjects.

Chapter 4 contains further detail of each of the mentorship schemes as they were operating at the time of the research. In this chapter I have attempted to show how the development of these has been gradual and interrelated.

Chapter 3

Researching Mentors and Schools: Background, Methods and Contexts

Irene Wooldridge

This chapter describes the background to the research project, the research design and the methods we used to gather and analyze evidence about mentoring in primary school settings. The mentors who participated in the research operated within a range of settings and course structures, so an outline of each of these is also presented in this chapter.

Background

As chapter 1 indicates, there is relatively little published work on mentorship in action in England and Wales in the field of primary initial teacher education. This being so, a group of six Bedford initial teacher educators submitted a research proposal to the Research Committee at Bedford College. The focus of the proposal was to research mentoring practice across the range of primary courses based at the college. Simultaneously, an application was made for further financial support to the Paul Hamlyn Foundation. Both proposals were successful.

The Teacher Education and Mentorship (TEAM) research project, funded jointly by Bedford College and the Paul Hamlyn Foundation, was an opportunity to examine mentoring within school-based phases of the teacher education programmes and to:

- make coherent what had developed in a piecemeal fashion;
- clarify the nature of mentoring in the context of primary teacher education;
- develop a theory of effective mentorship for school-based training;
- suggest some of the conditions which are conducive to successful mentoring outcomes, using insights derived from detailed analysis of research data.

It was felt that by researching mentoring practice the preparation for, and the quality of, mentorship within the school-based courses and mentor training would be enhanced.

Our key research questions were:

What do we mean by mentorship within school-based teacher education?
What do people called mentors do when they work with students?
What does it mean to behave in a mentor-like way?
What is the specific nature of the role that mentors perform?
What are the skills they demonstrate?
What problematic issues emerge?
What indications are there which point towards a theory of effective mentorship for school-based teacher training?

Mentor Training

Since all except two partnership schools had mentors who had undergone some form of mentor training from the college, we acknowledge (and indeed hope) that the mentoring observed may have been affected to varying degrees by the training experience. However, we have not attempted to take account of this effect. Rather, we have focused on how mentors and mentoring systems worked, given the range of variables affecting them. The nature, presence or absence of training is part of this range, but it also includes others which might be of greater significance — for example, school culture, size, mentor personal qualities, age phase, type of training to which the mentoring relates.

The Research Team

All the members of the research team had been primary teachers, two had also been head teachers, and each is now involved in primary teacher education at Bedford College. The roles and responsibilities covered by the team include, teaching students on primary BEd, and PGCE and Articled Teacher courses; supporting students and classroom teachers as a supervising tutor or as a link tutor for the school experiences in those courses; working with primary teachers on various in-service courses; writing, developing and implementing course structures; and coordinating and leading course teams. Each person on the project team had also had experience of undertaking research; some having been involved in localized or small-scale projects and others in national initiatives. Three had also spent eight weeks each, teaching full-time in different primary schools within the last two years. Thus, the team comprised people with multiple perspectives on teacher education, school-based experience, research and teaching in primary schools. From the outset we were excited about the project and keen to extend our experience of working together on courses by working as a team on this project.

The Course Structures Within which the Mentors are Operating

The Articled Teacher Scheme

This is a two-year school-based course for graduates who wished to enter the teaching profession. The course is a joint LEA and Bedford College of Higher Education venture and participants in the research were part of the first cohort for this particular education authority. Two articled teachers were allocated to each school. Schools were grouped into clusters of three and each cluster had a link tutor. The role of the college link tutor was to act as link between school, students and college. She/he dealt with organizational procedures and difficulties, and provided personal support for mentor and students as needed.

The Articled Teacher mentors received training and support before and during the course, which was run and accredited by the college. They were paid for their participation in the scheme and allocated twenty-six days supply cover. These were for attending training days, running some course sessions and for assessment and supervision of the articled teachers when they were on 'block experience'. During the first half term, three days supply cover for the mentor was used to allow time to be spent on IT-INSET.

Over the two-year period the articled teachers have work experience for a block of time in three schools including the one at which they are based — the 'partnership school'. They have a three-week block in an 'exchange school' in the second term of the course, five weeks assessed practice back in the partnership school during the third term, and six weeks assessed practice in a different exchange school in the fifth term of the course. Although the articled teachers take two of their three block experiences at the other schools in the same cluster, their partnership school is where they always return. Over the two years, 80 per cent of time is spent in school. Of that 85 per cent is spent at the partnership school.

During the first half term in school, most pairs of articled teachers were based with the mentor and her class. After the first two weeks they were in school two-and-a-half days a week and spent two of the remaining days in college.

IT-INSET is an integral part of the Articled Teachers scheme. The first part of this takes place during the first half term with the mentor and articled teachers forming a team to look at a specific classroom based issue. The supply cover specifically allocated for the IT-INSET is to enable the mentor to give time to study and reflection with the articled teachers.

The One-Year Primary PGCE Course: An Overview

The one-year primary PGCE course is designed for graduates wishing to teach within the primary age-range, either within the 5–9 or the 7–12 age range. There are two periods of 'partnership' experience: one in the autumn term and one in the spring term. For the autumn term, students spend two days per week in their partnership school, working in pairs with a class teacher. They follow a planned programme of activities which initiates them into the processes of classroom teaching and the primary curriculum. The remaining three days per week are spent in college on professional courses. In the spring term students have a diagnostic 'block experience' in a second school, before returning to their partnership school for a further four weeks of two days per week. In the summer term students complete a final school experience of six weeks in a third school. When added to a two-week observation period at the beginning of the course, this means that most students gain experience of four different schools.

As with the Articled Teacher Scheme, partnership experience is not formally assessed. But the experience forms a continuing focus for the professional work undertaken in college week by week. In other words, the process is essentially apprentice-like, with space for critical reflection on the changing classroom agendas presented by the periods in school.

During each of the block experiences, the supervisor and school staff provide feedback and advice to the student. The first block consists of four days in school and one day in college, and the students teach approximately 60 per cent of the time they are in school. At the end of the period, a report is written in consultation with the student. The final block school experience is the only one that is formally assessed. Then students take full responsibility for teaching the children, with the exception of some time each day for in-school preparation.

Schools which take PGCE students work with the college in one of two ways.

Partnership schools

These are volunteer schools who have usually been recommended by LEA officers as schools which offer models of effective primary classroom practice. There is no formal training for partnership teachers, though roles are defined in the College *Partnership Handbook*, and there is no payment to them or the school. Partnership teachers take responsibility for a pair of primary PGCE students within their classroom for the partnership experience. This occupies two days of each week the students are not on block experience. They may also have a student who is new to the school for one of the traditional block experiences — though a partnership school does not necessarily have students for a block experience.

The affiliated school scheme

Following the establishment of a course teaching base in Milton Keynes, and given the growing national impetus towards closer cooperation between schools and colleges for initial teacher training, it was agreed with Buckinghamshire LEA that some schools should have an augmented role in the school-based elements of training. Looked at from the school's point of view, this was a heavy commitment. Four students were placed in 'partnership' pairs with two teachers, with a further two individual students in two separate classes for each of the block experiences. A mentor was appointed from within the staff to take formal responsibility for the students. The mentors were paid a yearly honorarium of £300, in recognition of their contribution. This was used at the headteacher's discretion. The mentors attended a training course in the summer of 1991, run and accredited by the college. They were ready to receive their students, two in their class and two in a colleague's class, in September. To aid this pilot, the LEA provided each mentor with the equivalent of six full days of supply cover. The mentor was required to prepare reports on the students placed at the school for each block experience period and undertook the pass/fail assessment for the final school experience, in consultation with the link tutor.

Each affiliated school was visited by a college-based link tutor.

Primary BEd Third Year School Experience

As part of the four-year concurrent primary BEd degree course, third year students are required to undertake a four-week block school experience during the spring term. This is with the age range that the student has chosen at the end of the second year. During the first two years of the course they have ten weeks experience in three schools, including a five-week, assessed school experience in the summer term of the second year. The third year block experience is assessed as pass/fail, with one chance to retake. Students are expected to take class responsibility for 75 per cent of the time over the full four weeks. They receive two formal assessment reports which are given after week 2 and at the end of the four weeks.

At the time of the project, many third year students worked within a mentoring system (thirty-six of sixty-seven), although schools could opt for an orthodox college tutored arrangement. Mentors took part in a training programme, run and accredited by the College. Where teachers were undertaking the role of mentor for the first time, they were named as 'supported mentors', and received weekly visits from tutors during the school experience period. Full mentors were those who had been trained in earlier years, and had already successfully mentored on at least one occasion. Where full mentorship was undertaken the school was visited twice by a college tutor. The role of the tutor visiting schools operating a mentoring system, was to act as liaison and support for both students and mentor, rather than to act as observer and assessor of the students' work. The mentor took full responsibility for the detail of the student's assessment, unless failure was likely. In that event, access to a tutor was perceived by the college to be an additional support for the mentor's judgment, rather than a check upon it. A second opinion was normally required within the college tutored supervision. In the event of difficulties arising, the mentor was also able to call on the services of a 'flying squad' of tutors, who gave additional support to students and mentor. The schools of full mentors were paid an honorarium of £75 for two students. Wherever possible, at least two students were assigned to a school where a full mentor was operating.

Summary

The different course structures meant that there was a range of mentored and mentor-like settings. Mentors were working with and supporting students in a number of ways and contexts:

- The student worked with the mentor's class, with the mentor working alongside, observing, or elsewhere in the school. With PGCE students, this was for part of the week, over two periods of a term-and-a-half in total.
- Students taught the majority of the class sessions over four to six weeks, generally with the mentor not present, unless they were observing and evaluating the students teaching.
- Students were based with another teacher in the school or, as with the articled teachers, worked with different teachers and for different lengths of time.

Research Structure

Selection of Schools

The first selection decision for the project was to research mentorship across the range of primary initial teacher education courses. This meant recruiting four PGCE, four primary BEd, and four articled teacher schools as we wanted to research twelve settings.

The schools involved with the project were not a random selection of primary schools. As a first step towards locating schools which were suitable, the PGCE, Articled Teacher and BEd course leaders were asked to suggest schools which might be willing to participate in the project. These were approached to establish whether or not they might be interested. The leader for the Articled Teacher Scheme arranged for the project leader to talk to the mentors and students of the twelve schools involved in the Articled Teacher Scheme and issued an open invitation for them to take part in the project. Those who volunteered represented both the 'rural' and the 'urban' clusters of schools and became the articled teacher schools which were involved in the research.

All the schools which expressed some interest were visited by a member of the research team to clarify what 'involvement' meant. Then schools covering a range of settings were chosen from those volunteering. The decision to include research in two PGCE 'partnership' schools was made because the experience was mentor-like in structure. The student developed alongside the teacher and was supported by him/her over two terms. However, he/she was not involved in any formal assessment of the student and was not trained to undertake the task of working with the student(s).

Key selection criteria for school involvement were school catchment, type and size. A summary of significant details is given in table 3.1, which also gives some indication of the status of mentors in their schools, whether they had taken

Table 3.1: School contexts

SCHOOL	TRAINING CONTEXT	MENTOR FEATURE	MENTOR TRAINING	SCHOOL TYPE	STUDENT NUMBERS
Aimshigh	PGCE Partner	Deputy Head	No	Suburban Junior	4 as 2 pairs, then split
Bigtown	PGCE Partner	Deputy Head	No	Urban Junior	pair
Carlton	PGCE Affiliated	MPG	Yes — 1991	Urban, 8–12 Middle	4 as 2 pairs, and 2 singles
Deepvale	PGCE Affiliated	'A' allow-ance	Yes — 1991	Urban 8–12 Middle	4 as 2 pairs, and 2 singles
Endsleigh	Articled Teacher	'A' allow-ance	Yes — 1991	Urban 5–9 Lower	pair
Flenley	Articled Teacher	Deputy Head	Yes — 1991	Suburban 5–9 Lower	pair
Greenvale	Articled Teacher	Deputy Head	Yes — 1991	Rural 5–9 Lower	pair
Hillyway	Articled Teacher	Deputy Head	Yes — 1991	Suburban 5–9 Lower	pair for first term, then 1
Intake	BEd 3	Supported mentor; 'A' allowance	Yes — 1992	Urban Lower	3
June Lane	BEd 3	'B' allow-ance/full mentor	Yes — 1989	Suburban Junior	2
Kenleigh	BEd 3	Deputy Head/full mentor	Yes — 1989	Suburban Infant	2
Lonetree	BEd 3	Head as full mentor	Yes — 1989	Urban Infant	3

part in a training course and the number of students they were to mentor. The list of schools reflects a broad range of types of primary schools across three LEAs and represents the range of schools within the College's mentoring schemes. Though we cannot say that they were examples of effective mentoring practice, we can say that the schools and mentors were characterized by openness, self-confidence, and an interest in innovation, since:

- They were volunteers for their respective mentoring schemes, which were innovative.

- They were selected by recommendation from LEA's (articled teacher schools) and visits from PGCE tutors as suitable for partnership on the grounds of perceived effective practice.
- Mentors were willing to give time to be trained.
- They were schools where people were willing to open themselves to scrutiny. (Some mentoring schools initially approached were not willing.)

We do not suggest that these are typical primary schools. Nor do we claim the mentoring experiences in these schools are necessarily representative of all primary schools where mentoring of learner teachers is undertaken. Indeed, we consider it likely that these schools and mentors had attitudes and professional skills which were among those possessed by effective schools and teachers. However, we do suggest that the issues raised by this research reflects the range of issues likely to emerge within primary mentoring settings, and the similarities and differences between the different mentoring structures.

As part of negotiation of access, schools and students had received an explanatory leaflet. This outlined the project structure and purposes, and contained a code of 'Agreed Safeguards' for participants. Agreeing to participate meant agreeing to being observed and interviewed and to a case study being written. However, participants had control over the researcher's access to situations. The researchers agreed to anonymize the data, obtain participants' consent to use interview extracts, having shown them the interview data and explained how it was to be used. It was also made clear that the case studies would reflect the mentoring situations as understood by the researchers, having taken into account all the sources of information to which they had access. But participants were invited to add a further view of their own if they so wished.

The original project timetable provided for negotiation of research access during autumn 1991 with completion of field work and interviewing in twelve sites by the end of the spring term 1992. Case studies were written during the summer and autumn terms of 1992 which allowed necessary time for in-depth analysis of the outcomes.

Research Design: Multi-site Case Study

The research project was primarily ethnographic, essentially qualitative and hypothesis-generating rather than quantitative and hypothesis testing. It was undertaken in natural settings and used humans as primary data gathering instruments (Lincoln and Guba, 1985, p. 39). Thus, the methods we used for the collection and recording of evidence were considered in relation to the naturalistic research paradigm. The implications for research are that 'first, no manipulation on the part of the inquirer is implied, and, second, the inquirer imposes no a priori units on the outcome' (*ibid.*, p. 8).

The purpose of the Teacher Education and Mentorship (TEAM) research was to study twelve 'instances' of mentoring, and the 'case study' approach was considered appropriate because of our interest in understanding the phenom-enon of mentoring in a holistic manner. We worked within Stenhouse's (1978) definition that a case is an instance, an example of some phenomenon of interest, not a representative of a class. The 'case study' is an interpretative presentation and discussion of the case. A major strength of case study is that it makes use of multiple methods and those used are discussed later in this chapter. Team members were assigned schools from which to collect and analyze data, and each school was treated as a comprehensive case in and of itself.

Simultaneous to the study of twelve sites as individual cases of mentorship, we were seeking to build themes across the cases; attempting 'to build a general explanation that fits each of the individual cases even though the cases would vary in their details.' (Yin, 1984, p. 108). Thus the overall research design was that of multi-site case study which increases the potential for generalizing beyond the particular. 'By comparing sites or cases, one can establish the range of generality of a finding or explanation, and at the same time, pin down the conditions under which that finding will occur' (Miles and Huberman, 1984, p. 151). Projects of this nature have grown in frequency in recent years (Szanton, 1981; Elliott *et al.*, 1981; Lightfoot, 1983; Nias, Southworth, and Yeomans, 1989; Nias, Southworth and Campbell, 1991).

For each case in the TEAM project, data were gathered to learn as much as possible about each 'instance', its context and relevant variables. Our analysis for each case was a simultaneous activity to data collection and it continued, at a more intense level, after the data collection period. Cross-site issues were also explored throughout the course of the project, at regular TEAM research meet-ings. The nature of these is further discussed in the section on 'Making sense of the data'.

Researcher Stance

When in school, members of the research team watched, listened and interacted with children and staff of the schools. Hammersley and Atkinson (1983, pp. 93–7) draw attention to how the role of the observer in ethnographic research can be between that of a complete observer and a participant observer. With respect to the research process and the methodology undertaken, for the TEAM project, our research role was somewhere on the continuum between outsider-researcher and participant-researcher.

As researchers, we may be considered outsiders to the schools we were studying, because we were no longer full-time teachers in the classroom or mem-bers of the staff, permanent or temporary. However, it could not be said that we were complete outsiders i.e. strangers, with no understanding of the situations we were researching. All team members had an informed perspective on how schools operate due to experience of other primary staffs, school settings and related circumstances. They had all undertaken the supervisor/tutor role with students on school experience. This is a different role to mentoring students on a day-to-day basis, but does involve working with students in a school context. We, certainly, had to be aware of how such personal experience might influence the way we viewed various phenomena.

How we were perceived by the staff and students in school is also a consideration when examining the participant nature of our researching role. All of the schools taking part in the research were used to seeing College tutors regularly and having them in and around school working with students and talking to staff. They accepted students and tutors as part of the school year pattern. June Lane for instance had had third year BEd students for three years but had also had school experience students from the second and fourth year at different times. The schools involved in the Articled Teacher Scheme had all had students on teaching practice and, like PGCE schools, were also used to having the link tutors working in their school interacting with the mentors and student teachers. In some settings, the researcher was quite familiar with the school she/he was studying, since they had worked there as a school experience tutor.

From the perspective of the students involved, the researcher of their setting was also a familiar participant in their training. The researchers studying the PGCE and articled teacher settings were tutors on these courses, and though this was not the case for all the BEd settings, where it was not, the researcher was known to the student through their peers as course tutor and a school experience tutor. It might be said that, as researchers, we were participants, because school staffs and students knew us as college tutors, in the course of the schools' work with learner-teachers. This was because either the researcher had been in that particular school as tutor, or the school had experience of other College tutors as part of normal school life.

In the case of two schools (Deepvale and Flenley) the researchers were also course leaders for the course which the mentored students were undertaking. It was felt that the advantages of informed insight into course structures outweighed any possible disadvantages of being perceived in other roles by the participants. In practice, most of the six researchers experienced times when they were perceived as representatives of the college as well as researchers. These experiences are some indication of how far we were able to become 'insider-outsiders'. In only one instance was there any indication that course-related status might have had a temporary, and slight, adverse effect within a research setting.

From our perspective, we were aware that as researchers we had to try and suspend personal 'everyday knowledge' and any preconceptions of primary schools in general, and of the school we were studying. It was important to 'make the familiar strange' (Hammersley and Atkinson, 1983, p. 176) and yet try to understand the meanings, realities and intentions of participants within the observed situations. To some extent, researching in several contexts helped throw into relief the 'strangeness' of a particular school.

Methodology

As Adelman, Jenkins and Kemmis (1976) point out, 'case study' is an umbrella term for a family of research methods that:

are held in common with a wider tradition of sociological and anthropological fieldwork. Case study methodology is eclectic, although techniques and procedures in common include observation, (participant and non-participant) interview (conducted with varying degrees of structure) audio visual recording, field-note-taking, document collection, and the negotiation of products (for example discussing the accuracy of an account with those observed).

Thus the techniques standard to ethnographic, qualitiative research provided a framework for our study. They allowed for the description of, and analytical commentary on, the routine, everyday, unquestioned and, sometimes, taken-forgranted aspects of mentorship within the different course structures. We gathered a wealth of data, from which to select evidence, organized in terms of its relevance to issues of mentorship. Data was collected chronologically and, as we met to discuss what we had seen, issues and themes began to emerge 'across' the data.

The timing and length of the visits clearly affected the kind of data we were able to gather, and how much time was spent in each school setting was influenced by the mentoring context. The research phase for the PGCE and articled teacher settings was from September/October 1991 through to April 1992 and for the primary BEd schools it was the second half of the spring term 1992. Where the data was collected over two terms the time that the researcher spent in school ranged from between one and two hours to half-a-day in the school, at least twice in every three weeks. Colleagues researching third year BEd school experience settings visited at least once every week and generally stayed for at least half-a-day. Some visits included lunch time or after school.

Observations

Observations sought to gain a general impression, yet, achieve a comprehensive description of the setting. They were planned in terms of when and where they might take place but were not systematic. The development of a schedule for a systematic approach would have meant pre-judgments on what categories to consider. We considered that this was both restrictive and inappropriate.

Researchers took part in staffroom interactions and generated notes from informal contact and experience of the setting. In some cases they began to acquire a sense of the social structure of the setting and to interpret the organizational culture of the school (Nias, Southworth and Yeomans, 1989). Observation of the mentors in action meant that feedback sessions were observed, as well as classroom situations that involved the mentor and learner-teachers jointly and separately. The observations and personal thoughts were noted in brief form and unobtrusively in a field note-book. They were expanded upon away from the setting, and as soon as possible, while they were fresh in the researchers' minds.

Interviewing

The mentors were each interviewed, as were the students in all but one case (where they were reluctant). Where the schools were involved in the Articled Teacher Scheme or had PGCE students, the link tutors were interviewed as were the visiting tutors for the third year BEd students. In two of the cases the headteacher of the school was also interviewed.

According to Burgess (1982) interviews can be 'placed on a continuum with structured interviews at one end and unstructured interviews at the other' (p. 107). For this research the interviewing method used was the 'open-flexible type' (Ball, 1983) where each interview was developed in terms of the opportunities it presented to explore the interviewees' perceptions and related understandings of mentorship. Interviews became semi-structured in nature as issues and questions arose during the data collection period. Even when this was the case, neither the exact wording of questions nor the direction of the interview was determined ahead of time. The interviews were essentially exploratory. As Merriam (1988, p. 74) points out, 'This format allows the researcher to respond to the situation at hand, to the emerging worldview of the respondent, and to new ideas on the topic.'

Our interviews reflected Patton's view (1980) that:

> We interview people to find out from them what we cannot directly observe . . . We cannot observe feelings, thoughts, and intentions. We cannot observe behaviours that took place at some previous point in time. We cannot observe situations that preclude the presence of an observer. We cannot observe how people have organised the world and the meanings they attach to what goes on in the world-we have to ask people questions about those things. The purpose of interviewing, then, is to allow us to enter into the other person's perspective. (p. 196)

Respondents were asked for information about their mentoring arrangements as well as for their perceptions of, and thoughts on, mentoring procedures and processes. Each interview provided an opportunity to explore emerging ideas and themes. They were usually individual in a range of settings — a classroom, the staffroom, the headteacher's office — and often in the midst of a busy day.

The Study of Documentary Evidence

Some of the documents used for the research were those relating to course structures in the form of student handbooks, school experience handbooks and mentor handbooks. Members of the research team used them to make themselves aware of the specifics of the courses and the documented requirements of mentors within them. This information may have influenced the agenda of some of the semi-structured interviews, otherwise its use was quite limited. More significant, perhaps, to the purpose of the project was each researcher's access to a mentor's written assessment(s) of a student on school experience feedback forms, reports or articled teacher's professional competency profiles. Where used, this data was generally discussed as part of an interview rather than used in isolation. For example;

> If you make the interim report too glowing then the student will think 'I am doing all right' and sit back and not progress in the second two weeks. You don't want to make it too critical because there is nothing worse than somebody who is continually knocking someone. So it's a very fine line between praise and enough positive criticism so that the students still progress in their second half. (interview, mentor, June Lane)

Apart from stimulating thinking 'about important questions to pursue through more direct observations and interviewing' (Patton, 1980, p. 152), feedback forms and report forms also provided valuable information about the context of the particular case.

> He had had a briefing with each student and had given each student a feedback sheet full of questions and some tips. (fieldnote, Deepvale)

> Examples of the questions posed, not only give us an idea of some of the problems that the students had in the classroom but also show the way Dennis was trying to get them to think for themselves. (Sampson, 1993b, p. 15)

One of the researchers also had access to the mentor's diary which was kept for the first few weeks of mentoring. This provided a subjective and selective account of the mentoring situation over a short period of time, and might have suggested aspects to follow up in subsequent interviewing.

Making Sense of the Data

An essential feature of this project was that there were regular research-team meetings which served a range of purposes. We found that sharing a perspective from one case could throw issues into relief and thus inform further data collection for other individual cases. Also, as the analytical process is cumulative and we were starting with no explicit theory, discussions with research team members formed an important part of the analysis of data. Through collaborative analysis and 'progressive focusing' (Parlett and Hamilton, 1977), we sharpened our perception of the issues and developing insights were shared and tested against the range of cases.

We all tended to use the same general method in analysing the evidence we had collected, implementing the 'grounded approach' (Glaser, 1978), 'to build theory that is faithful to and illuminates the area under study'. It is also referred to as 'the constant comparative method of analysis'.

> Comparing as many differences and similarities in data as possible . . . tends to force the analyst to generate categories, their properties, and their interrelations as he tries to understand his data. (Glaser and Strauss, 1967, p. 55)

In our study we were trying to capture as much of the complexity of mentoring as possible. One aspect of our analysis was to use 'open coding' of data (Strauss and Corbin, 1990) which meant breaking down, examining, comparing, conceptualizing and categorizing data. In early discussion we referred to descriptive codes (Miles and Huberman, 1984, p. 56) such as 'roles', 'relationships', 'strategies' and 'skills', but each of the code-constructs generated through the process of analysis, subsumed a wide range of particulars so that sub-codes also emerged and developed from the data.

Cross-checking and 'pooled judgment' (Foreman, 1948, p. 413) were elements of triangulation between investigators (Delamont, 1992). In addition, insights were refined because concurrently four of the researchers were working as link tutors to other mentoring schools. The processes of puzzling over data and their interpretation, raising questions and seeking answers were important in establishing reliability and validity of developing theory (Lincoln and Guba, 1985, p. 288). These procedures emphasize 'dependability' and 'consistency' of the results obtained from the data rather than the extent to which findings can be replicated. Repeated observations of the same phenomenon over time and across the cases increases the validity of findings. The processes of 'within methods' and 'between methods' triangulation (Delamont, 1992, p. 159) also strengthened reliability and validity of data for each case, and across the cases. For example, corroborative and contrary evidence was searched for in the interview data. This meant looking at interview data, first, from the same session from different respondents; second, from the same and different respondents for different times. In these ways we might validate emerging issues from previous interview data or validate observation field notes and documentary evidence.

Referring the data back to the participants was not only part of the bargain struck when access was negotiated, it was also one of the validating strategies used by the research team. This means that the process was used by the researchers to clear their own data and to validate the case. Though we were aware that we could not assume that respondents had access to 'reality', they were being invited to check and comment on our interpretations and the meanings we had attributed to events and behaviours. As Lincoln and Guba (1985) point out:

> If the investigator is to be able to purport that his or her reconstructions are recognizable to audience members as adequate representations of their own (and multiple) realities, it is essential that they be given the opportunity to react to them. (p. 314)

Finally, debate with colleagues was crucial to establishing patterns in the data. Some issues were important across many cases while others were specific to particular mentoring arrangements. Through discussion we were maximizing and minimizing the differences and similarities of data across sites (Glaser and Strauss, 1967) to support tentative hypotheses while at the same time remaining open to the emergence of new hypotheses.

Cross-case analysis was complex. However, it was worth the effort, since it improved greatly the validity and reliability of generalized findings. We now turn to these in the following chapters.

Chapter 4

How Mentorship Happens: Evolving Procedures and Practices

Paul Frecknall

Speak the speech, I pray you, as I pronounced it to you trippingly on the tongue; but if you mouth it, as many of your players do, I had lief the town-crier spoke my lines. Nor do not saw the air too much with your hand, thus; but use all gently: for in the very torrent, tempest, and, as I may say, the whirlwind of your passion, you must acquire and beget a temperance that may give it smoothness. (*Hamlet*, Act 3 Sc 2)

This chapter attempts to look at how individual schools involved with the research developed their own procedures and practices when mentoring their students. It will attempt to explore the different approaches to mentoring within each course and begin to raise some of the issues related to them.

How Mentors are Chosen in Different Schemes

Who chooses the mentors?

Invariably the headteacher was the person who chose the mentor. However sometimes this was done directly, due to the headteacher's understanding of his/her staff and the needs and interests of individuals. The head then approached the member of staff and discussed it with them. Esther, a head, had identified what she saw as the personal and professional qualities that the role of mentor demanded. This, together with her knowledge of her individual staff members, helped her to make her choice.

The main thing is personalities . . . it is very important to identify the traits such as conscientiousness, patience, a liking for human beings, and the ability not to be offended easily, to be confident enough in what you do and what you say without overdoing it. (interview, headteacher, Endsleigh)

With regard to the professional qualities:

You have to be a good practitioner ... to be able to do a good job in the classroom ... have to be trusted by your colleagues. If you haven't respect then that affects things. It is also vital that she is sure of her position in the school — that she is actually valued herself. (interview, headteacher, Endsleigh)

Esther is the head teacher of a school on the Articled Teacher Scheme. As this runs over a two year period the success of the scheme relies heavily on the school's commitment and the appropriate choice of mentor for the role. Thus there needs to be a positive outlook on the part of the mentor. They often saw it as a part of their own personal and professional development:

Its about wanting to do it for a start ... (interview, mentor, Endsleigh)

Where the mentor wasn't approached directly by the headteacher the head often requested interested individuals to approach her/him for further information having first explained the role at a staff meeting. In some schools where the deputy headteacher had been responsible for students and/or probationary teachers they were asked to take on board the mentoring role. Some schools had a member of staff who previously had completed a mentor's training course with the college and therefore they took on the role.

In effect, then, the mentors across the schemes came from a variety of levels and experiences within the schools. All mentors had proven good professional and personal skills and appeared to want to do it at the outset. However out of the twelve schools observed six mentors were deputies, and one was a head. One held an Incentive B and three Incentive A allowances. The mentor's responsibility within the school sometimes made mentoring students problematic:

... Belinda as mentor — no problem — Belinda as deputy head teacher and mentor, a big problem because there were times when she was only there something like 65 per cent of the time, because on a Thursday afternoon she has always got a free hour, an assessment hour. (interview, student, Bigtown)

Choosing the deputy headteacher as the mentor throws up a variety of issues which perhaps need to be raised here. By the nature of their status within the school, deputies have fulfilled the criteria that Esther spoke of earlier in this chapter with regards to levels of personal and professional experience and skill; it is a high profile job and therefore gives a high status to the mentoring role. However the demands made of a deputy are special to that role and bring with it both advantages and disadvantages. For instance, when the headteacher at Aimshigh was away:

Alison seems to be working at fever pitch. She takes all aspects of her job very seriously but just how many pieces can she split herself into? (fieldnote, Aimshigh)

As the mentor on the PGCE partnership scheme Belinda, the deputy, had general oversight of four students and also of a probationary teacher. In her own classroom she had two of the four PGCE students. This did create some problems with regards to demands on her time. Similarly the situation was replicated in the other PGCE partnership school where Alison was deputy and mentor. However both managed to develop some strategies for juggling those demands:

> As deputy headteacher, I sometimes have to deal with behavioural problems around the school so, if I was interviewing any children I would do that just outside the classroom. (interview, mentor, Bigtown)

From experience of working with students in the field there is a great desire for feedback on their work. Many students who worked with deputies as mentors, especially on schemes other than the Articled Teacher Scheme, regretted that they didn't have more time with their mentor to discuss issues related to their teaching. However they did recognize that the sort of teacher who was a deputy was also a positive classroom model for them to be with:

> Because she is deputy we could use more of her . . . but she had a lot on her plate and she is rushing about and you are left getting a few flying words at a time — they are valuable. I think what I got from her was valuable in the end, the quality was high. (interview, student, Bigtown)

Another way of using time effectively was to include the students in aspects of school life which would not only develop their understanding of the broader role of the teacher but would give them opportunities to actively participate in discussions related to planning and evaluation.

> We hold weekly team planning meetings, weekly team evaluation meetings that the students are encouraged to come to and take part in to share their planning etc. So by working with other teachers within the team we saw it just as an extension of working with myself . . . I think what we offered them here is the opportunity to work within a team and that's the crucial part of it. (interview, mentor, Aimshigh)

Even though the deputy headteacher mentors recognized that they had a difficult job trying to fit in all the demands of mentoring with their other roles, they took both jobs seriously. As a deputy and mentor Belinda felt very strongly that she shouldn't be exempted from the scheme because of her existing role:

> I wouldn't have wanted to be told you can't have a student because you are a deputy headteacher. (interview, mentor, Bigtown)

and she goes on to explain why:

I think it is important to recognise within every member of staff within a school, there are going to be staff with various strengths and weaknesses, and I think the students need to appreciate that. (interview, mentor, Bigtown)

Differences in Course Requirements of Mentors

As there are different schemes in operation the requirements of the mentors varies. In simple terms the role is either supportive or one where assessment is built on to the supportive role. (A more detailed analysis of the role is given in chapter 5.) In the PGCE partnership schools, in the partnership element of the PGCE affiliated schools and in the partnership element of the Articled Teacher Scheme the role is largely a supportive one. The emphasis is switched more to assessment in the four-week BEd year 3 school experience. There is only one scheme where the mentor doesn't play a part in any formal assessment of the student and that is in the PGCE partnership school experience.

PGCE Partnership School Experience

In this scheme the mentor is usually responsible for two students in their own class, there may be other students placed in the school with other class teachers. Their role is to initiate the students into the school and its culture, to develop a programme of work to be undertaken with groups of children in their class, to oversee the planning and evaluation of sessions, to enable them to carry out routine activities like taking registration, playground duties etc. and to ensure that college defined curriculum tasks are carried out.

In practice the mentor plays an active part in the evaluation of the student as the college tutor will discuss the individual student's progress when visiting. However this part of the course is not assessed on a pass/fail basis but is seen as a way of introducing the students into the life of a school and the raising of awareness of the role of the teacher. In many ways the students are likened to that of apprentices and, as stated in the Partnership School Experience Handbook, the experience '... provides an opportunity for the college-based and the school-based elements of the course to mutually support and inform one another' (Bedford College of Higher Education, 1993).

Research shows that in the above situations where the mentor's role is clearly defined and communicated then the mentor-student relationships are very positive.

She (the mentor) wasn't like over friendly, but she was friendly. She was professional in organizing. You got the impression she was going to read through things and not just take it as it came, and think about what we were going to be doing ... She was very helpful about doing our first activity that we had to do. (interview, student, Aimshigh)

I have a lot of respect for her experience and I will listen to her. (interview, student, Bigtown)

PGCE Affiliated Schools — Partnership Element

This aspect of the Affiliated Schools Scheme reflected the partnership element in the one-year PGCE previously referred to except that the mentor had overall resonsibility for four students; two normally placed in their class and two in a colleague's class. This obliged the mentor to build a relationship with a colleague that was centred on the students. Following feedback from the reseached group of schools each mentor now only has responsibility for two students during the whole of the scheme.

Articled Teacher Scheme

This scheme uses four-fifths of the student's time on school-based work over two years. The mentor is 'responsible for the day to day professional and pastoral support for the articled teachers . . . Time must be found to meet this commitment and it is important that you meet with them each week (Bedford College of Higher Education, 1992). The course documents set out clearly defined areas that are the mentor's responsibility in the training of the articled teacher. It acknowledges that each articled teacher's experience in school will be different and sees this as a strength rather than a weakness.

The supporting role played by the mentors in this scheme is a very interesting one as the partnership has longer to develop and therefore there is the possibility of a more complex series of relationships which will be discussed later in the book (see chapter 7). Mentors on this scheme had a very broad supportive role to play. Naturally they were to evaluate their students throughout the course but their role as assessor during the research period was with regard to their own articled teachers on their block teaching experiences. This is an area that caused some difficulties in some of the schools studied and will be dealt with later.

From the research it appears that all the mentors on this scheme had both long and short-term goals with regard to their 'new colleagues'. As Eve commented:

I am trying to see a road through to a competent teacher at the end of two years. (interview, mentor, Endsleigh)

and in an interview with Hazel she also stated that,

Over the two years I want Heather to have as big a variety of experience as possible. (interview, mentor, Hillyway)

Because of these long-term objectives and because of course requirements, mentors of articled teachers needed to make arrangements for them to have a structure to their school-based work. However they also realized that within the course framework the articled teachers, like children in their classes, had specific learning needs. Therefore short-term strategies were needed.

Initial Support by Mentors for Articled Teachers

The four schools studied on this scheme began with similar ways of supporting their students in those first few weeks. It would appear from the data that the reasons for this were:

— to give the students a chance to acclimatize themselves to the school;
— to give them opportunities to observe:
  (a) the children; and
  (b) the teaching.

The following comments give some idea as to what the first few weeks were to be like for the articled teachers and one could predict that this is likely to be standard procedure as schemes develop. Similar experiences were had by students on other courses studied.

> It was a deliberate policy on my part, to not get them too heavily involved with any teaching to begin with, because I didn't feel that that was fair on the children, whether it was fair on the articled teachers or not I don't know, but I didn't want to just let them loose on classes for the first three weeks. (interview, mentor, Hillyway)

According to Eve, neither of the articled teaches had 'much idea about what to do about anything' when they first arrived so there was a need to direct them as well as respond to their questions:

> I have been getting them to tail me, observe me, talk to the children about their work and ask me questions. (interview, mentor, Endsleigh)

The pattern was similar elsewhere:

> I took her round the school on the first day and made sure that she met all the other members of staff so that she felt at home. (interview, mentor, Greenvale)

> The first week all I asked them to look at was how different children work and point out differences. (interview, mentor, Flenley)

As the scheme got underway the mentor/student relationship developed and the articled teachers realized that they were working with good role models in whom they could trust and learn from.

If we didn't believe in what she was doing we couldn't really talk to her about anything because there wouldn't be a lot of point. (interview, student, Endsleigh)

Mentor Support for Articled Teachers: Planning

The common pattern evolving from the case studies is one where the articled teachers took on board group work initially planned by the teacher.

They started to take groups then. First of all groups that I planned and organized and I told them exactly what to do, so it was more sort of a parent helper role. Then I gave them an outline of the type of thing I wanted to do. Such as I wanted to do symmetry and left them to find some ideas and when they'd found the ideas we discussed it and planned the group together. (interview, mentor, Greenvale)

No great demands were made of the students at this point. As the course developed there was a gradual development towards the articled teacher planning group and whole sessions more independently. A similar pattern of co-planning was followed by the mentor at Endsleigh. Eve felt that this was an effective way of developing her articled teachers' skills in lesson planning by feeding in her knowledge of the children together with ideas for activities:

We have planned some lessons together. For instance with a particular maths session we decided on a focus and I talked through the sorts of things I would expect the children to be able to do and the things that some would find difficult and why, and we discussed how it might be organized. (interview, mentor, Endsleigh)

In Endsleigh there were times when the co-planning initially involved the two articled teachers:

There were times when myself and Emily took team lessons where Eve said 'Plan about that and we'll talk about it tomorrow and then you can change anything you think is blindingly silly after we have discussed it.' And she gave us resources that would help us. (interview, student, Endsleigh)

At other times the co-planning was between one articled teacher and the mentor. Articled teachers were encouraged in all the schools to take more and more responsibility for their decisions. This was done by the mentors giving direct professional guidance which encouraged the students to reflect on, and consider, alternative approaches. This process appears to have enabled the students to become more self-aware. As Eileen recognized later on in the course:

I feel like I am functioning as myself more than I did. I used to function from asking Eve things all the time . . . but I am not now . . . I am more me dependent. (interview, student, Endsleigh)

This then appears to have been the students' build up. It was very gradual and consisted of a lot of observation and of working alongside the teachers under the mentor's direction.

Mentor Support for Articled Teachers: Broader Experiences

In planning a programme for the articled teachers the mentor is required to, 'Provide opportunities for an articled teacher to observe other teachers who have a range of teaching styles, and discuss these afterwards' (Bedford College of Higher Education, 1992). The reasoning behind this should be obvious if one is to gain a broader perspective on teaching, however, the way in which the mentor plans this is left to them as one needs to take into account the articled teachers' specific needs, personalities, as well as the needs or limitations of the school. Experience of working in other classrooms and access to a wider range of staff can help in the educative process because it means possible exposure to different teaching models and distinctive explanations. This alone may not lead to independence nor can it be assumed that these experiences facilitated critical questioning. Within the same school culture the practice may vary to some extent but the values and beliefs may not be significantly different. Hence Emily's comment, '. . . you get so ingrained into one way of thinking that its a real jolt to go into another school' (interview, student, Endsleigh). This area will be developed later in this chapter when I look at student placements.

To summarize this section on articled teacher mentors and the support given with regards to non-assessed areas of the course, our research shows that there was a very positive response from both mentors and students in this area. They had a feeling of belonging, and of being supported in the professional side of the job. A mutual respect was developing as the first block experience came on the horizon. Words like 'trust', 'respect', and 'openness' are used throughout the data to describe the developing relationship, however the mentor's role as assessor brought with it some difficulties that are issues to be raised in other chapters.

Support With Assessment Roles

There are three schemes that require the mentor to formally assess the student. The BEd third year school experience and the block school experiences on both the Articled Teacher Scheme and the PGCE affiliated schools scheme.

Articled Teacher Scheme and Assessment

The mentor is involved with three strands to the assessment of the articled teachers. These are:

(i)   The assessed practical school experience.
(ii)   The Professional Competency Profile and associated viva voce in Year 1.
(iii) Four linked written assignments with a reflective overview. (Bedford College of Higher Education, 1992)

The information contained in the Mentor Handbook 1992–1994 with regards to their role in assessment of assessed practical school experience can be summarized in the following points:

(i)   First block school experience term 2 diagnostic — the mentor in the exchange school (one of the other schools in the scheme in which the articled teachers are placed) will be responsible for the articled teacher.
(ii)   Assessed second block school experience (term 3) pass/fail — the partnership school mentor is responsible for 'support, supervision and for joint assessment of the student . . .' (*ibid.*)
(iii) Assessed third block school experience in the second exchange school — pass/fail — mentor based in exchange school has a 'supportive and supervisory role and will make a pass/fail judgment in conjunction with the link tutor' (*ibid.*). The partnership mentor forms part of the moderation body.

On this course the research highlights occasions when the assessment role of the mentor was under some strain, possibly due to the conflict with the purely supportive role established earlier on the course. For example, in Hillyway because the mentor was to play the part of assessor for Heather it appears to have had an effect on their relationship at that time as is reflected in comments like:

When you are assessed in the school its a bit different. (interview, student, Hillyway)

She goes on to explain why her feelings had changed.

Its rather an unfortunate part of the system, especialy with doing the teaching practice in the school where you are actually based. You are used to asking advice from the person who is going to be judging it all at the end. And you feel a bit, its very isolating. (interview, mentor, Hillyway)

The situation also had an effect on her relationship, or at least her attitude, with the teacher whose class she would be teaching on the block experience:

. . . even that's the same situation as well you see, because obviously they will exchange information and it will go down in the little black book at the end! (interview, student, Hillyway)

Heather's partner in this school had had to withdraw from the course due to a job move and so she was perhaps justified in feeling a little isolated as she felt that her mentor was going to be 'unapproachable for informal conversation about what she was doing' (Wooldridge, 1993b).

It is difficult from the case study material to state whether or not Heather's feelings were justified. However, in Endsleigh where there were still two articled teachers, a similar situation had arisen where feelings of isolation on the part of one student were very strong. This situation is well documented in the case study and does raise many issues relating to this dual process of support and assessor. According to the researcher it:

> . . . became a testing period of time because problems arose with respect to Emily's teaching. Feelings of anger emerged. From Emily's perspective she felt there was inconsistency in the way she was treated. (Wooldridge, 1993a)

The feelings from Emily about the situation are very strong.

> . . . all of a sudden from the beginning of the third week I got 'It can't be done. Change,' Which is very hard to do. I felt like the rug had been pulled from underneath me competely. Everything gradually got more formal and an atmosphere of assessment was created. Because there was concern about my teaching practice so all the attention was focused on me. (interview, student, Endsleigh)

The effect that this incident had on Emily influenced the way she viewed the staff, and her own personal dilemma comes out in the following extract:

> I did find it difficult to talk to anybody when I knew that I had to go back in that class and carry on doing it. I needed help with everything but I couldn't ask for it. Not during teaching practice because you are assessed on teaching practice. Nobody wants to know really. They just want to see what you are doing. (interview, student, Endsleigh)

Eve also felt that her relationship with Emily had changed during the assessed experience and blamed a lot of it onto the assessment issue.

> Relationships got very strained between Emily and myself because I was the one that was going to say 'yes' or 'no' at the end of the day. Emily's relationships with the staff were also affected at the time. But I don't think Eileen's were. (interview, mentor, Endsleigh)

In an interview Eve explains how she felt Emily responded to her advice.

> She seemed to ignore my advice and there were one or two little incidents where situations I knew for a fact that something had happened and I was told the contrary. (interview, mentor, Endsleigh)

Throughout the experience Eve tried to remain sensitive to the situation and was prepared to share some of the responsibility for the perceived change in the relationship, whether or not her reaction is justifiable in her view. However the relationship between Eve and Emily returned to what it had been during the partnership period once the assessed practice was over:

> *Eve:* But It seems OK now. They have gone back, I think, to where they were.
>
> *Emily:* Well its changed totally back now. (interviews, mentor and student, Endsleigh)

From the case study analysis in two schools it does appear that there are issues relating to the joint role of supporter and assessor in the Articled Teacher Scheme. In both cases the attitude towards the mentor and the whole base school staff appear to be changed. It isn't clear just how much of this 'change' is in the students' minds and how much is actual fact. However, the feelings were very strong especially when a student was considered to be having some difficulties, which may in themselves have contributed towards the student's perception of things.

BEd Third Year Mentored School Experience

This four-week block school experience was part of the four-year BEd programme. In June Lane Junior School the mentor was a very experienced mentor and was taking part in the programme for the third year running. He was fully trained and on a 'B' allowance. The fundamental difference of being a mentor on this course to one on any other was that these mentors were explicitly assessing students whilst they were performing other supportive functions which might be seen as characterisic of mentorship. According to Yeomans:

> There was some consistency between the idea of support and implicit assessment which was formative in intent and outcome. (Yeomans, 1993b)

Within the college's structures there were opportunities after week two for an 'explicitly formative assessment' — the interim report. This is a formalized feedback to the students. These comments were intended as an indication to students as to their performance at that stage. This report makes no contribution to official student records. The final report, however, is summative in nature and does form part of the student's records and leads to the judgment of pass or fail, which naturally has implications for the student continuing the course.

In June Lane Junior the students and the mentor appear to have few problems with the notion of mentor as assessor; in fact they were able to articulate the positive advantages of this type of assessment, mainly due to the fact that the mentor sees far more of the students' teaching and the way in which they develop relationships in the classroom and in the school.

> I have got a better idea of how they have performed over four weeks than somebody who will come in here and speak to them once every week for four weeks. (interview, mentor, June Lane)

> I certainly think it's better for the mentor to make the final assessment because they have got more of a look into how you have been getting on . . . (interview, student, June Lane)

This was also the feeling from Kenleigh, another school involved with the year three BEd students. This was especially the case for the student who was also in the mentor's class. In both these schools the student who had the mentor as class teacher felt they had a very good deal and their relationship with the mentor was a very positive one.

> I prefer mentorship to having a college lecturer because I think you are there all the time. Therefore you see everything that goes on rather than a tutor coming in and probably everything will go wrong then. (interview, student, Kenleigh)

The students with a class teacher who wasn't the mentor found the relationship a little less relaxed when the mentor visited their classroom and likened it more to the college tutor visits.

> *Jess to John:* Last week [Jenny] was worried about you being in, more so than me; she is used to me because I have stayed in there so often, so I think she is much better with me and I think because you have got the title of mentor she is a little bit more bothered about you . . . How does Jane react with you because you are her class teacher?
>
> *John:* Jane is fine. Jane has the same sort of relationship with me as you have with Jenny. (fieldnote of conversation, June Lane)

John, the mentor at June Lane, planned his work as a mentor very carefully. He believed that it was crucial to have a student with him in his class in order that he understood the nature of the beast and also in purely practical terms it freed him to visit the other student.

This issue as to the fairness of the system if the mentor is also class teacher should be raised. Research suggests that the positive elements of having an on-site mentor outweigh the fact that one student will have more time and opportunity to develop a relationship with the mentor if they are also their class teacher. The evidence would appear to be that the mentor is better placed to deal with both support and assessment. However the long-term relationship necessary for the articled teacher route can be very deeply affected by the assessing role.

The Placement of Students: The Principles of Pairing

All schools sampled for this research took in two or more students. Where possible this was done with pairs of students, or multiples of two. There are good reasons for this. There is the opportunity for the pair to be mutually supportive. This can be done through meetings back at college, lifts in someone's car to and from the school, and so on. The growing number of students means that it is also a practical solution to the increasing problem of placements in 'good' schools.

The main intention on the partnership phase of the PGCE courses as well as being one of mutual support, was one of mutual feedback and some integrated planning, especially in the first partnership phase. This appears to work in some situations better than in others. The main problem lies in the placements which are made before the students and the college have any real idea as to an individual's strengths and weaknesses. This can put a strain on a partnership experience if one student is strong and could benefit from, for example, planning for the whole class whilst the other has distinct weaknesses and is not yet at that stage of development. As Annabel observed,

> ... the two students were very different. One was capable of doing
> that from quite early on, one wasn't. You had to be careful as to how
> that went. Certainly you have to think on your feet because situations
> arise as you are doing it. (interview, mentor, Aimshigh)

In Deepvale, Dennis, the mentor, had to oversee four students during the first term, this in itself produced some problems:

> It can be quite difficult to get down to individual points with individual
> students if you are facing them as a pair, and on our Friday meetings
> I was facing them as a quartet, so the conversation, quite a lot of the
> conversation, was of a general nature. (interview, mentor, Deepvale)

So from the evidence presented in the case studies it could be assumed that the rationale behind the pairing has some very positive strengths but that there are, in effect, some difficult areas that are not helped by the multiplicity of students and their varying individual needs, especially where there is a limited amount of time available to both students and mentors.

How Mentors Observe and Feedback

Feedback of sessions taught, of planning and organisation is one of the crucial ways of learning how you are developing as a teacher. Inevitably the opportunity to spend time talking with the mentor or class teacher is seen as a high priority amongst all students on all courses.

They ate everything you told them. (interview, mentor, Aimshigh)

The opportunities for some students to have what they considered to be sufficient time for this type of feedback were not always seen as adequate,

I would have liked some more feedback — one way or another (interview, student, Aimshigh)

In order to provide good, constructive feedback it is necessary to have opprtunities for good observation. The Mentor Handbook for articled teachers lists guidelines for observing. Amongst the points made are ones that mention 'frequency of observations', 'sensitivity' and impartiality, familiarity with the planned lesson, the 'focus of the observation' written and oral feedback, immediacy of some feedback, opportunities for the student to choose what is observed, and to 'ensure that the observation is undertaken in a disciplined, focused and accountable manner' (Bedford College of Higher Education 1992). This Mentor's Handbook also lists 'Questions to ask when observing a lesson'. Similar questions to these appear in the school experience handbooks for other courses.

Observation

The evidence in the research would suggest that most of the classroom observations are done informally by the mentors. Most prefer to be a part of the activity in order that they don't present themselves as a judge. As Jane a student at June Lane Junior School commented:

If I was doing an introduction and he sat very much on the side facing me almost with the children. Not sitting behind me and watching me. Being more like 'Oh I will sit here and keep quiet, while Jane's introducing the lesson.' Not like — 'I am here to watch.' Which is nice and I have been able to switch off in a way and block him out. (interview, student, June Lane)

Of the same mentor Jenny commented:

He has been very casually observing. He hasn't come into the class and sat in the corner taking down notes which has made me feel relaxed in the classroom when he comes in. When he comes in he tends to obviously listen to what I am doing, watch what I am doing but at the same time he mixes in with the children and sometimes goes around and helps them as well so it doesn't feel as much that pressure of somebody coming in and sitting with a notebook taking down everything that you do. (interview, student, June Lane)

John's style of observing in June Lane has been carefully thought through and is based on his own experiences of being observed by his own college tutors and of his mentorship training course.

> When I am in there I try not to stay too long. . . . I try to vary when I go in, I try to look, obviously at beginnings, obviously at ends but I want to look at middles as well . . . Sometimes I will perhaps do two visits in one lesson with a break in between so that it gives the student a chance to recover as well . . . I try to build that more and more as the week goes on . . . When I go in I don't go and talk to them, I go to the children and help out. I am a second member of staff just like I expect them to be when they are with me. And by talking to the children, by listening obviously, by looking around, you can pick up things. (interview, mentor, June Lane)

These comments from John serve to show firstly, how sensitively classroom observations can be done, and secondly, that mentors across all courses adopted methods similar to this when doing some of their observations. Our research shows that mentors are better placed to carry out this type of approach than the traditional college supervisor because of their familiarity with the class, the school and the student.

Chapter 5

Analyzing the Work of Mentors: The Role

John Sampson and Robin Yeomans

Beryl: They all kept working and progressing, but I felt it was a bit hectic.

Belinda: Shall I go through my notes? Clear and precise instructions. Opening quiet — very good.

Beryl: I thought of that after you said. . . .

Belinda: Need to aim questions slightly lower, then other children become interested. I think you need to get the children closer together. Do you know who wasn't attending?

Beryl: No I wasn't sure.

Belinda: What you did do was to repeat points — you did say (I've got it here) 'What travels in straight lines?' Good knowledge. Good questioning. I'd like to hear some of your questioning in another subject where you are not an expert. Excellent resources.

Beryl: I have a house full of rubbish.

Belinda: The children enjoyed having it all at their fingertips — that was very good. You said, 'Go and get started.' Say, 'You have two minutes to read through the sheet — I want quiet while you are doing it.'

Beryl: I needed to be more precise.

Belinda: 'Tidy up' — give strategies.

Beryl: Give enough time.

Belinda: I've tried going round to groups — whilst some carried on working. Stop individuals and point to the activity they have to tidy up. What would you want to do next?

Beryl: I'd get mirrors and experiment with shadows. Then I'd give them more specific things to do. I'd need to structure it a bit more. (fieldnote of conversation, Bigtown)

The mentor (Belinda) is 'giving feedback' to the student (Beryl). But what does this imply? Is the mentor passing on tips? Perhaps there is an element of commentary on the action so that the student can modify her future practice? Are the mentor's questions designed to lead the student in an apprentice-like way, with the student intended to copy the mentor's practice? Or are they designed to help the student think independently and so devise her own model of effective practice? What then is the mentor doing?

One thing above all is clear from the conversation: the mentor's role is complex, multifaceted, and the way it is performed can change rapidly within the course of a few minutes. Our purpose in this chapter is to attempt to analyze how mentors performed their role, given their perception of what it entailed and the demands students and others placed upon them. Some aspects of the role were made explicit in the briefs agreed between the schools and college and clarified in training sessions, course documents, and conversations with link tutors.

In developing our analysis, we have attempted to make the complex accessible. In doing so we want to emphasize that though we describe mentorship in an ordered way, in action it retains its subtle nature.

An initial analytic concern is to clarify our terminology. Chapters 7 and 8 will refer to mentors' 'personal qualities'. In chapter 6 we shall describe strategies' and 'skills', whereas this chapter refers to 'role'. Yet such terms can be confusing. Is mentoring one role, referring to everything that mentors do, or should we think in terms of many roles, each describing a specific intention? For example, is 'observing' performing a role, selecting a strategy, or using a skill? In this and the next chapter we attempt to make our interpretations clear. Here we summarize our analysis of these terms, the meanings we ascribe to them, and their relationship to one another, insofar as they help to explain and make sense of the ways mentors' behave when confronted with different aspects of their task. The analysis is derived from our observations of and interviews with participants in mentoring settings in the twelve schools.

Role, Strategies, Skills and Qualities: An Overview

We have taken the view that we can most easily make sense of what mentors do if we describe mentoring as a single role. In the context of school-based initial teacher training, we take the mentor's role to mean the set of expectations placed on people called mentors, by students, college tutors, school heads, and other involved parties, in the course of seeking to ensure successful outcomes for students in training in school. The role requires behaviours which, though diffuse in nature, seek to serve that single end. However, some mentor behaviours seem to share the common characteristic that they are concerned with the mentoring context, with the students as people, or with their professional development as aspiring teachers. Hence we suggest that the role has three dimensions, each of which relates to one of these three broad areas of concern. We call these role dimensions 'structural', 'supportive' and 'professional'. We acknowledge that although the significance of a mentors' action may be predominantly within one dimension of the role, it may have implications for other dimensions too. In turn, each dimension has several 'elements' — though we recognize that in some circumstances, some elements may have implications for more than one dimension.

Each element reflects a specific purpose within that dimension, and may be related to a particular phase of a school experience or of a student's development.

We now analyze the role's dimensions further.

We suggest that the structural dimension involves acting to seek to ensure that conditions exist in the school which will enable students to perform as effectively as is possible, given the limitations of their current stage of development. The elements which we have identified within the structural dimension are: 'planner', 'organizer', 'negotiator', and 'inductor'.

The supportive dimension of mentoring is concerned with students as people, and with making them feel comfortable in or minimising the stress of situations they encounter in the school. We suggest that its elements are 'host', 'friend' and 'counsellor'.

Finally, the professional dimension relates to all those activities which are concerned with the students' development as potential teachers. Its elements are 'trainer', 'educator' and 'assessor'.

Within the particular purpose of an element of the mentoring role, mentors have to decide what to do to be effective. That is to say, mentors select the 'strategy' they deem appropriate. Of course, the effectiveness of the strategy selected is itself limited by mentors' ability to act in ways which will enable them to implement the strategy successfully. In other words, for a strategy to be effective, mentors have to have the relevant 'skill'. In turn, this skill may itself have one or more source. It may be a facet of the teacher as a person — a 'personal quality', or it may have been acquired through experience or through professional development of some kind, in particular through mentor training.

The relationship of role dimension and elements to one another is summarised in Table 5.1. This chapter will now focus on how mentors performed their role, in terms of its related dimensions and elements. We leave the following chapter to examine in detail how the elements of the role related to different strategies, how strategies were applied by mentors, and what skills they used in doing so.

The Structural Dimension

Mentors had a key role in preparing the way for students in the school and in the school-based part of their courses. Mentors created the conditions which would enable students to perform as well as they were able. In other words, within their structural role dimension, they were enablers, establishing and modifying social and organizational structures.

Planner

Particularly when the students first came to the school but also later as their and course demands change, it was the mentor who planned the students' programme so that they were deployed in the most mutually beneficial way. This is not to

Table 5.1: Dimensions and elements of the mentor's role

ROLE	ROLE DIMENSION	ROLE ELEMENT
	Structural	Planner Organizer Negotiator Inductor
Mentor	Supportive	Host Friend Counsellor
	Professional	Trainer Educator Assessor

suggest that mentors planned the last detail of the students experience. There were opportunities for students to initiate and to influence the detailed structure of their school experience. This happened several times. But whatever the student initiated, mentors played a part in the necessary organization.

To make the task more complex still in the Articled Teacher Scheme and in the one-year PGCE the mentor also has to be aware that the college-based course is to some extent dependent upon the students gaining certain experiences in the school at particular times. This means that the mentor and the students need to plan well in advance. Dennis, the mentor at Deepvale, explains the way he planned with the students:

> Well very early on, because they had tasks to do from the college they were coming in on the Thursday morning announcing what they had been asked to do and then saying how they intended to do it, they quickly come to the conclusion that they had to be prepared one week in advance for whatever the college demanded . . . So having announced the previous week what the college expected of them, and then fitting it in with other set things in the timetable like games . . . we would then work out who would be in charge of which group, or who would be in charge of the class at certain times during the day. (interview, mentor, Deepvale)

Organizer

Being planner and organizer were closely related. If planning dealt with intentions, then organization was concerned with the necessary conditions for favourable outcomes. However rigorous and ambitious the plans agreed, between students and mentor, effective implementation was more likely if mentors were able to organize conditions conductive to success. Mentors' organizational contribution was concerned with every facet of the student's life in the school. But the emphasis was on student's classroom practice, including the organization of curriculum tasks that related to the college element of the courses.

Mentors needed a clear view of the way ahead if they were to organize the student's day-to-day programme in the school. Typically the structure and detail of the students' teaching commitment was planned by the mentor and students, within guidelines produced by the College. The following examples show how mentors carefully planned and then organized the gradual involvement of the students in the rigours of teaching:

> They started to take groups then; first of all groups that I planned and organized. I told them exactly what to do, so it was more sort of a parent helper role. Then I gave them an outline of the type of thing I wanted to do. Such as, with this particular group I wanted to do symmetry and left them to find some ideas and when they'd found the ideas we discussed it and planned the group together. Then they started to take registration, following the procedure that I use in the morning — which is doing something from the blackboard. They ran through this with the children afterwards, copying exactly what I'd done; and they took stories. Then we developed them planning a group activity . . . (interview, mentor, Greenvale)

> They [the students] would be working with one child then maybe two then a group. Then planning a group and planning two abilities or the same activity with two abilities and finally to whole class planning of work in groups . . . you have this overall plan of where you want them to go. (interview, mentor, Aimshigh)

Negotiator

Mentors' ability to create optimum learning conditions for students also required that they negotiate with colleagues on students' behalves. Mentors' status and credibility within the school were important here. Being deputy head made negotiation easier for some, since making organizational requests to colleagues was an existing part of mentors' deputy head role. Similarly, deputy head mentors could use their close professional relationship with their head to the students' benefit. Non-deputy head mentors relied more on their personal credibility and existing relationships with colleagues.

Mentors had four main negotiating concerns. First, they needed to negotiate time for themselves and students to meet without the distraction of a class. This meant persuading heads or colleagues who had a student to take the mentors' class. Second, they sought opportunities for students to gain access to other classes, in order to observe colleagues at work, interrogate them about classroom practice, or have some teaching time with a different age group. Third, students might want to find out more about a particular curriculum area by talking to the curriculum co-ordinator. Fourth, since there was normally more than one student in a school, effective supervision of students required mentors to negotiate with host class teachers an unambiguous division of responsibilities for observing, reporting on, and debriefing any student not teaching the mentor's class. In one school, Deepvale, the mentor even arranged a visit to the feeder First School. Clearly there are implications for mentors' relationships with colleagues, their status in the schools and their own interpersonal skills.

Mentors also needed to negotiate with link tutors a shared perspective of the nature of effective teaching. Without such a common view, conflicting messages were likely. This tended to be a continuing process in which issues articulated in mentor training sessions were revisited explicitly and implicitly, when mentors and link tutors discussed students development. This subtle negotiation gained considerably when there was a continuing relationship of school and mentor with the college and a specific tutor.

Inductor

Mentors all took conscious steps to give the students insights into the ways of behaving within their classroom and within the school. They inducted them into the schools' systems, in terms of agreed procedures. But they also talked students through some of the informal habits which were part of the shared understandings which had evolved within the schools. Though important to the smooth running of schools and classrooms, these were often unacknowledged, seldom written down, and so could offer particular difficulties to unwary students. With such insights, the students could more rapidly learn to 'fit in', feel 'teacher-like' themselves, and convince the children and other staff by their authentic teacher behaviour. The mentor at June Lane Junior emphasized the importance of the students settling into the school. One way he tried to help this process was:

> To tell them the background of the school, because it's obviously important they know that. Let them know where they are going to be, give them some idea of the timetable, and how we work in the school . . . (interview, mentor, June Lane Junior)

Then the children in the classroom had to be met and the students had to get to know the way the classroom worked. This could be tackled in a variety of ways. Carole, at Carlton cum Chardley, gave the students the chance to:

> Talk to the children in just small groups . . . and that was quite useful because it gave us a chance to find out a little about the children and also for the children to find out who we were and what we were doing there and how long we were going to be there and other things that they were interested in about us, which worked quite well at setting the stage of things. (interview, student, Carlton cum Chardley)

Probably the most common way of dealing with early induction to the children and the way the class operates is that reported by Gail, the mentor at Greenvale:

> She observed to start with, although she joined in with what the children were doing I didn't expect her to do anything very much just to watch what I was doing, answer the children's questions, just generally get the feel of it. Then she went round the first week to see one or two other classes to watch them but generally we took a fairly relaxed attitude about the first week. (interview, mentor, Greenvale)

Gradually, by providing opportunities for the students to observe and to have discussion the mentor was able to induct the student into the class and to some extent the school. In the Articled Teacher and one-year PGCE schemes, mentors and students were able to give a little more time to this aspect than in the BEd scheme. While the induction part of the role happened mainly during students' first days in school, it was often revisited, particularly in connection with uncommon occurrences.

> Gemma (the student) had a case of a vomiting child. She had dealt with it herself as it was just at the start of playtime but both students wondered what you were supposed to do. Gail (the mentor) outlined the school system for dealing with such incidents and with nosebleeds, reminding the students of the importance of wearing plastic gloves if they had to do such clearing up. (fieldnote, Greenvale)

The Supportive Dimension

The supportive dimension of mentoring is closely linked to the nature of the relationship created between mentor and student (see chapter 7). A mutually open and trusting relationship was both the means to, and the outcome of, effective support. Mentors recognized that students' time in school could be stressful in several ways. First, they were outsiders, experiencing an unknown staff culture, whose rules and norms they needed to assimilate if they were to learn or behave authentically. Second, authentic teacher behaviour in the eyes of the pupils was itself an important condition of successful performance of the role of teacher, students could not take for granted pupils' sympathetic understanding. Third, students knew that however supportive they found the school context, their performance was under close scrutiny. Success and failure had a precise meaning and, in the assessed phases, carried career implications. In other words, school experience had many of the characteristics of a 'life' event.

Thus, the supportive dimension of mentors' role engaged them in minimizing possible stress for students, and ensuring that, when stressful situations were encountered, they enhanced students' self-awareness and became learning experiences.

Host

Mentors initially acted as a host when they welcomed students on behalf of the whole school. It was then that the mentor and student began to form a relationship, that students were introduced to school rules and procedures. These early moments were important and recognized as such by students in particular. They appreciated the efforts that were made to welcome them as can be seen from the comments at June Lane Junior:

> We came here the first day and actually being made to feel quite important because the mentor had the day off. Showed us around the school, spent time talking to us. He showed us round all the classrooms, showed us where all the resources were. So he had gone out of his way to help us . . . So from the start we didn't have a negative view at all. It was very positive from the start. (interview, student, June Lane Junior)

Similarly mentors saw the importance of a good start, the mentor at Greenvale remembered how she had tried to make her students welcome by acting as sponsoring member who initiated relationships with the staff in general:

> I took her round the school, on the first day and I made sure she met all the other members of staff so that she felt at home. She came in for the day beforehand which meant that she met the staff informally on a Baker day, which was very helpful because she felt she knew everybody. (interview, mentor, Greenvale)

The student, Gina, settled rapidly so that: 'I think by the time Gemma (a late student entrant) came I felt quite at home.' (interview, student, Greenvale).

Friend

Friendship as a description of mentor-student relationships is considered in chapter 7. Here it is relevant to note that some mentors were particularly adept at handling role conflict, and so managed to incorporate the extremes of assessor and friend within their role. Of course, friendship could be a consequence of always being a source of positive comment. Fiona was an example of a mentor who found no conflict between friendship and criticism, as the following extract shows:

> Fiona enjoys dealing with adults. She deliberately tried to get to know her students.
> 'I don't find dealing with people hard. I didn't find dealing with [students] at all difficult. I just treated them as though they were . . . more members of staff. I found out about them. They became friends.'
> She deals with them in the same way as she treats other members

of staff. 'I found it easy because they were friends to be critical. But again, that depends on the personality of the mentor. That is how I deal with other members of staff. I do it on a personal level. I am a person who likes the interaction with people.'

Fiona is like both personal and professional tutor. Her relationship with Florence and Freda [students] has to last two years. Like other mentors in the scheme she has had to deal with students in tears. Although she believes in training, for some aspects of mentorship, her view is that interpersonal skills cannot be taught. Some people are natural mentors.

'I think they have either got it or they haven't.' (Clarke, 1992a, p. 9)

Counsellor

The counselling element in the mentors' role had two sides. Mentors needed to help students cope with judgments on their teaching. The help was particularly needed when negative classroom experiences had undermined students' self-belief, or when circumstances required that they consider their long-term professional future. In an extreme case, a mentor might help a student deal with the consequences of short-term or long-term failure. For student and mentor alike, counselling phases might generate ambivalent feelings. The mentor who was the judge of success and failure also carried the responsibility of reconciling a student to the judgment and building from it.

Where closeness developed, particularly in long-term mentoring, trust could grow. Consequently, some mentors found that their role extended beyond immediate professional concerns. One link tutor commented that:

> I think the students at Greenvale feel they can talk to Gail about anything. She fulfils both a professional and a personal tutor's role with them. I know in fact that feedback from Gail and from Grace, the head, tells me some of the personal problems the students are having which otherwise I wouldn't have known about. (interview, link tutor, Greenvale)

Some mentors recognized the possible conflict between the supportive and professional dimensions of their role, and sought to adjust their relationships accordingly:

> They need to be able to talk to me about their problems but it could be a little difficult if I needed to be a little critical of something so I think there should be a slight distance. (interview, mentor, Endsleigh)

Here the mentor attempted to balance the apparent conflict stemming from the need for positive relationships with the distancing required for professional judgment.

The Professional Dimension

The primary purpose of the mentoring role was to help students towards becoming effective teachers. As chapter 10 suggests, the task carried different implications for each student. However, in broad terms the mentors' professional task had three facets. First, students needed to be helped to cope with the demands of the particular teaching situations they met. Second, some mentors tried to extend students' capacities to analyze and generalize from specific situations. Implicitly, they took Hirst's view that:

> It is by learning to judge accurately themselves their success and failure and by modification of their practice in the light of the characteristics of successful practice that they personally develop the necessary capacities. (Hirst, 1990)

They wanted students to gain a level of insight which would enable students to select from their own repertoire of skills. This could then be deployed to meet new situations with the same class, and ultimately in contests yet to be encountered. The third facet was that whilst helping students towards these goals, mentors needed to assess students' progress formatively, and in most cases also make periodic summative assessments. These three facets equate to the professional role elements of trainer, educator and assessor.

Trainer

Mentors acted as trainers when they took steps which enabled students to respond more effectively to current teaching needs. Of course, they hoped that if students successfully incorporated mentors' suggestions into their teaching, the students' long-term professional practice would also be modified. However, any such change tended to be derived from observing mentors at work or listening to advice, explanations or descriptions which reflected the mentors' own strategies for specific situations. In short, the emphasis in training was on successful implementation of the mentors' solutions.

Training was a necessary part of students' development, particularly in the early apprentice-like phases of PGCE and Articled Teacher Partnership. However, there was a temptation to extend training inappropriately. As experts, mentors drew on extensive experience, could identify underlying problems and suggest relevant strategies. As novices, students tended to recognize mentors' expertize, having observed their classroom practice, perhaps noted their status and credibility in the school, and knowing that the college confirmed their mentor status. Consequently students might expect to be told how to deal with their class, particularly if it was also the mentors' own. A mentor's legitimate concern for the needs of their class might also lead to a narrow interpretation of the mentor role. Strategies which a mentor used successfully with that group of children were safer for mentor, student and class than encouraging a student to experiment. Thoughtful commitment to students' development was needed for mentors to recognize that only applying short-term solutions carried long-term dangers for students. They might become unthinking and unquestioning adherents to all the mentor said and did, unquestioning followers of one model who found it difficult to meet new circumstances, a concern that chapter 9 considers more fully. Fortunately the TEAM evidence is that students and mentors were often aware of this danger. Mentors were concerned about the danger that by always telling students they inhibited students' capacity to think for themselves:

> I find it difficult not to give them answers, my answers. I try to suggest ways they can discover for themselves. Yesterday I suggested that they transform the library area into a shop. Should I have shown them or helped them? Am I giving enough guidance? Or am I giving them too many choices or possibilities. (fieldnote, conversation with mentor, Kenleigh)

Educator

To behave as educator was to be a mentor who enabled students to become autonomous, self-referential, teachers, capable of objectively analyzing their own and others' professional practice.

Summarizing the ideas of Handal (1990) and Smyth (1991), Day (1993) has described the relationship between constructing, deconstructing and reconstructing practice. He suggests that in order for teachers to move beyond 'Planning and acting (constructing practice)', they need to spend time on 'Observation and reflection (deconstructing practice)'. Day further suggests that the concept of reflective practice (Schon, 1983) is an incomplete recipe for effective professional development:

> Reflection will need to be analytic and involve dialogue with others. Thus Schon's (1983) notion of 'reflective practice' may itself be criticised for failing to deal with the importance of the discursive, dialogical dimension of learning, which can only emerge from the processes of confrontation and reconstruction. (Day, 1993, p. 86)

Mentors were well-placed to be students' dialogical partners. If as trainers they were largely engaged in helping students construct practice, as educators their concern shifted to helping students deconstruct teaching sessions so that they began to reconstruct their version of effective practice and ultimately to amend their professional schemata. In other words, reconstruction was concerned with students' long-term development rather than merely with the here and now. The intention was that students would develop their own, personal, flexible model of professional practice. This would enable them to adapt their teaching model to new circumstances. It was the mentors' skill in moving students towards independence characterised by self-generated reconstruction that was the essence of effective educative mentoring. At Endsleigh the mentor described her efforts to move students from dependence to independence as a weaning process:

> As there became less need to direct I encouraged them to think more for themselves and to take some responsibility for their own learning. My role has been to answer their questions, but it is also about focusing their minds on various points that they can observe, so that they learn for themselves, encouraging them. (interview, mentor, Endsleigh)

Chapter 9 explores further the implications of educative mentor behaviour.

Assessor

Mentors were also assessors. They had daily access to students' work in school and so were well-placed to make assessments of the students' fitness to teach. Formative assessment at an informal level was a continuous process in all forms of mentorship. Through regular observation and feedback, mentors explicitly assessed the students whilst they carried out the other dimensions of the role. TEAM research did not include the periods of assessed school experience in the one-year PGCE. Evidence of mentors acting as formal assessors is derived from the Articled Teacher Scheme and the third year BEd school experience.

Assessed blocks required formal written interim feedback from mentors half way through the block experience. It was intended as an indication to the students of their performance at that stage but did not become part of a student's college records. Since it provided a summary of the student's progress to date and gave clear indications of areas that needed further consideration, this interim report was both formative and summative. The final summative written report carried a pass/fail recommendation, so the interim report's written nature also carried intended implications of formality. It was an indication to students of possible success and failure. Chapter 7 explores the implications of assessment for mentor-student relations.

There were obvious advantages in having the mentor as assessor. They knew the school, the class and the children far better than any visiting tutor could. They were also likely to have an established relationship with other teachers students worked with, and so were better able to access other perspectives on students' school performance. Mentors were able to discuss with students their performance more frequently than could a visiting tutor. Of course, mentors lacked an overview of a range of students in a variety of settings, and so the final confirmatory pass/fail decision rested with the College. In practice, the arrangement created few difficulties, since there was regular contact and discussion between mentor and link tutor.

The student's view of the assessment element of the mentor's role is informative. How far the assessment element dominated their perception of their mentor seemed to be influenced by other aspects of the mentor-student relationship. At June Lane the mentor had one student in his class (Jane) but the second (Jenny) was in another class. The perception of the mentor and the other class teacher was that the students reacted differently to the mentor's presence in their classrooms. Jane was less affected by him because he was also her class teacher. The class teacher told John the mentor:

> Last week (Jenny) was worried about you being in, more so than me; she is used to me because I have stayed in there so often, so I think she is much better with me and I think because you have got the title of mentor she is a little more bothered about you. (fieldnote, conversation, June Lane)

On the whole, students seem to appreciate having a mentor as an assessor:

> I certainly think its better for the mentor to make the final assessment because they have got a better view of how you have been getting on. I keep stressing that point but I think it's really good. Because a lecturer maybe come in once a week and they see one lesson and it may go particularly badly and it may make you feel awful and the next time they come in it might go well. Having the mentor in all the time means he sees different parts of your lessons and sees how you are developing with the children I think they can see more and give you more. . . . (interview, student, June Lane)

There were tensions for mentors in being the assessors. First, when they reported to students on their progress face to face, mentors stated openly what might only have been tacit in other circumstances. Second, they managed the subtleties of reporting assessment, particularly at the interim report stage, so as to provide both warning or praise and stimulus for the student. There was skill in not making the report so positive or so critical that it was a disincentive to renewed effort and so limited further progress:

> If you make the interim report too glowing then the student will think 'I am doing all right' and sit back and not progress in the second two weeks. You don't want to make it too critical becase there is nothing worse than somebody who is continually knocking someone. So it's a very fine line between praise and enough positive criticism so that the students still progress in their second half. (interview, mentor John, March)

Third, such written confrontations of students with their strengths and weaknesses could be personally threatening to mentors and students alike. The mentor at June Lane had had to give a student:

. . . a good kick up the backside . . . but he needed it and if he hadn't had it then there would have been serious doubts about whether he actually passed . . . But as I say I didn't enjoy it. (interview, mentor, June Lane)

From a student's perspective the experience of assessment could be undermining:

I felt like the rug had been pulled from under me completely. Everything gradually got more formal and an atmosphere of assessment was created. Because there was concern about my teaching practice so all the attention was focused on me. (interview, student, Endsleigh)

Fourth, there was the responsibility of deciding whether the student should pass or fail. The role of a link tutor is examined in chapter 12 and has some bearing here. It is worth noting at this stage that mentors in the College's schemes made this decision once during the year. Mentors did signal some students as possible failures, link tutors agreed and the judgment was confirmed by external examiners. So although a failure decision was difficult, it was not shirked.

Conclusion

We consider that the complexities of mentorship can best be understood if it is seen as a single role. The role has structural, supportive and professional dimensions, each of which contains specific elements which reflect different modes of mentor behaviour. These are planner, organizer, negotiator and inductor (structural elements); host, friend and counsellor (supportive elements); trainer, educator and assessor (professional elements). Elements of the role were performed at different times in response to predicted needs and particular phases of school experience. But needs could also change from moment to moment. The emphasis within the role also varied with different mentors, so that not all mentors exploited all elements of the role to the same extent. We have suggested that closely linked to analysis of the elements and dimensions of the mentor role is an understanding of how these relate to the particular strategies mentors select and the skills they deploy. In the next chapter we shall examine the nature of this connection.

Chapter 6

Analyzing the Work of Mentors:
Strategies, Skills and Qualities

John Sampson and Robin Yeomans

The previous chapter analyzed the dimensions and elements of the mentor's role. In this chapter we explore how mentors implemented their role in terms of the strategies they developed, the skills they applied, and the qualities they displayed. Since our purpose is to clarify the nature of mentoring strategies, skills and qualities, we have not attempted to make comparisons between mentors, except where comparison would help understanding.

As with our examination of roles, we offer an ordered analysis of what was often complex and apparently random mentor behaviour. Before we consider that analysis more closely, we need to make several general points about the range of strategies and skills individual mentors used.

First, we suggest that our analysis reflects the dominant strategies and skills used by mentors in a variety of schools, but we do not suggest that all mentors displayed the full range of strategies and skills. Such uniformity was not to be expected. Mentors were individuals with their own strengths and weaknesses. Moreover, each worked within unique sets of circumstances, and with different students, all of whom had particular needs. Consequently some strategies were more appropriate to particular circumstances than others.

Second, to some extent the strategies and skills mentors used at a particular time often depended on which dimension of their role had relevance to a particular phase of a student's experience. For example, negotiating and informing were dominant strategies when mentors first met students, because this was a time when the structural dimension of their role was particularly prominent. Within the professional dimension, modelling and demonstrating strategies were conspicuous in the early partnership phases of PGCE and Articled Teacher courses.

Third, we suggest that there was a link of particular role dimensions and elements with specific strategies and skills, but that this was not an exclusive link. Mentors used an extensive range of strategies, broadly related to particular dimensions of the mentoring role. But we recognize that these overlapped significantly into other dimensions. Similarly, although some strategies necessitated particular skills, others were more broadly applied. In addition, mentors drew on particular personal qualities in relation to different role dimensions. Hence we refer to 'dominant' strategies, skill dimensions and elements, and personal qualities.

Within the chapter we now analyze mentor strategies before considering skills separately. Our analysis of mentors' strategies and skills follows the broad structure of 'dimensions' and 'elements' we have adopted for our discussion of roles. Finally we shall consider how far a mentor's capacity to deploy appropriate strategies and skills was dependent on their personal qualities.

Strategies

Here we attempt to explain our analysis of strategies by giving examples from our evidence. However, it is important to note that a single action may legitimately have several strategic implications. For example, the June Lane mentor sought to develop a student's understanding by focusing on specific aspects of her work, but he used that strategy to generalise from a particular incident:

> *John:* The key thing there in the appraisal is being prepared to alter things as you go along. It's thinking on your feet and being able to say to yourself 'why did that go wrong, how did it go wrong and how can I do it right?' As you found with the drama lesson particularly. You felt it went badly, I didn't feel it went as wrong as you thought it did. (conversation with student, June Lane)

We suggest that beyond the complexity of a single conversation was an overarching ordered structure. Certain strategies tend to cluster with each of the structural and supportive dimensions, without bearing any close relationship to particular elements. Within the professional dimension, the relationship was more specific. One group of strategies tends to cluster with the trainer element and a second with that of educator. However, there was a third cluster which related to either as circumstances demanded.

Table 6.1 gives an overview. The table is not able to show how the choice of strategies was affected by time in the long and short term. In the time-span of a whole school experience, there was a tendency for strategies related to the structural role to predominate in students' early days in school. They were also the dominant agenda of preliminary visit days. Students need informing about unfamiliar routines, teaching arrangements had to be made, and mentors spent time negotiating with staff who would be affected by the students' presence. The supportive dimension was important too in the early stages. As hosts, mentors tried to make students feel comfortable in settings populated by strangers by chatting to them about people, the school, and themselves and introducing students informally to their new colleagues. For the rest of the students' time in school, supportive strategies tended to be used in response to particular needs, but could also be important at times of assessment.

Table 6.1

ROLE DIMENSION	ROLE ELEMENT	DOMINANT STRATEGIES
structural	organizer inductor planner negotiator	negotiating informing
supportive	host friend/colleague counsellor	chatting encouraging praising joking
professional	trainer	demonstrating commentating prompting suggesting/advising coaching telling confronting
	trainer or educator	collaborating persuading explaining reviewing modelling
	educator	discussing focusing generalizing reflecting back questioning facilitating
	assessor	observing recording formalizing communicating feedback (confronting) (reviewing)

In the early stages of students' experience of school, the training emphasis was deemed appropriate to students' novice status, and so modelling, telling, coaching, suggesting seemed most appropriate. Educator strategies took much more time. They were based on the assumption that students needed to develop their own perceptual and analytic skills or needed to work out for themselves the specific implications of some generalizing statement, rather than being told or shown. Mentors were short of time, so it was always tempting to take a short cut, suggest to students possible courses of action — or even directly tell them what they should do.

In the time-span of a single feedback conversation there could be a complex pattern of strategies. Chapter 5 opened with a feedback conversation in which the mentor (Belinda) used a wide repertoire of strategies as she sought to develop her student's skill and insight.

Beryl:	They all kept working and progressing, but I felt it was a bit hectic.
Belinda:	Shall I go through my notes? (reviewing) Clear and precise instructions. (reflecting back) Opening quiet — very good. (praising)
Beryl:	I thought of that after you said . . .
Belinda:	Need to aim questions slightly lower, then other children become interested. (telling) I think you need to get the children closer together. (suggesting) Do you know who wasn't attending? (questioning)
Beryl:	No I wasn't sure.
Belinda:	What you did do was to repeat points (generalizing) — you did say (I've got it here) 'What travels in straight lines?' (reflecting back) Good knowledge. Good questioning. (praising) I'd like to hear some of your questioning in another subject where you are not an expert. (prompting) Excellent resources. (praising)
Beryl:	I have a house full of rubbish.
Belinda:	The children enjoyed having it all at their fingertips (reflecting back) — that was very good. (praising) You said. 'Go and get started.' Say, 'You have two minutes to read through the sheet — I want quiet while you are doing it.' (telling)
Beryl:	I needed to be more precise.
Belinda:	'Tidy up' — give strategies. (telling)
Beryl:	Give enough time.
Belinda:	I've tried going round to groups — whilst some carried on working. Stop individuals and point to the activity they have to tidy up. (telling) What would you want to do next? (questioning)
Beryl:	I'd get mirrors and experiment with shadows. Then I'd give them more specific things to do. I'd need to structure it a bit more. (fieldnote of conversation, Bigtown)

The complexity of the Belinda/Beryl conversation above is partly explained by Belinda's perception that Beryl was in a developing but still uncertain phase of her partnership. Consequently, Belinda shifts back and forth between trainer and educator elements of her role, interspersed with the praising strategy of supportive colleague, as she responded to the dual need to sustain short and long-term development.

Our analysis now considers briefly each strategy we have identified.

Strategies Within the Structural Dimension

Negotiating was an essential means by which mentors prepared the ground for students' experience at all stages, but was particularly important in achieving an orderly start:

> The first day they come in I always arrange with the Head that he will release me so that I can spend almost the whole day with the students in the school. Because I think its very important that they settle into the school. (interview, mentor, June Lane)

Informing: whilst negotiations with colleagues of all kinds helped prepare optimum conditions, students needed to acquire rapidly a considerable amount of information about the school, its' staff and children, before there was any possibility that they could convincingly adopt the guise of teacher within the school. Mentors needed:

> To tell them the background of the school. Let them know where they are going to be, give them some idea of the timetable, and how we work in the school . . . (interview, mentor, June Lane)

Strategies Within the Supportive Dimension

Chatting was a valuable way of helping students to rapidly feel part of a school. When the June Lane mentor suggested that students:

> Come down to the staffroom at playtime and just generally have a moan or just listen to what else is going on in the school itself.

He was concerned about more than a chance to unwind. Far from being trivial and unimportant, chat was 'a high level activity', by which mentors and others gave students access to the unspoken values, attitudes, beliefs and norms which were the cultural framework of appropriate behaviour in the school (Nias, Southworth and Yeomans, 1989, p. 79). Through casual chat, mentors shared with students something of the school folklore, introduced them to other sources of help, shared with them the current key concerns affecting the whole school, and enabled them to acquire the cultural knowledge which would help them through the hazards of unwritten understandings governing relationships with other staff and pupils in general. In short, mentors helped students acquire the means of behaving like an insider.

The casualness of chat was also an oblique means of commenting to students on their performance in circumstances where a mentor judged that confronting an issue might have been counterproductive:

If the penny doesn't drop . . . If it was something like, the children were not always listening, so they start getting noisy because of the lack of clarity of instructions perhaps, I would say 'you have probably noticed . . .' (interview, mentor, Bigtown)

In the uncertainties of their early weeks in school, at times when teaching sessions were particularly unsuccessful, students responded positively to mentors who were encouraging. The encouragement was especially important with an unconfident student who was apprehensive about a coming teaching session.

I was very lacking in confidence, so the mentor gave me some advice about how to go about it . . .

She was just trying to do her best for me — supportive and encouraging rather than being negative. (interview, student Beryl, Bigtown)

At other times too, a few words of considered approval could be sufficient to instil self-belief.

If I went into a lesson with Belinda unprepared, I could show her what I had planned, what I had thought about doing and how I was going to do it and she would say, 'Yes OK, go off and do it.' Because she knew I could do it, I knew I could do it. (interview, student Bill, Bigtown)

Similarly, praising was a widely used strategy for boosting students' self-esteem:

On one occasion, I did a particularly good lesson and Carole had obviously (noticed) because she came and stopped and congratulated me and said that was a very good lesson. I thought 'That was nice, positive.' (interview, student, Carlton)

They could then more easily accept advice and focus on areas for development:

When I was finished then the first things she said to me were positive and praising and then she could, without hurting my feelings, say 'Well, why don't you, how would it be if you tried such and such?' — So I was able to take that very well and I felt uplifted. It gave me some power. (interview, student, Bigtown)

You were good at picking out particular children and getting them to show the others. (fieldnote of feedback conversation, mentor, Kenleigh)

Joking was one means by which a mentor indicated to students that their mentor role could be open and supportive. A well-developed, supportive mentor-student relationship was both marked and further consolidated by the use of humour:

Belinda uses Bill practising at the board as a model for the children of how to do handwriting. To the children: 'Look at the concentration on Mr H's face. That's how careful you have to be.' Bill turns, grins, and simulates throwing the chalk at Belinda. (fieldnote, Bigtown)

Strategies Within the Professional Dimension

Since the professional dimension predominated within the mentor's role, the range of strategies within it was complex. We have followed our earlier analysis by separating into four groups strategies concerned with students' professional development (see Table 6.1). Three of the groups relate to the trainer, educator and assessor elements of the role. The fourth is a set of overlapping strategies. These could relate to training and education, depending on the mentors' intentions and/or students' perceptiveness.

Trainer Strategies

The purpose of trainer strategies was to use action and talk to help students deal with a specific situation. It was largely up to the student to generalize from the outcome. There were significant variables in how explicit help was. At one extreme, demonstrating or commentating might invite students to adopt a strategy by implication. At the other, telling students what to do, or confronting them with their limitations was sometimes an effective means of achieving short-term change.

Some mentors used demonstrating to provide students with a model that they wanted students to discuss afterwards. Typically a mentor might offer a demonstration lesson for a curriculum area like PE or teach a whole class session when that was not the mentor's normal teaching method. This was especially the case with early school experience blocks, when students were more likely to meet unfamiliar situations:

I have been getting them to tail me, observe me, talk to the children about their work and ask me questions. (interview, mentor, Endsleigh)

What she did was demonstrated how she would do a lesson that I have said I was frightened about. (interview, student, Bigtown)

Commentating was a strategy available to mentors who had two students in their own classroom, as in early partnership phases:

It was a good idea to have them both in the classroom to start with, because its much easier to talk about things as they are happening . . . (interview, mentor, Greenvale)

At Bigtown, a glass screen between the classroom and corridor meant that it was possible for the mentor, sitting outside, to share with one student a running commentary on the activity of the other working with the class:

> *Interviewer:* When Beryl (student) was teaching Belinda (mentor) seemed to sometimes talk to you about what was going on.
>
> *Bill:* Yes, that certainly happened; last week she was talking about what went on and she would share her notes of what she has said about Beryl. (interview, student, Bigtown)

Mentors sometimes delayed intervention and waited for students to become self-educating. Where such strategies were slow in succeeding, prompting could be an effective stimulus:

> In front of the student I would tell my class off; not in relation to the student, but by saying 'You know how to tidy up, you know where I expect you to put things, it doesn't matter who is in here.' Hopefully the student is then listening and thinking 'I should have told them to do that'. (interview, mentor, Bigtown)

Suggesting/advising was a strategy widely used when mentors were trying to move students towards making their own decisions about how to proceed, but with some ideas to work from. What was in the students' interests could be contrary to the mentor's inclination:

> I find it difficult not to give them my answers. I try to suggest ways they can discover for themselves. Yesterday I suggested they transformed the library area into a shop. (fieldnote on conversation with mentor, Endsleigh)

Advising a student to develop self-awareness could be an effective strategy:

> The most help I could give was to advise her to listen to other people who can (read aloud) and read into a tape recorder. The result was that she said 'yes, I did sound awful'. (interview, mentor, Hillyway)

When mentors dealt with the fine detail of imminent or current performance, they regularly chose coaching as the means of refining the nuances of students' teaching skills. Coaching required closely defined instructions or suggestions directing specific actions. Sometimes coaching happened during the stage of final preparation:

> You should just manoeuvre yourself so that you are next to S and very quietly you speak directly to him and say 'This is not acceptable. I want

you to do this and if you don't, this is the consequence' I think he will understand that you mean no nonsense. (fieldnote of conversation mentor to student, Kenleigh)

But if circumstances permitted, a mentor might coach unobtrusively whilst events were happening:

Belinda would always ask beforehand if we wanted her there. She would give you a nudge or a wink if you were obviously floundering, or give you ideas of what you could do. (interview, student, Bigtown)

In some circumstances mentors gave students direct instructions on how to deal with specific situations. Some of these were written down, leaving no room for misinterpretation, nor, perhaps, for the student to think things through for themselves. Mentors appeared to have several motives for telling, which often happened as part of feedback after a student had taught. Sometimes a student might not have used a minor but an essential teaching strategy:

Begin tidying up before 12.15 to avoid a slow start to the afternoon session. (fieldnote of written comment in student's file, Deepvale)

Some issues were too important for equivocation. Safety was one example:

Make sure that you are moving along all the time so that the children aren't queuing behind you. I have just put up a list of the rules in the hall, so they understand the codes of practice. Emphasize that if they don't follow it, it's dangerous. (fieldnote of feedback conversation, mentor and student, Kenleigh)

Moreover, mentors did not always wait indefinitely for spontaneous insight to be achieved, knowing that students tended to welcome teaching tips:

There does come a time when, as with children, you can see the frustration setting in, or if you can see the student doesn't know what they are supposed to be looking for, then you have got to tell them. (interview, mentor, June Lane)

Mentors tended to use sparingly the strategy of confronting, in response to situations where they felt they had no appropriate alternative, such as when students failed to prepare lessons carefully. Mentors did so knowing that the interview could be difficult for both parties:

It comes back to this: you are not criticising you are trying to help all the time. But it needed to be done sharply. Now I did find that difficult. Not pleasant. The student didn't enjoy the experience either. You could tell by his face that he wasn't a happy person. (interview, mentor, June Lane)

However being confronted with the implications of their own actions was seen as a necessary part of students' learning:

We had an incident with one of the students who had spoken quite sharply to a child. . . . Now unfortunately the very same child has a bed wetting problem. So consequently he wet the bed that night. Mum quite rightly phoned us up and said that he'd had a problem with a new teacher who'd snapped at her son . . . so obviously we had to speak to the student about this. To begin with she was very defensive and said had I (the mentor) not had to work with a different group of children in another class this wouldn't have happened because I would have known the children. So we had to really pull her back on that and say 'No that isn't the case in fact. Let's talk it through.' (interview, mentor, Aimshigh)

Consequently a cathartic experience could also be therapeutic:

I saw one lesson of Freda's where she was doing quite a few things (wrong), not major things, but things that had to be tackled . . . She said 'You are going to talk about the lesson aren't you?' and I said 'And you are going to cry.' (because I know Freda cries) 'I would cry if there was a reversal of roles. But the things I am going to say to you are not big criticisms, they're to help you.' After the talk she did cry. But she came back after half term a new teacher, and she had a brilliant time. Fantastic. Because she had listened. (interview, mentor, Flenley)

Trainer or Educator Strategies

The learning implications of some strategies depended on the context, the mentor's purpose or the student, rather than on the intrinsic nature of the strategies. There was a cluster of strategies which might have a training effect or an educative one, depending on one or more of these factors. Each was less or more educative according to how far it was intended to help students develop insight into fundamental teaching principles, or placed on students the onus of interpretation and decision. The cluster included collaborating, persuading, explaining, reviewing and modelling.

Collaborating took several forms. One form was co-planning of a student session. The mentor could with ease feed in their knowledge of the children to help the student match work and contribute ideas for activities, whilst leaving the overall planning responsibility with students:

We have planned some lessons together. For instance with a particular maths session we decided on a focus and I talked through the sorts of things I would expect the children to be able to do and the things that some would find difficult and why, and we discussed how it might be organized. (interview, mentor, Endsleigh)

An alternative form of collaboration was co-working. The value of co-working was that it established an interactive teaching relationship between student and mentor from which the student could gain insight. The more the student led, with the mentor the subordinate partner, the more co-working was educative.

Beryl and Belinda sit side by side talking to the children who sit around them on the floor. Beryl leads in the discussion, but Belinda listens and joins in at one stage with her own contribution. (fieldnote, Bigtown)

It could also be a helpful strategy for creating informal opportunities for assessment.

Co-working contrasted with parallel working, where students and mentor worked with separate groups concurrently. But this strategy had limited training or education implications, since its value as a way of giving limited teaching experience was offset by the lack of opportunity for the mentor to observe, or comment on the student's performance.

Mentors sometimes used strategies which were intended to point students in what the mentor considered the right direction, whilst still leaving the choice to the student. The first was persuading, whose essence was described by the June Lane mentor:

It's very easy to persuade a student to use word processing, — but that's the right word, it's persuade. It's not 'you will use a word processor with the children,' . . . It's 'Have you thought about doing this?' (interview, mentor, June Lane)

Such persuasion is here seen in action in a feedback session:

The next stage now is to look at some of the other things you can use the computer for; maybe some art package; maybe some data handling. See how you can fit those into your plan. Try and do it before you start, rather than thinking, 'Oh gosh yes, I can fit it in then' I know it's not always easy but it's something that you need to have done. (fieldnote of conversation, mentor and student, June Lane)

The second was explaining, when mentors gave reasons for particular teaching decisions, confirming the appropriateness of students' choice of tactics:

She felt that if I had spent a long time with [the less able children] on Thursday morning, I would have had to spend exactly the same amount of time with them on the Friday morning and the result would have been that the rest of the class would have suffered and the quality of work might not have been so good. (interview, student, Bigtown)

or clarified general principles:

> If you are going to work out in the corridor, make sure the doors are wide open so you have got your eye on the children all the time. It only needs something silly to happen — somebody sticks some scissors into somebody or a pencil into somebody and you can then end up in all sorts of trouble. So long as you have taken reasonable precautions then you have covered yourself. (fieldnote of conversation, mentor, June Lane)

Both the above extracts also show reviewing in progress. Reviewing was a form of coaching after the event. Mentors confirmed or recommended student strategies by talking through the detail of a student's lesson.

The effects of modelling are aptly expressed through a student's experience:

> It's like spending time with anybody; if you spend an incredible amount of time with them you find that aspects of that person do become part of you. (interview, student, Endsleigh)

Mentors provided a role model for students, sometimes as a planned outcome of initial phases such as partnership in PGCE and Articled Teacher schemes. Some mentors were aware of the student audience, and deliberately provided an unacknowledged demonstration. Equally, the impetus to adopt the mentor's model might come from students, who consciously based their classroom behaviour on that of the mentor, so that they 'learnt by being in her classroom, watching what she does and absorbing things' (student, Endsleigh). Students relied on their mentors as role models for issues such as judging appropriate noise levels (Endsleigh), or moving around the room and how to talk to children (Bigtown).

Students' own perceptiveness, sensitivity and experience were the main limitations on how far students learnt by working with mentors who were themselves skilled teachers. In one instance:

> That (organizational skills) partly came through watching what she was doing. It was largely observation on our part. (interview, student, Carlton)

Modelling was an especially important way of acquiring the classroom management skills, which would enable students to work effectively within mentors' classrooms. Mentor and class had evolved shared understandings about appropriate behaviour. Students who wished to operate successfully in that classroom needed to be aware of and build on these. For example, following a lesson in which he had some difficulty with control, a student at Deepvale seemed to be working appropriately as far as the children were concerned, when he copied his mentor, Dennis, to gain the class's attention:

> Derek asked for quiet by putting his hand up. Gradually the class re-
> spond by putting their hands up. Then Derek asks them to tidy their
> papers . . . [I] checked with Dennis, and this is his usual way of asking
> for quiet and attention. (fieldnote, Deepvale)

Educator Strategies

Educator strategies were those whose intentions were to reduce student dependence on support and advice and develop their capacity to think for themselves.
Many mentors tried to ensure that students emerged from the teacher education
process as articulate, largely autonomous professionals, who possessed the means
of achieving further self-generated learning, and had a broad perspective on the
nature of professional practice. The predominant strategies used to achieve these
outcomes were of two kinds. Through dialogue, discussing, focusing, and generalizing were concerned with helping students to move their perspective from
immediate classroom means and ends to the wider and longer-term applications
and implications of everyday solutions to classroom needs. Reflecting, questioning, and facilitating had a similar purpose, but by progressively reducing intervention from the mentors' perspective, imposed on students the growing responsibility
for self-analysis.

Discussing implied that mentor and students engaged in constructive dialogue about teaching. The strategy assumed a mutual exchange of experience and
perspectives. In short, such dialogues had the quality of a conversation between
colleagues about professional issues:

> John: I do that as well. I get totally involved with one child and I forget
>   that there are twenty-seven others in the room.
> Jane: I was conscious of it anyway, but when you actually said to me,
>   I thought well yes, I was getting involved with a group. (fieldnote
>   of conversation, mentor and student, June Lane)

The process required that students articulated views about the detail of effective
classroom practice. The intended outcomes were refinement of students' thinking about their teaching skills, the nurturing of a philosophy of teaching and
education and an enhanced capacity to articulate:

> If a child is to learn then they need to have time to think and talk about
> that experience, making the experience a lot clearer in your mind. Well
> there's no difference between them learning and us learning. There's a
> need to talk about things. (interview, student, Endsleigh)

It was also important that students develop the capacity to discriminate within
the vast quantity of information emerging from teaching contexts:

As there became less need to direct, I encouraged the students to think more for themselves and take some responsibility for their own learning. My role has been to answer their questions, but it is also about focusing their minds on various points that they can observe and learn for themselves. (interview, mentor, Endsleigh)

Focusing was also a means of broadening students' perspectives beyond the detail of classroom practice:

The key thing in evaluating is being prepared to alter things as you go along. It's thinking on your feet really and being able to say to yourself why did that go wrong, how did it go wrong and how can I do it right. (fieldnote of conversation, mentor and student, June Lane)

Focusing was regularly used in conjunction with generalizing. When generalizing, mentors attempted to move the students' frame of reference from the detail of specific incidents to consideration of the broad principles which they exemplified. They addressed key professional concerns, such as children as individuals:

You realise that each child is an individual and you can't deal with all the children in exactly the same way. (fieldnote of conversation, mentor and student, June Lane)

teacher 'withitness'

They talk about teachers having to have eyes in the back of their head. You have got to be very alert and aware of what needs doing or what needs picking up. Or if there is something that is potentially dangerous like for example if a sharp pair of scissors have been left lying around. (fieldnote of conversation, mentor and student, Hillyway)

how teachers improve:

You have built on what you have done so far each time. You have looked at what's gone wrong and tried to analyse where it's gone wrong and tried to see how you can improve it. (mentor to student, June Lane)

Reflecting back was an important means by which mentors enabled students to see themselves. We use the term to describe how mentors acted in a 'mirror-like' way. They attempted to develop self-awareness by giving a description of the student's performance from an outside perspective. The description might convey praise or disapproval:

You do work well with the children actually. You have got a nice tone of voice. You never seem to raise your voice much, but you are there all the time. But I can tell from the inflection in your voice how you feel about the children — whether you are happy, or whether you are pretending to be annoyed. (fieldnote, mentor feedback to student, June Lane)

A continuum links the comment of a mentor who gives the student an encouraging description of themselves in action, with an analytical critique that has longer term implications. The mentor as reflective agent helped students acquire a clear perspective on, and if necessary modify, the principles by which they are operating. For example, at Deepvale the mentor was able to see things that the students had completely missed:

I know a couple of lessons were lousy and you think why was it lousy? You might make a couple of points but then Dennis will come along with half a dozen more that you haven't thought of. You can't always see. (interview, student, Deepvale)

One outcome of adopting a reflecting strategy may be that it encouraged the student to consider modifying classroom practice, as the following exchange suggests:

John: . . . you tend to stick [your voice] at that one level with the children. Sometimes, rather than shouting at children the opposite can help. By talking quietly.
Jenny: By talking quietly.
John: Then they have got to listen.
Jenny: I haven't tried that actually. (fieldnote of feedback meeting, mentor and student, June Lane)

Questioning was a significant means of promoting student independence, since it placed on them the responsibility for analytical deconstruction of professional practice. The mentor's contribution was to direct students' attention and by implication, to offer a self-analytic strategy. By questioning, mentors acted as a second voice which raised issues that the student might in time be able to raise for themselves through reflective analysis.

By letting the student talk it through. Not me saying, 'Right you went wrong, how did you go wrong', but, 'Can you tell me about the incident. What actually happened? What did you do?' and then he actually came to fill it out 'Ah, I left him sitting on the bench'. And I put the question 'was there anything else you could have done?'. 'Well I couldn't leave the whole team because there was nobody else and . . .' — and he went on this way. (interview, mentor, Aimshigh)

Examples of the questions posed by the Deepvale mentor show how he tried to induce students to think for themselves.

> If you had wanted to summarize the activity of the first thirty minutes how easy would it have been to get their attention? Is it necessary at this stage or are you continuing tomorrow?

> Perhaps you were too quick in introducing the session before assembly. What could be done as an alternative activity during those few minutes?

> How do you get the attention of the whole class — not just the mathematicians? (fieldnote, Deepvale)

When mentors used facilitating as a dominant strategy, they appeared to do least for their students, yet often achieved most. Rogers suggests that when facilitating predominates,

> Students make no particular mention of their teachers, but simply of the psychological climate in which they were enveloped. The rewards of an excellent facilitator are different from the rewards of a brilliant teacher. (Rogers, 1983, p. 145)

He refers to the Chinese philosopher Lao-Tse's maxim:

> A leader is best
> When people barely know he exists,
> Not so good when people obey and acclaim him,
> Worst when they despise him.
> But of a good leader, who talks little,
> When his work is done, his aim fulfilled,
> They will all say 'We did this ourselves.'

The essence of facilitating was that students were helped to carry out ideas they had in mind, and encouraged to become self-sufficient by the absence of close direction:

> You had to leave the opportunity for them to actually express themselves and try things out. (interview, mentor, Deepvale)

or the progressive removal of direction:

> Fiona places the students with care, knowing what she expects to happen, yet not putting them in situations where she feels they will fail. She withdraws some of her support to encourage the students to become more independent:

> I put her into a class where I knew the teacher could not communicate with adults, and which was an awkward class — and I saw the student absolutely 'go'. I just left her. The students both came through, but I knew they would. (Clarke, 1992)

Mentors could be at their most effective when they merely watched, and by doing so, encouraged students to be constructively self-conscious:

> Without raising voice significantly, and without prompting Bill [student] asks children to listen to him. He starts to count 10, 9, 8 . . . This seems to be his own style of calling for attention . . . The mentor, sitting on chair, models for the children how to listen — face and body turning to Bill, gaze directed at his face. (fieldnote, Bigtown)

Assessor Strategies

With the exception of the partnership phase of PGCE and Articled Teacher schemes, all mentors made and reported to students summative assessments of their teaching. In addition formative assessment was part of the continuing agenda of all phases of school experience. In both instances trainer and educator dimensions of the mentor role became relevant to the process of communicating mentor assessments, with reviewing the dominant strategy at such times — although it has been noted that confronting had to be used occasionally.

Communicating feedback was an essential mentor strategy which ensured that students were made aware of strengths and weaknesses, and encouraged to extend and deepen knowledge, skills and insights, and examine attitudes, beliefs and values. Feedback was regular, both written and oral, and usually both. Many examples have already been given of mentor-student feedback. But it is worth noting that informal feedback by class teachers was one of their most valuable contributions to student development:

> I know Dan and Diane have spent quite a considerable amount of time talking to Deirdre (non-mentor class teacher), both before school and after school. (interview, link tutor, Deepvale)

As has been suggested in chapter 5, some mentors and students found the assessor part of their role mutually stressful. The physical and psychological distance between mentors and students who did not work in the mentor's classroom made communicating assessment easier. In other instances one strategy successfully used to create a helpful distance was formalizing the relationship, often by consciously choosing a context and adopting modes of behaviour which conveyed formality:

> Beryl and I went to the staffroom and I actually took on the role, sitting next to somebody and saying, 'Right show me your notes, yes, yes, yes.'

Almost, if you like, as an expert. Whereas I wouldn't do that normally. (interview, mentor, Bigtown)

Observing was the chief means by which mentors came to conclusions about the students' development, both in the classroom and as a member of a professional group. Observation was also important as the basis of evidence which they used to make formal assessments. For this reason observing was often complemented by recording in some written form the details of observations and the analysis drawn from them. There was a double benefit. First, students were able to share details which they might be unaware of, but mentors had observed:

She'd sit out a lot and she would write little notes down for us. I found that very useful because when you are doing it you cannot see certain little things. (interview, student, Aimshigh)

Second, the record of observations was valuable evidence both of the frequency of supervision by mentors, and of student performance on identified occasions. Consequently the record was a safeguard to mentor and students alike, when summative judgments had to be made about passing or failing a school experience.

Having analyzed mentors' strategies we now consider how they relate to the skills mentors demonstrated when seeking to apply appropriate strategies.

Skills

We suggest that there is a broad relationship between particular mentor strategies and the dominant skills needed to implement them. In many cases the relationship is of such a direct nature that the strategy itself aptly describes the skill it requires. We suggest that the structural, supportive and professional dimensions of the mentor role have corresponding dominant skill dimensions. The structural dimension called upon enabling skills, the supportive dimension on interpersonal skills, whilst the professional dimension required both pedagogic and analytic skills. Each skills dimension had several elements which related to particular needs. This part of our analysis is summarized in Table 6.2.

Enabling Skills

The enabling skills were those which created the optimum structural conditions for students to perform and learn effectively. The nature of planning, negotiating and organizing skills has been exemplified when discussing their corresponding strategies. Implementing skills were concerned with the capacity to ensure that well-planned, carefully negotiated and meticulously organized arrangements were carried through to fruition in the face of any obstacles which might threaten to undermine them. These might be external constraints such as college transport,

Table 6.2

ROLE DIMENSION	DOMINANT SKILL DIMENSIONS	DOMINANT SKILL ELEMENTS
structural	enabling	planning negotiating implementing organizing
supportive	interpersonal	empathizing listening communicating
professional	analytic	observing analyzing (situations) interpreting analyzing (needs) objectivizing generalizing
	pedagogic	demonstrating articulating facilitating questioning

temporary rearrangement of school timetables, or unexpected demands from other responsible roles mentors performed within the school. In essence implementation skill bridged the gap between general expectations within the arrangements of a scheme and their realization in an individual school context:

> We have tried to arrange for all four students to get the chance to go into different classes, talk with teachers and see their types of organization. (interview, mentor, Bigtown)

> Belinda said that the set up would be (meeting on) Friday lunch times. (interview, student, Bigtown)

Mentors then have to use considerable organizational skills. Not only have they a class of children to manage but they also have to organize the students' work in that classroom. In the examples above this can be seen to be a complex task requiring the mentor to take account of the students' gradual involvement as their confidence grows and also an awareness that this confidence will grow at different rates for different students.

Interpersonal Skills

As chapters 7 and 8 show, the successful outcome of students' school experience is dependent on the mentors' capacity to form productive relationships with their colleagues and with their students. Mentors interpersonal skills had some influence on their capacity to negotiate helpful arrangements for students' school experience within the structural dimension of their role. However, their capacity to be supportive to students relied on establishing a relationship characterized by the skills of empathizing, listening and communicating.

The significance of empathizing skill was that mentors need to be able to 'take the part of' students in order to know how best to advise and support them. Empathizing could mean that a mentor had to be prepared to share all aspects of the experience of being a student:

> We've had discussions on what's happened at College and any gripes they've had, or about their assignments or problems about money coming through. The problems of transport, because it's a long way, especially for Gina to get here in the mornings. (interview, mentor, Greenvale)

Given time, students' perception that a mentor was empathetic helped students deal with their difficulties:

> If you've got a mentor who is sensitive then they should be able to help students build up their confidence. I think it's very important to have these times when you can talk to them on their own. Just to be able to let them talk about their problems. (interview, mentor, Intake)

As this mentor implies, mentors' listening skill was closely linked to students seeing that mentors were empathetic.

> I have learnt to listen with the counselling training I had. So I'll listen very carefully to what people are saying to me. Watch people. You can tell a lot from body language. The listening skill, probably because I have had to sit in when somebody is being counselled and just listen and learn to be silent and not react. (interview, mentor, Intake)

However, she recognized that often the skill of being an effective listener was itself the means by which students became receptive to the support and advice mentors were able to offer. Hence, communicating, in the sense of possessing the skill to establish a relationship which allowed for mutually open dialogue, was the end for which empathizing and listening were the means.

> I have got to do a lot of the talking too . . . I suppose the counselling has helped me to say, 'Perhaps you could look at it this way. How about, have you thought about doing it in such and such a way.' (interview, mentor, Intake)

The capacity to make openness acceptable benefited mentor and student alike when inadequate student performance had to be faced and shared:

> One of the horrible things about being a mentor is being completely honest with someone when you really wish to say [difficult] things. You think, 'oh dear, I would really rather not have to say things like that', but of course you have to. (interview, mentor, Hillyway)

Professional Skills

In this discussion, we treat separately those professional skills concerned with understanding, diagnosing, and clarifying students' learning needs. These form a dimension of professional skills which is analytic in nature, informs pedagogy, but is distinctive from it. By definition, pedagogic skills were concerned with the mentor working in a teacher-learner relationship with students.

Analytic Professional Skills

Analytic mentoring skills concern a related sequence of activity from observing students at work, through analyzing teaching situations, interpreting student behaviour within them, to analyzing student needs, so as to determine how best to proceed in learning terms. When mentors moved from training to educating, they then became more concerned to detach themselves from the immediate teaching situation and their subjective perceptions of the class and school, and considered long-term implications for student development. We have called this skill 'objectivizing'. Objectivizing, led to generalizing, when mentors began to interpret the long-term developmental implications of students' classroom performance, and identified the key lessons to be communicated and learnt.

Observing effectively was a skill which led different mentors to experiment with different styles. Most worked on the assumption that if they were to gain an authentic version of student-class interaction, uncontaminated by the mentor's intervention, they should seek to be as unobtrusive as possible. For example at Intake:

> She's kept out of the way, and because the children know who she is, and they are used to lots of people coming in and out of the classroom, they haven't taken much notice really. (interview, student, Intake)

At Lonetree, however, the headteacher mentor, who used several methods of informing herself about students' classroom performance, initially indicated her purpose clearly:

> At first it was clear that she was specifically watching me . . . she'd stand away from the other children with her clipboard and she'd be watching me. I could feel her watching me. But after a while she'd be sitting with me and talking to the children about the work they were doing and

perhaps even talking to me . . . (Now) she will work with the children that I have got going on something or other. Then she'll ask questions. Presumably she asks questions back to them to find out if they understand what I am going through with them. (interview, student, Lonetree)

Analyzing situations was linked to direct observation of students in the classroom, and indirect analysis of students' descriptions of their teaching. The observational process itself refined mentors' analytic skills. By looking with the intention of analysis, mentors often became aware of the nature of a skill implicit in taken-for-granted classroom procedures:

> She came about another two hours afterwards to dissect the day as it had gone. But that's fine . . . you learn a lot yourself from doing it . . . the things you take for granted, like, how you dismiss children from the classroom area. The student said 'Go', and you think 'Oh no!' (interview, mentor, Aimshigh)

Interpreting the meanings of students' classroom behaviour, in order to analyze their needs, were also closely related skills:

> How I feel, in terms of what I expect in their files, my expectations of them and how they should develop, all comes from me watching them in the classroom and trying to perceive their needs. (interview, mentor, Endsleigh)

> You are helping and assessing at the same time. So you help, then you assess, then you assess where you are going to help. I think it is a difficult skill. It is almost like dealing with children. You have to watch for the signs. (interview, mentor, June Lane)

We have already suggested that attempts to analyze students' performance led to self-awareness on the mentor's part. This process of seeing oneself and familiar classroom practices from an outside perspective contributed to development of objectivizing skill. By this, mentors helped students to isolate their immediate experience from its context, and so enable them to assess the long-term value of teaching strategies.

> I have spent a lot of time telling them why I did things, even what might seem the most obvious little things about management. It has really made me think about the things that I do automatically almost — with questions like, 'Why am I presenting this activity in this way, how else could I have done it?' (interview, mentor, Endsleigh)

In turn, achieving an objective perspective helped mentors move students from an awareness of concerns which had a specific implication to an awareness of wider meanings. Often they were able to do so because of their skill in generalizing from the particular experience:

> (The student) said, 'Although we've planned the work together, when we get in the classroom we do it completely differently.' I said, 'You've hit the nail on the head there. That's what teaching is all about, it comes down to the individual in the classroom.' So that's why I like them to go round the school and see how other members of the staff work. Because although we have got a school approach, we are individuals. (interview, mentor, June Lane)

Pedagogic Professional Skills

Chapter 7 will indicate some overlap of the nature of mentors' relationships with child pupils and adult students. To some extent, mentors drew on skills developed from working with children when they dealt with students. Demonstrating, articulating, facilitating, and questioning were all part of the agenda of classroom teaching skills which mentors explored with students, and were also the dominant elements of pedagogic mentoring skills.

Demonstrating, facilitating and questioning have already formed part of the discussion of strategies. Articulating was a skill which was not an inevitable consequence of being an effective teacher of children. There was no guarantee that mentors were sufficiently self-aware to be able to describe skilful teaching with clarity, analyze the nature of students' teaching skill, and so be able to explain to students how they might improve their performance. Many examples have already been included of mentors describing and analyzing teaching. Mentors unused to articulating the nature of teaching skill became increasingly able to do so. It seems that the more they observed sudents, the better mentors were able to understand their own performance, and convert that insight into analytical descriptions of teaching skill. In other words, in observing others, they became better able to see themselves, and then describe skilful teaching in general.

Questioning has also been discussed as a strategy. Here we note that questioning skill centred on careful selection of an appropriate degree of openness in its structure. Mentors might direct students' attention to specific aspects of performance with focused questions such as:

> At what point do you use threats i.e. the loss of games time? (fieldnote of feedback, mentor to student, Deepvale)

Or they used more open questions to encourage students to examine the basis of their decisions about broad issues such as methods:

> That was often a question I would ask 'well would you do it the same next time, how would you change it, if in fact you would?' So that is something they can learn, looking at themselves. (interview, mentor, Bigtown)

or purposes:

> I would say a lot of the time we have been asked quite open-ended questions. So we had to actually look at what we wanted to get out of the lesson in the first place and see how it didn't really meet the aims that we had set at the beginning and look at why. (interview, student, June Lane)

In short, questioning, was a way of stimulating self analysis, and so achieve the move from dependence on the mentor to student self-reliance.

So far we have analyzed the structure of mentoring strategies and skills and the relationships between them. We finally consider how mentors' capacity to apply appropriate strategies and skills was itself influenced by mentors' personal qualities. Chapter 7 will suggest that there is a core of personal qualities which effective mentors possessed to some degree. We now consider how these were related to dominant mentor skills.

Personal Qualities

Just as there seems to have been a direct relationship between some strategies and particular dimensions of mentoring skills, so there further existed a connection between some skill dimensions and related personal qualities. The nature of that connection is summarized in Table 6.3.

Table 6.3

DOMINANT SKILL DIMENSIONS	DOMINANT QUALITIES
enabling	efficiency reliability flexibility warmth
interpersonal	open-mindedness straightforwardness sensitivity
pedagogic	confidence
analytic	self-awareness perceptiveness

As the table suggests, each dimension of mentors' skill benefited from particular personal qualities. Their detailed nature is discussed in chapter 7. We acknowledge that there may be some truth in the assertion that there are 'natural mentors':

> We are not used to this kind of support. It's so positive, and I think that's because you are an early years teacher, that you are so used to being positive with children and building up self-esteem that you are doing it naturally with us. (fieldnote of conversation, student to mentor, Kenleigh)

These are mentors who are effective through qualities which seem to be part of their 'self', or have been developed through mentors' teaching training and experience. But we do not suggest that the absence of some quality necessarily prevented a mentor from acquiring a particular skill. Our analysis has implications for mentor training, an issue which will be explored further in chapter 13.

Summary

In this chapter we have explored the nature of the strategies, skills and qualities that mentors used, applied and demonstrated. We have suggested that mentors made extensive use of strategies we have described as 'dominant', when they worked within particular dimensions of their role, and that each role dimension had its own dominant strategies. Role dimensions also tended to draw on particular dominant skills, and we have suggested that those skills can be analysed in terms of skill dimension, each of which contained further skill elements. Finally we have suggested that mentors' skill was informed and enhanced by certain personal qualities, each of which tended to relate to a specific skill dimension.

In this and the previous chapter we have presented a complex picture of the mentor's role, and of the strategies and skills which contribute to it. Yet we have suggested that the complexity was ordered. An important determinant of how mentors interpreted their role was the relationships context within which they were able to work. The next two chapters analyse the nature of the mentor-student relationship and of the set of relationships within which it was located.

Chapter 7

Relationships: Mentors and Students

Robin Yeomans

Chapters 5 and 6 have described the work of mentors in terms of roles and skills and make clear its complex nature. The evidence from our twelve schools is that success in sustaining a complex web of relationships was a key component of effective mentorship. In addition to the central relationships with students, being a mentor required negotiations with a range of professionals, each with unique personal characteristics and professional pre-occupations. These include other teachers who had students in their classes, other colleagues, the Head and the College Tutor. Students in school were not their only concern. Consequently, gaining cooperation and support made heavy demands on mentors' own personal qualities. To understand the complex nature of the relationships contributing to the students' experience means considering the contributions of all partners.

This chapter and the next will analyze these contributions. This chapter focuses on the mentor-student relationships. Chapter 8 will then examine other contributing strands.

In this chapter I shall consider first how individual personal qualities of mentors and students affected their relationships with one another. Then I shall discuss the nature of these relationships and consider how they affected the mentoring process. I am concerned here and in the next chapter with individual relationships, rather than with the influence on students of the whole staff, or of individuals behaving in ways representative of the staff as a whole. (Discussion of the influence on students of staff cultures and individuals as 'culture bearers' (Nias, Southworth and Yeomans, 1989) will contribute to chapter 9.) I shall suggest that establishing harmonious relationships with other adult participants in the mentoring process appeared to be a major determinant of students' professional success. Positive relationships helped students to focus on developing their professional skills in a supportive atmosphere. Consequently, harmonious relationships tended to foster professionally effective ones. By 'professionally effective' is meant a relationship within which the mentor was able to provide students with access to the means of developing teacher skills relevant to classrooms and schools. In only two of the twelve mentoring settings were there phases when mentor-student relationships met difficulties. In both instances the apparent causes (Deputy Head's workload, and temporarily uncertain professional credibility with students) confirm evidence from other settings about the conditions which promote effective mentorship (see chapter 10).

The Importance of Personal Qualities

Establishing harmonious relationships with individuals in their school, especially their mentor, was of considerable concern to students:

> I was thinking, Oh, I have got two years here. What if I don't like someone or they don't like me. Or what's my relationship with the mentor going to be? What's my relationship with the other articled teacher going to be? (interview, student, Endsleigh)

This concern was typical of many students, and was affected by knowing that they had little or no control over who they were to work with. Decisions about who went where were usually made by the College, taking into account students' travelling and age phase needs, but there was little scope for matching people.

Students were particularly concerned about the sort of person their mentor was. Our evidence is that their concern was well-placed, since the personal qualities of mentors contributed significantly to their effectiveness as mentors, were a strong influence on the relationship which developed between mentor and students, and contributed to the quality of students' wider experience within school. The explanation of this last point is that the mentor's relationships with colleagues affected their negotiations with colleagues on the behalf of students. For example, the researcher at Endsleigh noted that there:

> The students' sense of inclusion and belonging was partly to do with them being strongly associated with the mentor. Her 'place' within the set of staff relationships seemed to influence the set of relationships for the students. (Wooldridge, 1993a, p. 32)

Mentors as People

'Who' a mentor was mattered because:

> It communicated a positive impression to students and others, and encouraged them to respect her professional standards and place their trust in her. (Yeomans, 1993a, p. 32)

One mentor acknowledged that:

> I probably didn't appreciate or I hadn't sat down and really thought the personality of the person was going to play such an important part. (interview, mentor, Hillyway)

Another suggested that some people were 'natural' mentors and that:

> They have either got it or they haven't. (interview, mentor, Flenley)

Credibility with their students did not depend on mentors having the same personal qualities. At Bigtown the mentor was:

> Just bouncy and bright about it, she gets excited about good results and nice things produced. (interview, student, Bigtown)

Whereas at Hillyway she was considered:

> Good-natured . . . a very dedicated teacher . . . a diplomat, but she always gives her point of view. (interview, student, Hillyway)

However, mentors who achieved effective relationships tended to share a core of qualities. This leads us to suggest that some personal qualities are desirable if mentors are to promote relationships which effectively support student development, even though mentors may differ significantly in other ways. These desirable qualities were first, friendliness, which expressed itself as interpersonal warmth, second, confidence, third, openness, expressed through self-awareness, open-mindedness and straightforwardness in telling the truth, however diplomatically, and fourth, perceptiveness, which emerged in the capacity to analyze situations and through sensitivity in the way mentors performed their role. Finally, mentors who were efficient, reliable, and flexible, were appreciated by students for their ability to smooth paths and create optimum conditions for learning.

Mentor's Personal Qualities

Mentors tended to be actively friendly towards students, tried to know them as people, and colleagues, and so establish warm relationships.

> I didn't find dealing with them difficult. I just treated them as though they were — more than members of staff. I found out about them. They became friends. (interview, mentor, Flenley)

They conveyed relaxed confidence through various aspects of their behaviour:

> I have met her before in another context two years ago. She conveys an impression of smartness and confidence — a dress with a jacket and heels, a regular smile, direct gaze, and she talks with an easy and rapid delivery. (fieldnote on mentor, Bigtown)

> Alison is warm, open, but business-like, very confident and a good ambassador for the school. (fieldnote on deputy head mentor, Aimshigh)

A significant outcome of mentors' confidence was their openness with students, a dimension of colleague-like relationships discussed later. Because they were self-aware, many mentors felt comfortable with and were ready to acknowledge their own strengths, failings, and past difficulties:

> (The mentor) was open about his own weaknesses, he told all the students about a disastrous science lesson he had had involving caustic soda. This followed an art lesson that Debra had taught, which she described as disastrous. (fieldnote, Deepvale)

> I remember my first PE lesson, and I said, 'Right, get your pumps on.' The children looked at me as though I was an idiot, and they didn't do anything. So I said 'We are going to get changed for PE', and they all started putting on what I would call their pumps. So I said 'What on earth do you call those?' and they said 'Oh, they're trainers', or some such word. (fieldnote of conversation, mentor and student, June Lane)

and sufficiently secure to be open-minded in their discussion of professional issues with students.

> I just feel that the beauty of mentorship is that I am here all the time and we have got a two-way dialogue. So it's not me feeding out what I would like to see as a mentor. It's also a chance for you to feed back as a student. (interview, mentor, Kenleigh)

Consequently, many mentors encouraged students to express their own perspectives rather than uncritically accept mentor comments:

> (of a written report) If you want to put in your ticks and I will put in my ticks in a different colour if you want. Don't feel mine is the right answer. I think it's important you put down what you feel as well. (interview, mentor, June Lane)

Openness was also a characteristic of the way mentors expressed their views of students' performances. To be effective, a mentor needed to help students acquire a realistic view of their teaching, and yet do so in a manner which the students found acceptable and so could stimulate subsequent learning. Achieving this outcome required that the mentor could be straightforward, like Hazel:

> A straightforward sort of person. She doesn't offend people, though she will say if she thinks something is wrong. . . . She will tell you. But it's usually things that you know anyway. I think that's a nice thing though. At least you know where you stand with her. (interview, student, Hillyway)

Being straightforward and yet not causing hurt also made demands on mentors' communication skills and affected their own feelings:

> It's hard having to confront someone with something that they have
> done that's not correct, and finding the right words. To be able to say
> it without hurting them, yet making sure they really have got the message.
> (interview, mentor, Hillyway)

Knowing how best to support an individual student required that mentors were
perceptive in their analysis both of a student's performance, and of the student's
likely response to critical comment. Perceptive analysis of performance required
that mentors identified the underlying causes of success and difficulty, and
selected those aspects of student performance they judged most responsive to
change. Perceptive analysis of students enabled mentors to identify the feedback
strategy most likely to gain a receptive response from a particular student:

> Very early on Belinda decided on different strategies for dealing with
> the two of them; different kinds of experiences that they needed, even
> to different kinds of ways of telling them things and then she would
> discuss that with me. (interview, link tutor, Bigtown)

as the following instance achieved:

> When I finished, then the first things she said to me were positive and
> praising, and then she could, without hurting my feelings, say, 'well, why
> don't you . . . how would it be if . . . so I was able to take that very well,
> and I felt (it was) really more uplifting. It gave me some power, and I
> felt a lot better. (interview, student, Bigtown)

> From the start we didn't have a negative view at all. It was very positive.
> He always said to us first 'Well, this point is good.' So he praised us a
> lot and then brought in the other points. (interview, student, June Lane)

Mentors' perceptiveness in matching strategies to students explains why students
in most of the schools felt that their mentors were supportive and encouraging:

> She's so nice and so helpful. You feel you can ask her anything and
> discuss it. She says things in such a nice way and she's so positive.
> (interview, student, Intake)

At a school where relationships took some time to become relaxed, one of the
earliest signs of change was a student acknowledging and valuing encouragement
from their mentor:

> On one occasion I did a particularly good lesson, and Carole obviously
> noticed, because she came, stopped and congratulated me, and said
> 'That was a very good lesson', and I thought that was very nice and
> positive. (interview, student, Carlton)

Since the relationship of mentor to student was implicitly and often explicitly judgmental, sensitivity on the part of the mentor was a prerequisite of a constructive relationship. Students needed to feel comfortable and relaxed with the mentor to perform effectively. The mentor's behaviour could help to achieve that outcome:

> He has never said, 'Oh, I am coming in this next lesson to watch you.'
> He just comes in and helps with the class. He has always come in and
> been working with some children and observed from a distance always.
> (interview, student, June Lane)

As learners, students' acceptance of constructive criticism was crucial to their development. The capacity to help a student accept an unwelcome truth depended largely on the sensitivity which mentors showed in selecting times, contexts and phrases:

> I do find that I have to hype myself up to be able to say some things and
> also think about the right way to say it and pick the right moment. If you
> can almost touch on it in conversation, it comes a bit easier than bringing
> it in out of the blue. (interview, mentor, Hillyway)

Sometimes sensitivity meant not overwhelming students with too many truths too soon:

> I think formal feedback can make the student worried and under unnec-
> essary pressure, and so sometimes it is better left for me to comment as
> we go along. Then for them to feel comfortable enough, having achieved
> good control, to enable me to relate back to something that was previ-
> ously a weakness. (interview, mentor, Bigtown)

A sensitive mentor was able to justify a student's novice skills to a potentially critical audience without the student losing face, and so legitimise some aspects of being a learner:

> (The mentor) quietly outlines the afternoon's programme to the class.
> 'Mr B is going to do your spellings He has to learn the writing style you
> use, just like I did. Remember when I first came I did the looped writing
> and had to learn yours? Well, so does he.' The student is defined as
> learner, but learning is justified as a natural, legitimate and appropriate
> activity for newcomers, including teachers. By implication, being an
> apprentice is a phase even experts have to pass through, and should not
> diminish status or imply weakness. (fieldnote, Bigtown)

Finally, decisions about when or whether to intervene relied on sensitively judging a student's level of self-confidence:

During Debra's art lesson Dennis just sat and watched and let the students get on with it. Debra said that she was made to feel it was all right to have a disaster. (fieldnote, Deepvale)

Efficiency, reliability and flexibility were mentor qualities which students appreciated because it enhanced their feeling of security, by enabling them to predict events and so anticipate and prepare for them.

Efficiency meant having well-planned organisation which created a supportive framework which enabled a student to be well-organised:

(The mentor) would say 'Right, you are doing the Thursday session. I will need your lesson plans the week before you are going to do it so that I can see them and we can talk about them.' That was good because it gave me the opportunity to try out different ways of planning lessons. (interview, student, Carlton)

A reliable mentor avoided last minute changes and so enabled students to carry out their own plans, free from avoidable complication which might confuse a novice:

(Student refers to his first block school experience)
We were doing a topic on the Victorians, we then talked about the speed of the early railways, and the class teacher said 'You have got an ideal opportunity to do speed for tomorrow.' So I did it, and I lost my impetus on the data handling work. . . . with Belinda (mentor), that would never have happened. I would have gone in with a plan that was on data handling over the two weeks, I would have said how I was going to do it, and it would have been accepted that that was how I was going to do it. (interview, student, Bigtown)

Whereas mentors who were flexible were ready to accommodate their own plans to students' needs, rather than vice versa:

I shall be around in the room first thing this afternoon, if that's all right. But we haven't got any times for the rest of the week. Are there any things happening that you'd like me to come in to? (fieldnote of conversation, mentor to student, Kenleigh)

Mentors' Professional Credibility

The advice somebody gets from a mentor is as good as the student is prepared to accept. But if they don't rate the mentor, they are not going to rate the advice. (interview, student, Lonetree)

Mentors also depended on professional credibility to convince students that the advice they gave was worthwhile, and to gain the respect of colleagues. Evidence of some aspects of mentors' professional skill can be seen in the way they performed the mentoring role and managed the complex web of relationships, but two general points can be made about their professional credibility. First, it was the mentors' actions rather than what they said that convinced colleagues and students alike of mentors' skill as teachers. This meant that being seen in action was as important in establishing a mentor's credentials as it was in providing a model for students. At Bigtown, for example, the mentor deliberately used classroom opportunities to convey to students messages about herself:

> I felt I needed credibility, and also I felt it was important that they saw what my class were like with me. They are very well behaved, motivated and I have got them how I would want them. I also wanted them to see what expectations I had of the children and that in terms of work as well as behaviour. (interview, mentor, Bigtown)

Second, professional credibility also came from being perceived to have professional values and standards observers admired, since:

> If we didn't believe in what (the mentor) was doing we couldn't really talk to her about anything because there wouldn't be a lot of point. (interview, student, Endsleigh)

A Hillyway student's view of someone she described as 'a good mentor', was that:

> She's good-natured. She is quite politically aware. She is a very dedicated teacher. She is usually very busy and she sets herself a huge workload, as well as her class. She is a very good and conscientious teacher. (interview, student, Hillyway)

Whereas a student's unease about the mentor's skills and professional values contributed to initially uncertain relationships at Carlton, where:

> One thing we found very difficult was that the grouping in the class was very complex. We found it difficult to understand because the children were grouped differently for maths and for English and for science and for humanities so they would be in colour groups or friendship groups or name groups or ability groups, depending on what activity they were doing. The children were very confused about it, and so were we to be quite honest. Eventually she scrapped it altogether. (interview, student, Carlton)

In time, the emergence of 'A change of attitudes, far more professional', coincided with growing student appreciation of 'What I am trying to do in my class', so that 'He now sees the value of integrated day, that you can teach small groups' (interview, mentor, Carlton).

Students' Personal Qualities

The interactive nature of relationships meant that however approachable mentors might be, students' own personal qualities also contributed to effective working relationships with mentors (as well as those with other staff and students).

Friendliness, willingness, openness, and a positive attitude were student qualities valued by mentors. They were more concerned that students should have clear views of their own than that they should necessarily follow their mentor in all respects. The Endsleigh students were seen as being:

> Nice people, friendly, positive, adaptable and willing. They have both got their own character, are reasonably strong personalities . . . are pre-pared to say if they disagree with something or are not happy about something. They are both willing to ask if they don't know. (interview, mentor, Endsleigh)

At Flenley the mentor contrasted her previous experience of a student, who:

> Demanded of me and didn't give back.

so that:

> I found it draining. I could have cried at the end of every debriefing session.

with her present students who:

> Have got a lot to say for themselves. Got a point of view, will stand up for themselves . . . Florence is very quiet. But that doesn't mean she's not got a strong will and a lot of positive ideas. (interview, mentor, Flenley)

The Hillyway mentor was concerned about one student because:

> I wanted her to be lively and enthusiastic and the problem was you see, I think really she is enthusiastic about doing the job, but it doesn't come out, it doesn't come out at all. (interview, mentor, Hillyway)

Finally, the mix of personal qualities affected relationships. One mentor suggested that similarity of personality helped to explain the positive working relationship she achieved with her students, because:

> I quite like 'head-on' people who will say 'Well I think this'. I don't know
> if I could have coped with somebody who kept saying 'Oh I don't know'.
> (interview, mentor, Flenley)

However at Hillyway, the link-tutor suggested that the mentor's concern that
'If she didn't make the suggestions the questions wouldn't come', derived from
a mismatch of mentor and student qualities:

> I think it's partly to do with Hazel being an extremely clear thinker and
> experienced in foresight and Heather's laid-back approach. (interview,
> link tutor, Hillyway)

Since the mix of mentor-student personal qualities was a matter of chance, it was
important to be aware that mentors might need to develop different strategies for
different students, as chapter 10 will discuss.

The Nature of the Mentor-student Relationship

Having examined the contribution to mentor-student relationships of the qualities of individuals, I shall now consider in depth the professional and personal
dimensions of the relationship, and suggest that these became fused in many
instances. I shall discuss mentor and student perceptions of their relationship. I
shall then examine how and why relationships differed to some extent in different
contexts and under different conditions. Finally I shall discuss how mentor-
student relationships tended to change over time and in response to new phases
such as assessment.

In almost every instance overall relationships between mentors and students
were positive and mutually valued. An Endsleigh student commented that:

> We have a special relationship with Eve. If there were any problems I'd
> always go back to her. (interview, student, Endsleigh)

Her view is representative of the experience of most of the students in the twelve
schools. By definition, the mentor-student relationship was an essentially professional one. Students' presence in the schools had a professional purpose, and
mentors acted in an explicitly professional supervisory and assessment capacity.

Although the relationship was necessarily characterized by an imbalance of
power and experience, in several instances it also acquired some of the qualities
of a relationship between equals. One was that it was often characterized by trust
and openness:

> They need to feel that they can say virtually anything to me about
> anybody or anything and it won't go any further if they don't want
> it to. . . . The confidence keeping is important. (interview, mentor,
> Endsleigh)

A further aspect of an equal relationship was that both partners contributed:

> If you can glean things off them as well and they know you have learnt something from them, it helps. Heather lent me a book that had got some ideas in, and I think that's getting things going two ways. (interview, mentor, Hillyway)

A second aspect was that both mentor and students were exposed in the classroom. Students' learner status made them vulnerable, even if it acted as a protection against unrealistic expectations. Similarly, the mentor could become vulnerable from the need to demonstrate expertise and justify actions. The Carlton mentor described such feelings when she expressed her preference for not having a student attached to a mentor's class:

> There are advantages in that you are one step removed from them and you are not available for criticism as well. So having students in my classroom as their mentor was quite stressful for me because I was thinking 'I have got to be striving or justifying', when I feel I shouldn't be justifying to them — because I know the reasons, but I have to explain it to them. (interview, mentor, Carlton)

Vulnerability felt by one partner in a relationship required sensitivity from the other. Its absence could lead to strains:

> I was making notes on observations and I had just made this little note at the end: 'Why are there so many worksheets?' And she (mentor) was quite angry about this. Saying 'Well, you shouldn't put things like that in your file.' She was obviously upset that I put that in. We talked about it afterwards and it was OK, but I was surprised. (interview, mentor, Carlton)

Such a reaction illustrates the point that the personal and professional dimensions of the mentor-student relationship were inseparable. A mentor who had participated in the articled teacher selection process emphasized that personal qualities were important in choosing students:

> Being involved in interviewing was an interesting experience because you want someone who will fit in, seems likeable, pleasant, and has a sense of humour. (interview, mentor, Endsleigh)

The contribution made to the professional relationship by its personal dimension could work in two ways. The personal dimension of the relationship might facilitate professional growth, as at Flenley, where the mentor 'Found it easy to be critical because they were friends'. Alternatively, effective professional relationships could themselves promote rewarding personal ones, so that at Endsleigh 'We were all here to do a job, and things have developed from there', so that 'work relationships have developed into friendship' (interview, student, Endsleigh). In practice, once a mentor-student relationship became professionally effective and personally harmonious, its two dimensions tended to be mutually and positively reinforcing. For example, at Greenvale, the mentor felt that:

> That's the most difficult thing, finding people that click . . . I feel that I've been fortunate because they've been very easy people to get on with. and to have in the classroom. (interview, mentor, Greenvale)

The link tutor there observed that similarly:

> (The mentor) fulfils both a professional and personal tutor role with them. (interview, link tutor, Greenvale)

It was often difficult to separate the professional from the personal dimension of the mentor-student relationships, since they emerged as dual interpretations of single actions or events. This duality took several forms. First, when mentors were supportive, advice was welcomed, self-esteem sustained, confidence improved and professional performance enhanced. At Bigtown, returning to a supportive relationship renewed a student's confidence bruised by experiences in another school:

> It is just knowing the children and knowing that Belinda is there really. The children are children, so it wasn't like suddenly going from a class of devils to a class of angels because they are not angels — some are right little sods. I am fairly sure it must be going back to Belinda. If I went into a lesson with Belinda unprepared, I could show her what I had planned, what I had thought about doing and how I was going to do it and she would say, 'Yes OK, go off and do it', because she knew I could do it, I knew I could do it. (interview, student, Bigtown)

Second, in most instances, respect for the person permeated professional negotiations between mentors and students. Examples included readiness to negotiate the timing of classroom observations:

> Are there things happening that you'd like me to come into now that I have come to various reports? (interview, mentor, Kenleigh)

the form of feedback:

> He did ask us if we felt he was neglecting us by not actually writing down comments for us, because a lot of the feedback we have had apart from the formal reports has been verbal. (interview, student, June Lane)

the content of written reports:

Have you any comments about the final report, anything you disagree with? (fieldnote of conversation, mentor to student, June Lane)

and emphasizing to students the mutual gain from mentoring:

It is for your benefit, but it's also for my benefit, in that I hope I will have staff that I will be doing appraisals with. (interview, mentor, Kenleigh)

Third, statements of professional values, attitudes and standards often reflected deeply-held personal ones. Relationships where values were shared tended to be personally close and professionally effective, because:

What you value yourself, if you can see that in other people, then often that's relationship-forming in itself. (interview, student, Endsleigh)

Yet:

It was not a matter of students simply accepting the values of a more experienced practitioner. Rather their perception of Belinda was that they observed someone whose attitudes conformed to those they considered were important. (Yeomans, 1993a, p. 35)

At Bigtown the central shared value for one student was that:

I have a lot of experience with children and I like to respect them . . . (The mentor) likes children. She has a respect for children. (interview, student, Bigtown)

Whilst the dual personal and professional dimensions of the mentor-student relationships were part of their strength, mentors needed to remember that their responsibility was predominantly professional, and that they would ultimately make judgments about success and failure. Awareness of the assessment role may explain why mentors and students who often spoke warmly of their relationship, nevertheless perceived it differently.

Pupil/Teacher or Child/Parent?

Mentors' and students' perceptions of their relationships indicated parallels with 'teacher and pupil' learning relationships. Some mentors referred explicitly to the teacher skills within their mentor roles, describing as 'The same as with children' such actions as providing students with weekly timetable sheets so that they would not feel threatened by uncertainty (Kenleigh), feeding back positive points from observation first, or treating students as individuals (Bigtown). For the Endsleigh mentor, moving-on from the relative tensions of the assessed phase of school experience was analogous to working with children:

> This term was problematic and resolving the set of problems was complex. Getting the teaching practice over with, was the aim, really, though it's like with children . . . they are naughty one minute and then they do something good and you forget the other. (interview, mentor, Endsleigh)

One of her students too, recognized similar overtones:

> Eve questions us rather like she does the children, in a way, trying to get us to think and question for ourselves. She sometimes provides us with some thoughts but says we should make up our own minds about things too. (fieldnote on conversation, Endsleigh)

However, the Hillyway mentor acknowledged the need to remember:

> They are still adults bringing their various experiences — I think that's what makes it difficult actually, you can't treat them like a child. (interview, mentor, Hillyway)

Though some mentors 'Felt a bit like a teacher, like a parent' when students left them (Kenleigh), others were aware of the dangers that pupil-teacher overtones might become parent-child ones, so that:

> It's like having a couple of kids really, watching them grow, and standing back to let them get their independence, though as with children, how much do you let them find out for themselves, how much do you support them? (interview, mentor, Endsleigh)

This mentor also stressed the need for 'A weaning process' within the relationship, and in making the same analogy, one of this mentor's students emphasized the danger that such mentor/student relationships might reinforce dependence rather than stimulate independence:

> The cut off period (separation to other classes) seemed to be at exactly the right point. I suppose it's like having children really, in a way- to say 'Just get on and do it, you will be all right'. (interview, student, Endsleigh)

The theme will be revisited more extensively in chapter 9.

Colleague or Friend?

An alternative description of the mentor-student relationship reflected the personal/professional duality. When the relationship had had time to develop effectively, it was often described by some as having the equality of friendship, by others that of colleagues. Students tended to value particularly the former:

> We've got to know Eve. We've been with her a lot, and friendship has developed. (interview, student, Endsleigh)

Of course, a student might value the friendship at one moment:

> It's quite easy to talk and ask questions, it's more like a friend. (interview, student, June Lane)

yet recognize at another that the relationship had another dimension:

> When he has talked to us it has not been 'Well I am here to assess you.' It's been more as working with a colleague. (interview, student, June Lane)

At Lonetree, however, one student best expressed her approval of her mentor-head by suggesting that in discussing the student's work, the Head treated her 'Just like a teacher.'

Mentors were more likely than students to emphasize the colleague-like nature of relationships:

> Friend is perhaps the wrong word I think, colleague is a better word, yes more of a colleague, more of an equal, the students think they are not equals, but I would rather treat them as an equal. (interview, mentor, June Lane)

> I think it is important to have a friendly relationship but not too familiar . . . a professional relationship, I suppose, rather than a friendship. I think I would call it being a critical friend. (interview, mentor, Endsleigh)

The mentor-student relationship at Hillyway confirms that treating a student like a colleague did not necessarily imply friendship. There, a colleague-like relationship which was professionally helpful was not personally close, possibly because the mentor was much older than the student. At Carlton also, valuing professional advice did not imply friendship:

> I felt the criticism that I got from (the mentor), being the class teacher, was more practical because she knew the children I was dealing with and she knew that . . . to actually get them all involved was very good news. I thought over that period of time I would have developed some sort of friendship, but I didn't. (interview, student, Carlton)

I have suggested that personal qualities significantly affected relationships. But relationships were also affected by the contexts in which they were formed. One set of such influences was the particular mentorship arrangements for different teacher education schemes. A second arose from the choices schools made about how mentoring happened and from which level in the school's organization the mentor was chosen.

Differences Between Schemes

Mentor-student relationships could be affected by the teacher education scheme the student belonged to, because of differences in how much time was spent in school, differences in levels of student experience at a particular course phase, and the different designs of the school-based parts of each scheme.

At the time this research phase was concluded articled teacher mentors had spent fifty-eight days with their students in their own school, and had visited them during their three weeks in a second school. PGCE students spent two days per week over 18 weeks in their partnership school and four four-day weeks of diagnostically assessed school experience in another school. BEd mentoring was for four preliminary days and a specific four week period, being twenty-four days in all. Inevitably, longer time together tended to mean more contact, more talk, greater familiarity, and a more intense feeling of belonging. For example:

> The length of time working together makes a difference to relationships. I'm the person who is learning from them, but on the level of personal relationships I don't see myself as inferior to anybody here just because I'm learning. We feel very included here and feel part of the staff. (interview, student, Endsleigh)

Since time affected frequency of interaction, it seems probable that relationships of articled teachers and their mentors reached the point where they achieved a constant relationship, with the added impetus of knowing that articled teachers were to be based at the school over a two-year period. For PGCE partnership students and BEd students, relationships tended not to achieve the same depth, since BEd students' relatively short stay meant their relationships might be still evolving when the students left. PGCE partnership students' intermittent pattern tended to mean that at best, they achieved the 'semi-detached' relationships akin to those of part-time teachers.

For the articled teacher course and the PGCE partnership phase a 'teacher-pupil' relationship was encouraged by students being at the start of their course when they first met their mentor. Their relationship was intended to be apprentice-like in its early stages. Students normally worked in mentor's classrooms, observed mentor's as teacher models, and spent time working collaboratively with mentors or with groups under the mentor's overall direction. However, BEd mentors worked with students who had already completed three school experiences, and were in the third year of their college course. There was an explicit requirement that the BEd students teach for two-thirds of their time and that 'By the end of their first week, students would normally expect to be responsible for the whole class for substantial periods of time' (Bedford College of Higher Education, 1992). Consequently their relationship included both support and assessment, but was less likely to become a dependent one unless there were particular difficulties.

Differences in course design also affected the context of the relationships, by encouraging articled teacher course mentors and PGCE mentors to adopt a strongly supportive and collaborative relationship during the partnership phases. These students normally stayed in the mentor's classroom, so forming a working trio at a formative stage. Moreover, during PGCE partnership, mentors were not required to make any summative written assessments, and articled teacher mentors did not do so for their own students until the third term. However, BEd mentors completed an interim formal written feedback after two weeks, and contributed to pass/fail decisions at the end of the four weeks.

Time itself and the presence, absence and timing of assessment may also explain why some relationships changed as students' competence developed and the emphasis changed within the mentors' role, particularly where articled teachers were concerned. By the time they had reached their third term, articled teachers had often developed growing confidence and a relationship of trust. But anticipation of their mentor assessing them during the impending school experience affected how some students saw their relationship and how ready they were to approach a mentor for advice:

> I think it's partly the assessment. It has formalised the responsibility she has. I think you now have to be more careful talking to the person who is the mentor. (interview, student, Hillyway)

and that it was easier to ask advice from a class teacher because:

> It's nice to talk to somebody who is not actually assessing me. (interview, student, Hillyway)

Similarly at Endsleigh:

> Relationships got very strained between Emily and myself because I was the one that was going to say 'yes' or 'no' at the end of the day. (interview, mentor, Endsleigh)

Both articled teacher and mentor at Endsleigh said that once the assessment phase was complete, relationships returned to their earlier harmony. In contrast, the relatively distanced relationship between Cecile and her mentor made being criticized feel less disturbing:

I got no inkling of any other life from her. So the criticism came quite naturally anyway. (interview, student, Carlton)

Differences Between Schools

The choice of which teacher became mentor was an important decision made by the schools (though there was some LEA consultation where articled teachers were concerned). Personal qualities may have been one criterion, but others seem to have been experience and position within the school's own organization. The need to have positive role models who were able to make objective judgments, meant that experienced teachers with incentive allowances were chosen in four schools, with the Deputy Head acting as mentor in six schools, and the Head in one (see table 3.1). Only at Carlton was the mentor a 'main professional grade' teacher. In several instances the decision was a natural extension of existing job descriptions which gave a Deputy Head overall responsibility for all students and new teachers (for example at Aimshigh and Bigtown).

There is no evidence that dealing with a Deputy Head or incentive holder in itself led to a more or less effective relationship. Position in itself did not prevent deputy heads from developing and sustaining constructive relationships with students. The deputy heads were experienced teachers, with their own classes, and so were able to provide models of classroom practice. However, there is some evidence that deputy headship could carry such extensive responsibilities that sustaining an effective mentoring relationship meant that students competed with other pressing demands for a finite supply of time: such as dealing with deviant children, curriculum development and liaising and deputising for heads:

Belinda as mentor — no problem. Belinda as deputy head and mentor, a big problem. . . . If there is a disciplinary problem, once somebody had been reported to the head of upper school or lower school they go to see the deputy head. (interview, student, Bigtown)

The mentor and head . . . tend to spend time together on issues like school development, funding, appointments and so on. So that wouldn't be an issue if she was not the deputy. (interview, link tutor, Bigtown)

At Aimshigh, students mentored by the Deputy Head had less access to her than those with the second mentor. The researcher recorded that the students:

Genuinely valued their (Deputy Head) mentor's observations, criticisms and discussions, but it seems that the time factor can, even with the best will in the world, become a problem. (Frecknail, 1992, p. 8)

In patches she was very busy . . . I would say that it just seemed to me she was overloaded. (interview, student, Aimshigh)

Whereas the second Aimshigh mentor would:

> Sit out a lot and she would write little notes down for us. Each week she
> made sure we were happy about what was going on. (interview, student,
> Aimshigh)

The Deputy Head herself realized the dilemma, and arranged that her students
transferred to two other separate classes, under the day-to-day oversight of class
teachers, though the students felt that they still suffered to some extent from
uncertainty about who carried what responsibilities for their supervision, particularly since their class teachers were themselves probationers.

It is a tribute to the personal qualities sensitivity, professionalism and time
management of the Head as mentor at Lonetree that the three students there felt
well-served by her:

> I found that she's so easy to get on with, which is good because I have
> met heads who don't really want to know about the students, they are
> the teachers' business . . . You can talk to her, which you can't usually.
> She's not like a normal head, in that you don't feel uncomfortable.
> (interview, student Lonetree)

It is interesting to speculate whether the relative inexperience of the Carlton
mentor explains her unease with students as observers.

Mentor-student relationships were also affected by whether students had
the mentor as class teacher and whether they worked as a pair. Articled teachers
were based in their mentor's classroom, for thirteen of their first fourteen weeks.
For the partnership phase, PGCE mentors had a pair of students in their class,
with another pair in another classroom, except for Aimshigh and Bigtown. But
BEd students worked in separate classes. The schools could decide whether one
student should be in the mentor's classroom, which was the arrangement in three
of the four BEd schools, partly for organizational reasons. In the fourth BEd
school, the Head who mentored had no class.

Class teacher mentors tended to develop a closer relationship with the
student in their class than when the student was in another classroom:

> I think it's easier to be mentor and class teacher than mentor to some-
> body else in another room. Because you have got a closer relationship.
> Certainly last year and the year before I felt that I built a closer relation-
> ship with my own student in my own room — we ended up laughing and
> joking with each other and that made it much, much easier to be able
> to talk with them about what was going on. (interview, mentor, June
> Lane)

> From speaking to Ivy (the student in the mentor's class) I would think
> that she's found it quite helpful that I have been around so much and
> that I have been the mentor. (interview, mentor, Intake)

However, frequency of contact did not necessarily imply closeness:

> Having the mentor as a class teacher might not always work out. Maybe if there's a personality clash, if you don't get on with him, having him around all the time might not be a good idea. (interview, student not in mentor's class, June Lane)

Nor did being a head without a class prevent Lesley being perceived as accessible to students:

> I have always felt that if we disagreed with her she would listen to us. She's been very approachable, and if I didn't think that something was as she had seen it, then I could tell her. (interview, student, Lonetree)

The explanation of the differences between class teacher and non-class teacher mentors seems to be in frequency of interaction, form of contact, amount of talk, and shared activity, whether as a pair or singly. When a student was in a mentor's classroom there were more unplanned opportunities for discussion, whereas a mentor had to plan carefully access to students in another classroom.

> Because the mentor is there all the time, or nearly all the time, they can actually see you, or you talk to them a lot saying, 'Well yesterday, music was a disaster.' So although it's not a matter of sitting down for twenty minutes every day and having a chat, it's comments at the end of a lesson. (interview, student in mentor's class, June Lane)

Mentors allocated time to observe students in other classes and to talk to them about their work, but the informal support and comments of a class teacher-mentor came from the additional support of the class teacher.

> You can't get down to them so therefore you have to rely on that teacher being prepared to put some time . . . Although we plan meetings all together you don't build up your knowledge of that person as much as you do if they are in your own room. But again because Cecile (the class teacher) has been so willing that has not been too much of a problem. (interview, mentor, Carlton)

Summary

I have suggested that personal qualities of mentor and students had an important influence on the nature of the relationships which emerged. Whilst mentors and students were individuals, there were particular qualities which seemed necessary for mentors to be effective. They also needed professional credibility. The mentor-student relationship was mutually valued. Its personal and professional dimensions were fused, and in spite of an apparent imbalance of power, it had some of the characteristics of a relationship of equals. Although participants sometimes used the analogy of 'pupil-teacher', or even 'child and parent', such assumptions presented some dangers. A more helpful characterization was 'friend' and 'colleague', although the two were not inevitably linked.

Mentor-student relationships were also affected by the circumstances of particular teacher education schemes. In general, more time spent in one school tended to lead to closer relationships. The choices schools made influenced relationships, because they tended to affect the amount of contact and nature of support. Where deputy heads were designated as mentor, students had to compete with other deputy headship responsibilities which demanded time and attention. Students who had their mentor as class teacher tended to have a closer relationship with the mentor than students whose class teacher was not the designated mentor.

This last point indicates the contribution of other people to students' success in school. Indeed, the mentor-student relationship was at the heart of a complex web of relationships which is the concern of the next chapter.

Chapter 8

Relationships: Exploring the Web

Robin Yeomans

> The mentor discusses with the link tutor a student's timetable. She says she will find ways to raise with the teacher how the student can be given responsibility for a greater amount of time. She is the ideal bridge, saying, 'That's fine ... I can tell the teacher that's what the College wants the school to do'. (fieldnote, Intake)

Whilst we have recognized that the relationship between mentor and students is at the heart of mentorship, the success of the mentoring process was the outcome of a complex set of interdependent relationships involving mentor and students jointly or separately. Four points need to be made here. First, the term 'web' is used to suggest a complex, but patterned and interdependent closed system, which was nevertheless flexible and responsive. Within that web, some roles were formally defined, others evolved in response to needs, but all contributors were connected. Although some connections were more episodic than others (for example, between students and some staff members), each relationship in some way affected all other relationships and contributed to the process as a whole, since individuals belonged to several relationship clusters. Second, within the web, some aspects of particular relationships were in tension under particular conditions. The most significant of these were support and assessment. Third, there were parallel web-like systems in addition to the one intended to facilitate student mentoring. These sometimes involved the same individuals, operating in different roles and responsibilities — for example, the school-college institutional relationship, the school's pupil-oriented organization, and its internal adult social system. Fourth, when participants tried to fulfil the perceived obligations of their multiple roles, it was sometimes difficult for some participants, particularly mentors, to isolate mentoring obligations from their other roles. 'Webs' might become 'entangled', and role conflicts sometimes emerged. Tutors also had to balance concern for students' needs with recognition of the school's organizational priorities, and the importance of sustaining a constructive college-school relationship. Class teachers balanced obligations to students with children's needs and staff membership. Several staff had to manage the multiple perspectives and obligations of mentor, deputy head, colleague and class teacher.

Given the relatively small size of primary school staffs, relationships were often characterized by interdependence (see Nias, Southworth and Yeomans, 1989) and chapter 9 will consider how induction in particular was affected by the nature of whole staff relationships. Mentors and students were participants in a series of triangular relationships, in which the third vertex was, at various times, class teachers, college tutors, and other school colleagues. Fellow students were an important source of peer support. For clarity, and in order to make sense of the complexity, I intend to examine separately how students and mentors were affected by their relationships.

Class Teachers as Student Hosts

For PGCE partnership students, mentor and class teacher was the same person but during the diagnostic block experience, students in PGCE affiliated schools were usually not placed in mentors' classes, to avoid overloading the children with students. Most BEd students had a separate mentor and class teacher: of our group, three BEd students had their mentor as class teacher, compared with seven who did not. The eight articled teachers spent long periods in their mentors' class, but also worked in other teachers' classrooms too, and had to form several class teacher relationships in their host school. Consequently, in many schools, relationships with host class teachers who were not defined as mentors, had an important influence on student development.

As far as students were concerned, host class teachers were an important source of influence, advice, and support, since they were usually in more frequent informal daily contact than were mentors. At June Lane the mentor recalled the importance of the class teacher's contribution to a previous panicking student who:

> Because she'd built up this other relationship with the class teacher, it was much easier when she was in there than when I was in. (interview, mentor, June Lane)

Frequent interaction meant that student and class teacher often developed a close relationship. Closeness may have been encouraged by student perception that the mentor rather than the class teacher was the principal assessor. One outcome of the closer relationship of a class teacher to a student was that:

> It's much easier for a class teacher to help and support because the student thinks that the class teacher isn't assessing. (interview, mentor, June Lane)

Moreover frequent contact and a shared professional interest in the same group of children encouraged closer relationships. Certainly class teachers regularly fed back to students how they had performed. But class teachers shared their thoughts on students with the mentor, and usually contributed to assessment reports. They tended to be seen by students as a constructive and supportive presence.

In some respects class teachers became surrogate mentors, in that they performed parts of the mentoring which designated mentor-class teachers would have carried out (see chapter 5). Class teachers were prominent in developing and supporting initial planning, since it was they, rather than the mentor, who had detailed knowledge of the children and their stages of development:

> We arranged that the first day next term for their final visit, a supply will do half a day in each of the classes so that the class teacher can actually sit down and go through the folders in detail ready for block month. (interview, mentor, Deepvale)

> It was the class teacher that I asked, 'Where do I gauge this and what things have they already done? What level?' Looking through the curriculum, it was all class teacher. The mentor looked at the plans and was happy with those. But really I don't think even she could say whether they were at the right level for that class. (interview, student, Intake)

In the PGCE and articled teacher schemes, students also gained from co-planning with class teachers:

> She is going to take Henrietta's class next term so Henrietta has already given her a very, very sparse outline of the topic and the articled teacher is going to choose which parts she wants to tackle and they will get down to the fine planning as a team. (interview, mentor, Hillyway)

Class teachers gave routine day to day informal feedback:

> I get on really well with my class teacher, we are always talking. She's really helpful . . . She gives me constant feedback. (interview, student, Lonetree)

Sometimes they provided expertise and a model, especially in curriculum areas where some students tended to feel insecure, such as physical education:

> I have done so many things that I wouldn't have tried because I have a class teacher who's so good at game skills and P.E. and things like that . . . I think that's one thing we don't get enough of at all and that's watching good teachers in action. (interview, student, Intake)

or music:

> We have had [class teacher] help anyway on a lot of things, especially the music. We went to her more than the mentor, because she is the Music specialist and said 'What can we do? How best can we do it?' (interview, student, June Lane)

However, acknowledging that a class teacher's contribution could itself be mentor-like did not mean that the roles were interchangeable. The responses of students, class teachers, and mentors were affected by knowing who had formally defined responsibility for students. Mentors tended to be particularly conscious of a dual responsibility for the development of students and children:

> There is a difference, because the class teacher is responsible for the class that you are in. They haven't got a responsibility for me. They have agreed to have me in the class but I would go out of my way not to ask them questions which take a great deal of their time . . .
> It was slightly different in (the mentor's) classroom from being in others. (The mentor) would always come across. Everything she did she would explain what was going on. (interview, student, Hillyway)

Class Teachers and Mentors

> There's a little boy who is a bit of a problem and I said to (the class teacher) 'I really don't know what to do with him'. I told my mentor about it and they both gave me advice and suggested things I did. Then I tried something and sorted the problem out. So my class teacher went and told my mentor. And said that I'd solved my problem and everything was fine. (interview, student, Lonetree)

The incident the student describes typifies constructive mentor and class teacher relationships. Mentors' view of host class teachers' contributions to mentoring can be summed up by the comment that:

> It's a three-way thing. There's the student, the class teacher and the mentor all the time, except obviously the student in my room. But it is a three-way thing and a three-way partnership that works, I think very well. (interview, mentor, June Lane)

How effectively it was 'a three-way thing' tended to depend on the mentor ensuring that respective contributions of mentor and class teacher were clearly negotiated, that communication was sustained, and that class teachers felt their contribution was valued. June Lane provides a model of an effective relationship between mentor, class teacher and student. The mentor's and class teacher's respective contributions had been mutually agreed:

> We work together John and I. He has asked me to be in the class situation, listen to Jenny, how she approaches the lesson and how she deals with it. (interview, mentor, June Lane)

Consultation between mentor and class teacher at key moments showed that the class teacher's contribution was valued, enhanced the quality of mentoring, and was a check on the system's smoothness:

I saw the lesson plans. The students came in first of all and they planned together. We had actually decided a certain area, based on the National Curriculum, and then we allowed them to go away and plan, given parameters. Then they brought it back to us and we both looked it over . . . He asks my opinion — he asks fairly regularly before he writes his report. We do work together quite well . . . It's down to John to finalize with the report — I haven't actually written the report but I have contributed my comments. (interview, class teacher, June Lane)

Students were aware of the mentor-class teacher collaboration:

My class teacher has been in the room a lot and I think they've had a lot of discussions about how I have been getting on and John has been coming in and out maybe once or twice a day. (interview, student, June Lane)

and the mentor encouraged them to look to their class teacher for help and advice:

Get Jess to fill you in on that definitely because she hasn't got the best of home backgrounds. Now I am not saying that's the be all and end all but it's just something that you need to bear at the back of your mind when you are dealing with her. (interview, mentor, June Lane)

In most of the other schools, mentors showed considerable interpersonal skill in ensuring that students with host class teachers were effectively supported. It was part of the mentor's contribution to ensure that class teachers provided classroom conditions in which students could perform effectively. In doing so, mentors sometimes needed the sensitivity noted in the previous chapter:

The mentor discusses with the link tutor how best to resolve a mis-understanding between a student and her teacher. The teacher wants to give plenty of ideas, but the student is reluctant to deviate from plans she has already developed. She recognizes that both are trying to do their best, and then says 'I know what to do now.' Her knowledge of the people involved enables her to choose the best way to deal with the difficulty. (fieldnote, Intake)

With the other class teacher it's been a bit more difficult because she's such a strong character that there have been one or two occasions when I wanted to say 'Look, you must let your student have enough time. She's got to have overall responsibility for the class'. But I have had to try and word it in a way that wouldn't upset her too much and would help the student. (interview, mentor, Intake)

Being mentor to articled teacher students meant particularly complex relationships with other teachers, since several teachers were likely to host students at some time during their stay in the school. Difficulties in communication could affect students adversely. Consequently:

> When the students go into somebody else's class I have to mentor the class teacher first of all, and then the class teacher has to be a 'mentor'. . . . I have learnt you must prepare the students and the teachers thoroughly. Your can't say 'Oh, just go in with her.' (interview, mentor, Flenley)

Creating an effective network of support depended also on a mentor's close knowledge of their colleagues:

> Most of the teachers [the student] will go to are experienced teachers. I know how they work. I have worked in parallel with them at some time or other . . . So I know how to interpret their word for what has gone on. (interview, mentor, Hillyway)

Such familiarity helped mentors deal with class teacher-student problems when they occasionally arose, although it did not avoid the possibility of role conflict between being a student's mentor and a teacher's colleague:

> At the end of the day the teacher came into the classroom to distribute reading books to the children, although the student had already done so. The teacher's intervention may have been unnecessary, and created minor disruption. It seemed that she was anxious to maintain contact with the class she perhaps felt she was in danger of losing. It needs particular sensitivity from a mentor to establish a successful learning opportunities for the student in such situations. Whilst the mentor's understanding of the situation and her relationship with her colleagues may be helpful, here she may also feel inhibited by the prospect of harming colleague relationships, especially when the school prides itself on supportive staff relationships. A mentor must look after the student's interests, yet cannot easily be seen to take sides. However, she may not willingly put herself in a position where it is difficult to live with her colleague after the students have gone. (fieldnote, Intake)

When problems arose in other classes, mentors then considered the responsibility theirs:

> Freda went (from me) to a teacher who was finishing her probationary year . . . and teaches in a totally different style from myself. So the articled teacher went from my structured way to a teacher who appeared to be more unstructured. The articled teacher couldn't see any work, she didn't

understand why they were doing what they were doing. It was not the articled teacher's fault. It was not the class teacher's fault. It was my fault I hadn't briefed them. (interview, mentor, Flenley)

When their contributions were clearly understood by all parties, class teachers made a significant contribution to student mentoring. They regularly fed back to mentors comments on students' classroom performance, sometimes taking notes, as at Carlton and Hillyway. Where there were four students to mentor during partnership, as at Deepvale, the class teacher often became the mentor in effect:

> There isn't the time or the opportunity for you to leave your own class too often, to actually go and watch the students in other classes. The monitoring aspect, with my cap on as mentor, my monitoring was very much talking to the class teacher on Friday after school, or pre-school Thursday morning or during the rest of the week, in terms of how Diane and Dan were doing and what they were intending to do. (interview, mentor, Deepvale)

However, when a difficult situation arose, it was mutually understood the mentor rather than the class teacher deal with it:

> It's a bit hard to ask somebody else to say 'Look here, you must do this that and the other.' That's what I have got to do whether I like it or not. (interview, mentor, Hillyway)

When a class teacher's role was not clearly defined both student and mentor might be disadvantaged. At Lonetree, the headteacher was anxious not to over-burden her staff. As mentor, she efficiently conducted daily observations of three BEd students. The class teachers' contributions were initial discussion of plans and any informal advice or support they chose to give (as they regularly did). The students' evidence suggests that whilst these teachers were a major support, their frequent classroom contact with students meant that they had an informative view of student performance, which they would willingly have contributed in a planned way had they been asked to do so:

> My class teacher read my interim report, she said it didn't do justice to what I had done. I just think the class teacher should be more involved with the mentor. I think that's really important. Because ten minutes (observation) out of the day isn't really an awful lot. Because you could have been having a hell of a ten minutes or you could have been having a really good ten minutes. (interview, student, Lonetree)

On another occasion a class teacher's perspective, helped by the mentor's openness and accessibility, encouraged the student to be assertive, and corrected incomplete impressions which even this diligent head could not prevent:

Over the weekend I had it, my report, and I looked at it and gave it a good going through and I found the thing about me having a limited imagination or something along those lines — I can't remember the exact wording. I was really quite upset about it. I don't feel it's true at all about me. So on Monday, I showed my report to my teacher and she couldn't see it either and she said she thought that I should ask my mentor what she'd meant by it. So I did ask my mentor about it . . . She said she could now put on my final report that I did show evidence of imagination and she did. The fact that I was able to ask her about it said an awful lot. (interview, student, Lonetree)

Mentors and Tutors

Chapter 12 is particularly concerned with the College tutor's role in ensuring that mentorship happened effectively. At this point it is appropriate to note that doing so meant ensuring that mentors understood administrative procedures, and monitoring the quality of support and assessment, particularly when mentors were in their training year. However, it would be a distortion to suggest that the College alone gained from tutors' participation. Mentors and students also valued their contact with College tutors. Their comments suggest that the relationship was often beneficial professionally and personally, and the reasons they gave demonstrate that both groups had a legitimate interest in effective mentorship, and were concerned that its quality should be maintained.

Relationships between mentors and tutors were dominated by two interacting themes. First, as experienced educators, mentors often developed clear views about students' classroom needs. They were ready to interpret their role actively, justify how they did so and sometimes went beyond their formal brief if they thought it helpful for students and College. Second, however, as relatively novice adult educators, they had a concurrent need for reassurance and support from tutors, because they wanted to have 'Confidence that my performance is right' (mentor, Carlton). For example:

I have actually written [to the College] because although it's an un-assessed practice, I feel quite strongly that College needs to know how I think. I am clearing myself really aren't I, because I feel that articled teachers need a tremendous amount of help? (interview, mentor, Hillyway)

I have written my own notes down to work from, particularly when I write the report. But I have always given it verbally. Can I ask you how do you feel about that? Do you feel I ought to be giving written reports? A written report to me would be very impersonal. I couldn't just give somebody a written report and say here you are, go away and read that . . . Have you found anybody else who does not give written reports?

Am I alone in this? (fieldnote of conversation, mentor and tutor, June Lane)

The June Lane mentor's analysis of his relationship with tutors is particularly informative, because he was in his third year as a BEd mentor, and so was in a position to begin to generalize about mentorship. In his first year as mentor, his relationship with the College tutor mirrored his own with students in that:

He was there for support for me, a bit like a mentor in many ways.

This support had been especially helpful in his second period as mentor, when a student was underperforming and the mentor needed to know that there was consistency in the messages the student received:

I desperately needed it last year because I think it was vitally important that the student actually was told from two sides that he needed to pull his socks up.

But personal encouragement and the reward of being told you were doing a job well were important too:

I write my report and I think, have I missed something out. Am I doing something wrong? It's this pat on the back all the time again, isn't it? I need it just as much as the students need it. (interview, mentor, June Lane)

Now, as a full mentor, in his third mentoring year, John felt he still wanted contact with the tutor as a sounding board:

It's somebody to generally chat to about them and to crystallise my own thinking on the students. (interview, mentor, June Lane)

In the current mentoring round the tutor's dealings with the mentor had themselves been a model of ways to question and prompt students' thinking:

He was writing down notes all the way through, and I thought afterwards 'My goodness me, why didn't I do that?' Because he was asking the right sort of questions which were making me think about the students' performance. (interview, mentor, June Lane)

An important ingredient in effective mentor-tutor relationships was the sustained relationships which had been possible with several mentoring schools. When mentors and tutors had previously worked together, they were able to build on shared understandings of the school, the process, and one another:

I know Greenvale because I have done previous supervision work at Greenvale. I know the staff quite well. I have been quite at home at this school and I meet Gail also in mentor meetings out of school. (interview, link tutor, Greenvale)

The same was true of most of the other schools. Indeed sustained contact with a specific tutor throughout one or two years was part of the structure of the PGCE affiliated schools and articled teacher schemes.

Students and Tutors

Where the main responsibility for observation, feedback and assessment was shifting to the mentor, contact with the tutor was still valued by students as a source of reassurance and encouragement:

The second time (the link tutor) just came — I think actually I grabbed her from the staffroom because I wanted her to come and see something that we had put on display. We'd understood all along that we'd only talk to Doris if there was some major problem along the way. (interview, student, Deepvale)

Both students have been keen to show the tutor what they have been doing. (interview, mentor, June Lane)

They valued the tutor's objective view, given that there was always the possibility of discordant student-mentor relationships:

I think if you had a personality clash with your mentor, for any reason, I still think you need a tutor that you can go to if that happened. If you hated the school or you hated the class or you couldn't cope with either the class teacher or the mentor, it would be very difficult because they have got to work in the school, and you are the outsider. (interview, student, Intake)

Students wanted to feel that they had not been abandoned by the College:

When you are out on teaching practice you aren't having so much contact with the other students, you aren't having so much contact with the College. There was a couple of times when people popped in and you heard they'd been and they'd not popped in and seen you and you felt a bit lonely. (interview, student, Deepvale)

The students need that other shoulder that they can turn to and cry on if necessary or just feel that there is somebody else there that they can talk to who isn't directly related with the school. (interview, mentor, June Lane)

Students and Other Staff Members

Given the presence of a named mentor with defined responsibilities, it might be tempting to undervalue the contribution of informal support from other adults within the schools to the success of a mentoring process. However, the evidence is that individual teachers not directly involved with students made significant contributions to their development and were a substantial help to mentors.

Chapter 9 will examine the implications for training and education of students feeling 'at home' in their school and part of its staff. Here it is important to note that when individual staff made a point of including students in informal interaction such as staffroom talk, feeling accepted and welcome tended to relax students and enhance their sense of security. Inclusion was particularly likely to be a feature of the sustained relationships of the Articled Teacher Scheme. The following exchange is characteristic of the student-staff relationships found in articled teacher schools:

> The staff start appearing in the staffroom for lunch. There is a general level of conversation then one teacher says 'Don't the children make a terrific jump this term?' The class teacher looks across at an articled teacher and says, 'Yes I think we've found that as well, don't you?' The articled teacher agrees. (fieldnote, Greenvale)

One reason for feeling part of the staff may be that articled teachers worked with several teachers in the school, and so developed a working relationship with several staff:

> I had an awful lot of support from the year one teachers in the year one unit which was nice and I had quite a few ideas from them as well, because there were three teachers there. We planned together and that was helpful. (interview, student, Endsleigh)

Support from teacher colleagues took several forms, and could come from several sources in the same school. One form was as practical advice:

> *Student 1:* One teacher was very good in that he gave me lots of ideas and how to go about them.
> *Student 2:* The head of my year was very helpful and very friendly.
> *Student 1:* I did once ask about Art and Music, in the beginning and that was, 'Oh, well go and see somebody else,' and literally you could just go off and see whoever it was to find out. (interview, Aimshigh)

Occasionally, the advice was offered as an alternative supportive professional view, when a teacher felt that the mentor's advice was open to debate:

> A teacher happened to come through to make a drink or something and Mrs X had been saying something about hearing people read. She suggested me hearing children read while we were getting changed for PE. The next day, we were doing PE and the same teacher came through and she said to me, 'I am not being rude or anything but . . . if you are going to spend every minute, every spare second that you've got, hearing people read or doing this or doing this then you are just going to drive yourself up the wall'. (interview, student)

Discussion with other staff could help broaden students' understanding of the school and its educational strategies:

> Well, for example, the English co-ordinator actually spent half an hour of her own time at the end of the day explaining to us about the school's ideas on reading and how it should be done, ideally, and how that was having to be modified because of the difficulties that the children were coming in with and how they were using various schemes in various ways. She spent her own time doing that, it wasn't school time. (interview, student, Carlton)

Mentors and Their Colleagues

In addition to the close relationship between mentors and host class teachers, there was evidence that successful mentors sustained and were themselves sustained by an extended network of staff who contributed to the effectiveness of the mentoring role. Maintaining such a network made demands on mentor's negotiating skills, and could lead to situations in which there were conflicting calls on their loyalties.

The complexities of negotiation could make working directly with students seem a relatively minor part of the job:

> I'm organizing timetables . . . working with class teachers. I'm learning about responding to adults and assessing adults. The role is not just about teaching the articled teachers to teach, it's also about dealing with other professionals. There's networking involved — contact with heads, mentors, tutors, teachers and other articled teachers. (fieldnote of conversation, Endsleigh)

The researcher at Endsleigh gives an authentic flavour of the negotiating skills of the mentor there:

Eve uses a range of interpersonal skills to undertake her role. She is
sensitive to the professional needs of the articled teachers when negotiating for them to spend time with colleagues and their classes, and yet
she was also sensitive to the pressures upon her colleagues. When Emily
and Eileen are in with the classes of the colleagues, 'I go round and say,
"Is everything okay?" and thank the member of staff for their help'.
(Interview) She also involves the headteacher in some of the decisions
related to the mentoring process and has to consider when this is appropriate. (Wooldridge, 1993a, p. 27)

Effective negotiation with colleagues enabled mentors to secure specific benefits
for their students:

The mentor asked me if there was anything I needed for this assignment
or anything I needed to observe in the school. I said 'Yes', and what it
was, and she arranged it all for me — and the teachers actually came to
me and said to me this morning 'Come and see me whenever you want.'
(interview, student, Kenleigh)

So that mutual understanding and esteem could lead colleagues to support a
mentor who they respected professionally:

I have never heard the staff say anything that was a criticism of her. I
know when she was off sick most people were betting odds that she
would be back after a day, but she actually had two days off and that was
really unusual. (interview, student, Hillyway)

The importance of support as an ingredient of mentoring has already been
emphasised. But several mentors commented on the valuable support they too
received from colleagues:

It's been a team approach and I have appreciated that because it's taken
some of the load off my shoulders as well. At the end of the day it's
always been my responsibility, but I know there are others I can turn to
for help and I have appreciated that tremendously. (interview, mentor,
June Lane)

Heads were prominent in this respect. It was often sufficient for mentors to know
that they were trusted to take responsibility and get on with the job:

She is important because she is there. She leaves it to me. She trusts me
to keep her informed of anything that she ought to know, which I do.
(interview, mentor, Endsleigh)

The Head has said, she's left everything to me. She hasn't interfered at
all. She said she thinks the students have got enough people worrying

about them without her interfering as well. So she's kept very much in the background but has been there if I've needed her. Which has only happened once. (interview, mentor, Intake)

When necessary, other senior colleagues could be helpful. The Carlton mentor used her deputy head to resolve a tension with one of her students:

I said to the deputy head you are going to have to talk to her, because everything I said, the fence was immediately up. Whereas he could come in a lot more softly. (interview, mentor, Carlton)

Mentors' appreciation of the contribution their colleagues made to the mentoring process recognizes the value of peer support. Discussion of the network of relationships would be incomplete without considering how peer support helped students too.

Student Peer Support

Students were allocated to schools in pairs or threes whenever possible, with the deliberate intention of preventing isolation. They tended to speak warmly of the help they received from other students working with them:

I think the students support each other a lot. I think it's quite important really that you are with somebody else. It must be awful to go to a school on your own. (interview, student, Intake)

It was exceptional to have only one student in a school, but when one articled teacher left the district, the student at Hillyway was left on her own and felt a loss:

I found it easier when Harry was there actually, I found it easier having two of us in there. Because you're nothing like anybody else who is there. Not a mum or a non-teaching assistant or the teacher and it's nice to have more than one of you.

Indeed, she looked for sympathetic support elsewhere:

I talk to my boyfriend about it. I mean he's a teacher as well. So that's quite helpful, especially as I say, since Harry left, I needed to talk. (interview, student, Hillyway)

In several schools mentors encouraged students to collaborate by ensuring that conditions facilitated such behaviour — particularly planning and working together. There were phases of both Articled Teacher and PGCE courses when it was the intention that students worked as a pair in one classroom. Amongst the BEd schools, collaboration was particularly emphasized at June Lane. There the mentor had arranged that the students taught parallel classes, and actively encouraged them to collaborate:

> When we were told that, I suppose our faces gave it away. We just thought 'This will be really good', because we knew each other before we came into College anyway. (interview, student, June Lane)

The outcome was that they were able to give one another much of the support they might otherwise have sought from their mentor:

> We were able to sit down and plan all the work together and bounce ideas off one another. We were able to do that and then sit with the mentor and say 'Well, this is what we have thought about. What do you think? Is it the sort of thing that you were hoping we would do?' We talk together afterwards as well — [saying] 'How did that go?' To be able to say 'Well, I think it was better than last week because we did this', that has been really good. (interview, student, June Lane)

In addition to such planned co-operation, students eagerly grasped opportunities to share and solve problems informally:

> Well we share the resources and the books and throw ideas at each other and have a good winge or a laugh. I think it's quite important to be with another student actually, I think it's good. (interview, student, Intake)

> Even things like display. [We say] 'Come and have a look at the display. Do you think the lettering is right?', and stuff like that. Even helping you put the frieze paper up. (interview, student, Lonetree)

Similarities of age, gender, attitudes, encouraged closely supportive peer relationships. Friendship and contact away from school were an important additional impetus to professional sharing, as was having complementary experiences. For example, the relationship of the two Endsleigh students was one of mentor-like mutual support and learning. Peer support there was based on growing friendship, and was valued because it came from someone at the same level and sharing the same experiences:

> Emily [student in the school] has been part of the learning. By having someone who is in the same situation as you, who's going through the same experience and being able to talk to them about anything that happens to you — that's vital. I am not sure how I would have felt about things if there wasn't another person in the school with me. For example

there are certain things that we can work out ourselves without having to go to someone who is an authority on the situation. There are things that we can contain amongst ourselves which is really useful because you're so much more independent. (interview, student, Eileen, Endsleigh)

If you have got someone on the same level as you, you can say anything to them. But you don't want to make yourself look really daft by saying the obvious to somebody who's been doing it years and years . . . We are at the same level really, because everything one has done the other had done as well. So especially now that I am in the year that Eileen was with, and Eileen is in the year that I was with, we can ask each other things. Sometimes the car journey isn't long enough to last a conversation, so we sit in the car a bit longer . . . Sometimes we don't need to ask our mentor, because we have discussed amongst ourselves. We might go to her when we have sorted out what we think rather than with just a vague idea at the beginning. (interview, student, Emily, Endsleigh)

A comparison of peer support at Endsleigh with student relationships at Bigtown confirms that if peer support was to be mentor-like, more was needed than a sympathetic, non-judgmental ear, valued though that was. Differences of gender and personal styles may explain why Bigtown students gave one another less support than elsewhere. Teaching credibility seemed to be a further issue. Bigtown was a partnership school where each pair of students was in one classroom. One student's success made it harder for the other to accept peer support when she had classroom difficulties, and then affected the value placed on her comment:

The chance to share classroom experiences with a sympathetic colleague had the possibility of avoiding a sense of isolation in what could be a potentially stressful set of circumstances.

We would talk about things. You get a lot of value from other students. . . . Just mutual support and mutual understanding from the students' point of view. (interview, student)

However, for support to develop to that beneficial, yet personally supportive feedback and analysis which might be defined as peer mentoring, the relationship between students needed to display that same mutual trust and respect, together with openness tempered by sensitivity, which characterised the relationships the mentor herself had worked to establish. Whilst the relationship between students was amicable, it only achieved the sophistication of peer-mentoring 'A little bit' (student), and interviews suggested that students' readiness to accept self-exposure depended on 'If its worth it or not'. In this instance it was 'a very sensitive area I guess' (student). (Yeomans, 1993a, pp. 46–7)

Summary

I have suggested that interacting with the mentor-student relationship was a web-like system of interdependent relationships which connected them to other participants in the mentoring process. In particular these were, students' class teacher hosts, College tutors, and other staff in the school. Fellow students provided regular peer support. The obligations of multiple relationships could lead to role conflict.

Class teachers gave information and support which helped students work effectively with their classes, so that close relationships often resulted. The triangular relationship between mentors, class teachers and students provided complementary support and advice. There was greatest benefit when spheres of responsibility were clearly agreed, though responsibility rested firmly with mentors.

College tutors monitored the mentoring structure, and provided valued support for mentors and students. Mentors referred to tutors for confirmation that they were performing their mentoring role appropriately, and tutors' involvement was seen by students as a safeguard in the event of difficult student relationships with mentors.

Other school staff helped students by making them feel welcome, included in the staff, and by giving encouragement and advice in specific contexts, such as when curriculum expertise was needed. Mentors were able to draw on an extensive network of support from their colleagues, including the head, for themselves and for their students.

Finally, students working in the same school supported one another, sometimes by collaboration, but most frequently by problem sharing and solving and by providing empathetic understanding. In some instances, peer support was mentor-like in the nature of its contribution.

The previous and present chapters make clear the important contribution of the relationship between student and mentor in ensuring that students performed effectively. However, they also confirm that 'mentor' and 'mentoring, were not synonymous. First, 'mentor-like' actions were performed by a range of surrogate mentors — especially by host class teachers and by students' peers. Second, mentors performed other roles concurrently, so that the obligations of mentorship were sometimes brought into conflict with other expectations.

A further point we have made is that within the schools we studied, effective relationships tended to be harmonious ones. Chapter 6 suggests that under certain circumstances, confrontation could be an appropriate part of an effective mentor-student relationship, and we suggest that harmony and confrontation were not inconsistent, where mentor-student relationships were characterized by openness and trust. Indeed, relationships which do not allow for confrontation may disadvantage students. In the next chapter we consider the effects on students' learning of circumstances where mutual wish for harmony, characterized as 'fitting-in' is the dominant concern.

Induction, Acculturation and Education in School-Based Initial Teacher Education

Irene Wooldridge and Robin Yeomans

In this chapter we consider how school-based initial teacher education is affected by a student teacher's close link with a mentor, especially in course structures where there is also a dominant relationship with one school. In particular we examine how mentors and school staffs contribute to students' induction to an individual school, to their understanding of classroom processes and skills, and to their induction to the teaching profession. We then examine the relationship between induction and acculturation. We suggest that the emphasis on 'fitting-in' meant that induction was extensively concerned with acculturation, a process which, being often tacit, presented some dangers. In particular, the influence of a school's culture on students who, through sustained contact, become 'temporary' staff members, could mean they might become narrowly acculturated to one school's ways rather than educated beginning teachers. By 'acculturated' we mean having internalized the 'beliefs and values; understandings, attitudes, meanings and norms (arrived at by interaction); symbols, rituals and ceremonies' (Nias, Southworth and Yeomans, 1989, p. 11) shared by a particular staff. These features of an individual school's culture, including its dominant model of classroom practice, did not necessarily reflect the general professional culture of teaching. In terms of learning to teach, by 'educated' we mean having developed a set of values, attitudes and beliefs about teaching which are independent of specific contexts, and inform and sustain an individual's practices as teacher. They are grounded in, and encourage a reflectively analytic response to the individual's experience and that of other professionals. We suggest that whilst induction and training are a necessary part of students' preparation for teaching, that preparation is incomplete without an educative dimension.

Induction and acculturation are not synonymous, since acculturation implies more than understanding and learning prevailing norms in order to fit in with them, and so ensure continuity and social harmony (the purpose of induction). The norms of a specific staff culture are the outcome and embodiment of personal and professional values, attitudes and beliefs which are implicit in classroom and staffroom behaviours, yet often unarticulated. Consequently acculturation can have an unacknowledged yet profound influence on the development of students' own values and attitudes, emerging as beliefs and then being reflected in their classroom and staffroom behaviours.

Mentors carried the major responsibility for ensuring that students gained from induction into the culture of a particular school. They needed to ensure that students were able to use their experiences to help them become skilled beginning teachers with an objective professional perspective, rather than one framed by the culture of a particular school. However, we suggest that to achieve this outcome, mentors need skills and perspectives which their school situation does not inevitably provide or even encourage.

Induction and the Mentor

Chapter 5 has suggested that being inductor to the formally defined, informally articulated, or tacitly understood school and class procedures, structures and norms was an important element of mentors' role during students' early weeks in school. Induction had three facets. First, it familiarized students with the social, organizational and pedagogic norms of a particular school and class. Second, it initiated students into the nature of general classroom teaching processes. Finally, students were initiated into the wider professional culture of teaching, including the nature and obligations of the job within an institutional framework.

Induction to school norms was intended to ensure that students anticipated and so avoided foreseeable difficulties and that disruption was minimised. Whilst much of this knowledge concerned procedures, informal understandings could also be part of the agenda. For example, at one school students needed to be aware that:

> This is what we expect in the school. The women wear trousers at school but we wouldn't expect anybody to turn up in trainers and jeans, not on a teaching day. All the male members of staff wear ties. (interview, mentor, June Lane)

Induction to teaching processes was explicitly part of the agenda of the initial apprenticelike partnership phase of the articled teacher and PGCE schemes, which was students' first planned and sustained primary school contact within the courses. In this phase, mentors provided students with an influential model of how a teacher organized learning, controlled children, and created a classroom environment:

> You need to see somebody in action. What I really like seeing about her is the way she starts lessons and gets the children. She has a terrific way with them (saying) 'Something surprising is going to happen, listen carefully'. (interview, student, Bigtown)

The thinking behind the model could then be articulated through a context-related commentary on, and discussion of, classroom phenomena and students' teaching experiences (see chapters 5 and 6). However, the rationale for partnership was that in working closely with an experienced teacher, students were given access to an instance of skilled teaching, rather than to a definitive exemplar. The implication was that the model was to be considered critically in order to aid the student's own development, rather than to be followed slavishly.

Induction to the wider implications of the teacher's role, including the professional values of teaching was a continuing part of experience in school. Being given access to a wide range of school situations was important here. Students might feel disadvantaged if they were unable to experience fully the obligations of the job:

> (of their previous school experience)
> I think it would have been of value to have been invited to the planning meetings, just to sit in and watch. To see what happened and how they worked. It would have been interesting to go to a staff meeting as well. (interview, student, Carlton)

'Professionalism' in relationships with colleagues was an important induction concern in several mentor-student relationships.

> I have to be careful what I say to Emily and Eileen because we are all professionals here and I can't undermine another member of staff. I have to be careful to help them to see both sides of the coin. Just support them, answer their questions, discuss the educational issues and theories . . . (interview, mentor, Endsleigh)

> You can't criticise the teacher. Now they have got a little bit of knowledge and they see things they don't agree with, my job is to point out all the styles of teaching, and why they're done that way. (interview, mentor, Flenley)

Induction and the Staff

Mentors were not the only source of student induction. The process which led to schools' participation in school-based training meant that whole staffs were often supportive to students. The invitation to take part in the schemes had gone to schools which were thought to be supportive to students by reputation and past College experience. These schools had then chosen to participate. Consequently they tended to be ones where students were welcomed. Whole staffs contributed by trying to ensure that students feel supported. For example, at June Lane:

> The day visit before we started our block they all said, 'If there is any-
> thing, don't be afraid to ask'. The mentor said, 'We have all got different
> areas that we consider ourselves better at. So perhaps if you ask me
> something I may not be able to help you but I can put you in touch with
> somebody that can'. (interview, student, June Lane)

At Greenvale:

> The fact that they have included them in everything and taken them as
> other members of staff, has helped. When the students have gone into
> their class, each member of staff has been very willing for them to
> observe and to join in with groups if they wanted to. (interview, mentor,
> Greenvale)

One aspect of support for students was that staff tried to ensure that pupils
perceived students as teacher-like. In one school, reminding a child to hold open
a door for a student indicated their staff status:

> It's just a norm here that children actually hold the door for the mem-
> bers of staff. There have been lots of little instances where you have
> thought staff are actually saying to the children 'Do with these "teach-
> ers" as you would to us.' (interview, student, June Lane)

In another, the judgment that 'If you let the children see that that person is a
lesser teacher then they are going to treat them like a lesser teacher' (interview,
Head, Hillyway) accounted for students' breaktime routine, 'Because in the children's eyes students were staff if they were on playground duty' (interview, mentor,
Hillyway).

In such circumstances students' perception was that 'The staff are seen to
treat us like two extra members of the staff in everything' (interview, student,
June Lane). At Hillyway it was 'Partly to do with the staff here; people don't find
it difficult actually to fit in. They are seen as part of the staff' (interview, mentor).

Much of students' understanding of the wider professional implications of
becoming a teacher emerged through informal staffroom interaction. Sometimes:

> You can't have a conversation in the staffroom with a student without
> someone else butting-in. (interview, mentor, June Lane)

The more students were treated as members of staff, the more open was the
staffroom talk they heard and shared, and the greater their access to opinions,
and the values, attitudes, and beliefs implicit within them.

A frequent outcome of working with a supportive staff was that in such
schools students often reported that they felt and behaved as if they 'belonged':

> Part of how welcome we have been here is we have felt we have
> belonged. (interview, student, Kenleigh)

It's perfectly obvious [the student] is very accepted and when there are things to laugh at she'll get the giggles. (interview, mentor, Hillyway)

A student's sense of their staff membership could be of an intensity which justified the metaphor of 'home'. Deepvale provides such an example:

> The students were quickly absorbed into the general life of the school. This was not confined to the normal school day. The relationship then was reciprocated by the students who gave their own time to support extra curricular activities. Dan participated in the cross country on Saturday as an extra-curricular activity (fieldnote). This also shows how the students gradually became absorbed into a school culture in which all members of the staff were involved in extra curricular activities.
>
> Denise, the student who joined the school after Christmas to do a block placement, also felt the welcoming warmth of the staff and was, again, involved in extra curricular work. (she said) 'I think it was the nature of the school. I felt far more at home at Deepvale than I did' (at my previous school). (Sampson, 1993b)

However, although 'belonging' was valued by students, and could be both an encouragement to and a symptom of successful experience in school, there was an inference that students who belonged did so because they had demonstrated in some way their acceptance of the staff's essential values and attitudes, partly by adopting the school's norms. The expectation that students should 'fit-in' with these core elements of the school's culture carried implications which will be discussed in the next section.

Fitting In and Acculturation

A previous paper has analyzed the subtle and complex processes of 'Hearing Secret Harmonies', by which newcomers appointed to primary school staffs gradually achieved staff membership (Yeomans, 1986). The processes described there also have implications for the induction and professional learning of primary school student teachers. In that paper a probationer teacher acknowledged the powerful influence on newcomers of the desire to achieve staff membership when, on being appointed to the school, she expressed her anxiety to 'fit in' with the ways of working and behaving of a group of people whose professional standards she admired:

> I was absolutely over the moon because as soon as I came to look round the school I thought 'This is really the school for me, I could really see myself working here.' . . . I thought 'Gosh, I could never ever aspire to anything like this.' But I just thought 'I want to be as good as this, the work's brilliant.' (Probationer, Sedgemoor, *ibid.*, p. 1)

The initial stage of achieving membership was through induction into the explicit rules and agreements and tacit norms governing the professional and personal activities of a school staff. It was explicit insofar as there was formal induction by staff, including the head, when agreed procedures and arrangements were explained. Information acquired over a period of weeks gave newcomers guidance about how staff members behaved in their relationships with children and one another. Explicit induction was supplemented by understanding acquired tacitly through watching how members behaved and listening to what they said.

Superficially, understanding how to behave meant knowing what to do. But in time, newcomers came to 'assimilate the framework of values which members share and which gives coherence to their actions'. Finally eligibility for membership meant 'Demonstrating that they share membership beliefs, values and attitudes when they behave in ways which harmonize with them' (*ibid.*, p. 5).

Whilst induction into planned and agreed procedures was an open process, where meanings were explicit, induction which was achieved through the tacit processes of acculturation carried hidden implications. First, the newcomer might learn new behaviour without being aware that they had done so. Second, whilst norm-led induction might reflect the complex negotiations of a particular staff culture, it did not necessarily express ideal outcomes. Indeed, there might be a rhetoric/reality gap between the statements of explicit induction and the inferences of induction achieved through acculturation. Third, induction through acculturation, being usually unacknowledged, except perhaps until after it has happened, was difficult to resist. Moreover, there were considerable pressures on any newcomer to behave in culturally appropriate ways within the classroom and staffroom when these were expressed through the everyday behaviour of members and were the coinage with which everyday relationships within the staff, and between staff and children, were transacted. In short, rather than acculturation being the legitimate means by which induction was partly achieved, induction could become the means by which acculturation was unwittingly achieved.

It was particularly likely that newcomers would experience acculturation because most had a strong wish to 'fit in'. The present study suggests that this possibility was greater when the newcomer was a student teacher. Then, the anxiety normally associated with joining a new staff was intensified by the stress of being perceived as a novice amongst experts, yet being formally assessed within that school's context.

Student teachers' wish to belong had both professional and social roots. Their professional need to understand school systems, timetables and curricular arrangements was matched by their personal need to feel secure and psychologically comfortable in a strange environment. Since, as Maynard and Furlong have suggested (1993), survival was the student teachers' initial concern, they were relieved if they joined a staff where they could fit-in easily:

> We fitted in straight away really. . . . I wanted to. I liked the school, I liked the people I was working with and it came naturally that I fitted in whereas at the other school it was a little bit more like working in an

office or a factory — the atmosphere just wasn't the same. (interview, student, Deepvale)

Survival at classroom level dictated that even when given the chance to modify ways of working, students tended to want to leave familiar routines undisturbed:

> You don't want to step on anybody's toes and you don't want to totally disrupt the class because that's what the children are used to. We have been told 'Don't feel that because we do it you have to. It's your teaching experience'. But I think we felt because that's the way they do it we would rather carry that on. (interview, student, June Lane)

Schools also were concerned that students should fit in. In the Articled Teacher Scheme, where school staff had participated in interviewing potential students, the prospect of a two-year involvement with students made one head suggest that:

> It was so important that we were actually involved in the initial stages of people being selected, to consider whether that person would fit into the school or not. (interview, head, Endsleigh)

Similarly, on a four week BEd school experience, it was clear that:

> The student has got to fit in with the school, not the school fit in with the student. If the student doesn't come up to what the school wants then there are problems, not the other way around. (interview, mentor, June Lane)

References to 'fitting-in' confirm that both students and schools believed there were school-specific ways of behaving which needed to be learnt, that these concerned personal attitudes as well as matters of routine, and were crucial to a successful experience for students and the school. Although the school's 'culture' was not referred to, induction seems to have been concerned with ensuring that students fitted in with dominant values, attitudes and beliefs, as well as adopting school norms in classrooms, staffrooms and elsewhere. The comments of three students at Intake illustrate the tacit processes and range of acculturating experiences at a school where collaboration, openness and mutual support were dominant staff themes.

Learning how things are done here.

> Well I think you pick things up all the time, just by being in the school. The whole life of the school, the routine and how things are done. Because each school is different. (interview, student Ivy, Intake)

Learning how teachers teach by watching.

> I am always just watching what they are doing. Not necessarily just the mentor. I think you are very aware of what everybody's doing. For example, if you walk through somebody's PE or assembly. (interview, student Ivy, Intake)

Feeling supported and secure.

> Well you are just part of the team really. Everybody talks to you and can ask people things without feeling embarrassed or shy about it, because everybody is friendly and helpful. (interview, student, Iris, Intake)

Learning from mistakes.

> If the staff are more relaxed and let you learn by making mistakes then it comes a lot easier. You feel that you can try out these things. (interview, student, Iris, Intake)

Acquiring professional values (collaboration).

> They all work as a team. I think since the National Curriculum came in within the planning in schools you can see them really gelling as a team. (interview, student Isobel, Intake)

In other words, even without the active encouragement of mentors, as well as learning how to fit into their particular school, students were likely to develop understandings, often unarticulated, about how teachers behaved in general, and how they taught. These were then reinforced, because the measure of fitting in was that students confirmed their understanding by adopting culturally appropriate behaviours 'absorbed' from the staff models they encountered:

> It is almost like learning to teach by osmosis — by just sort-of absorbing everything round you. . . . I feel, at the moment, that whatever type of teacher I become, I will have facets from every member of staff in me somewhere. I'll be an Endsleigh-hybrid, I think. (interview, student, Endsleigh)

but, as the image of osmosis implies, did so without necessarily being aware of how the process happened:

> It is quite difficult to know how it happens. It is something that happens without you realizing. I think initially you do think about it but as time goes by, it's like spending time with anybody, if you spend an incredible amount of time with them you find that aspects of that person do become part of you. (interview, student, Endsleigh)

Such an intangible process and its outcomes was not easily susceptible to scrutiny.

The earlier comments of Intake students suggest that even though BEd students spent only four weeks in their mentored school experience, they too might experience acculturation. When students spent far longer in a school, as in the case of the two-year attachment of articled teachers, the effects of acculturation were likely to be still greater, especially since staffs had usually been involved in the decisions to be part of the scheme, and so were committed to it, and prepared for students.

> The staff were involved in the decision to be part of the Articled Teacher Scheme and knew we were coming. They were very well prepared for us and most of the staff knew our names when we started. Evette sees us as permanent members of staff for a couple of years at least. (interview, student, Endsleigh)

Long-term attachment cemented the relationship of students to their 'home', gave ample time for acculturation to happen, and so encouraged the acceptance of students as colleagues and members of the staff as a social group:

> The length of time working together makes a difference to relationships. We feel very included here and feel part of the staff. (interview, student, Endsleigh)

Situations could develop where students were anxious to fit in, were welcomed to a staff, inducted, and felt they belonged. Under these conditions, acculturation was likely to be a particularly powerful influence on students' development. Indeed, the more supportive the school, and the more wholehearted its acceptance of students as staff members, the more powerfully acculturating its influence on students. That is to say they were more likely to take for granted the 'rightness' of the school's practices and less likely to critically examine what seemed like the self-evident truths of a school's culture. Indeed, to question practices would be to question by implication the values, attitudes and beliefs which underpinned them. To do so would be to challenge the basis of the school's culture and the values, attitudes and beliefs of the staff who had created and sustained it. A cycle could develop in which students who were able to adopt effectively a school's ways of working, were accepted into staff membership as a consequence, and were thus further encouraged to internalize the school's attitudes, values and beliefs. This effect could be especially pronounced if professional talk was not a prominent feature of staffroom, and learning came largely through watching and adopting models offered by mentors and other staff:

> The students learnt how Gail's classroom operated by being involved in the everyday organisation and teaching rather than by having lengthy explanations. When asked how they learnt how Gail operated Gemma

replied '. . . just by being involved really.' Gina extended this answer to include observation by saying, 'Demonstration and being involved.' As they were working alongside teachers and learnt by watching and copying, Gina and Gemma gradually came to work in the same way that the teachers did. This process of taking on the prevailing mode of teaching was a form of acculturation; the adopting of the way of doing things without necessarily a large amount of explanation or reflective analysis. (Sampson, 1993a)

Such acculturation was an effective method of learning how to do things the Greenvale way, but in itself did not necessarily develop in students a critical and self-analytic stance which could inform their learning in other teaching contexts.

Dependence: Learning to be Blinkered

Although encouragement to fit-in could lead to an emphasis on acculturation, most mentors and school staffs did not rely on example alone to influence student development. They were at pains to explain the reasons behind their choices of teaching strategies. As chapter 6 suggests, strategies such as commentating and explaining helped students begin to understand the rational basis for classroom decisions and encouraged them to develop similarly rational criteria. Of course, for such strategies to be influential, mentors needed professional credibility in students eyes, since:

> If we didn't believe in what the mentor was doing we couldn't really talk to her about anything. (interview, student, Endsleigh)

However, professional competence was a basic criterion for choosing mentors, and explanations which justified courses of action typifying the dominant professional culture of the school were likely to be confirmed by other practices within it. Consequently, explaining was likely to further reinforce students' approval of mentors' and schools' ways of doing things.

Therefore two elements were particularly important if students were to develop an independent perspective and self-sustaining skills. First they needed to be helped to 'learn to see' (Dewey, 1974; Schon, 1987; Maynard and Furlong, 1993). Chapter 6 emphasizes the contribution to mentors' perceptual development of the specific analytic skills of observation, analysis of situations and needs, interpreting, objectivizing and generalizing. These were skills which students also needed. Second, students needed encouragement to articulate the outcomes of analysis, in order to become self-aware, since:

> When enquiry into learning remains private, it is also likely to remain tacit. Free of the need to make our ideas explicit to someone else, we are less likely to make them explicit to ourselves. (Schon, 1987, p. 300)

Without such support, there was a danger of dependence, particularly when students were placed in those situations which were designed to be apprentice-like. As Nias (1987) suggests,

> Situations which encourage adult learners to be authority-dependent will increase the difficulty they experience in accommodating to new ways of thinking and behaving. (pp. 12–13)

Students in our research schools tended to confirm the view that 'They feel under pressure to adopt a similar teaching style to their mentor', and that 'This is partly an attempt to gain credibility in the pupils' eyes' (Maynard and Furlong, 1993, pp. 77):

> When you first go into the class it's very much 'How does this person work, am I going to be able to do this?' (interview, student, June Lane)

When they had spent the early part of their training in a mentor's class, students tended to use that experience as a yardstick for subsequent teaching:

> I think we both tend to judge everything from this class. We know we have a very good example in Erica (mentor) so that we can compare everything to that. (fieldnotes on conversation with student, Endsleigh)

Limited experience of alternative models of teaching, and the blocks of time with the mentor and her class may explain why one articled teacher described herself as 'having dependence on somebody', namely, the mentor:

> There are always many occasions where I think, 'Oh, Erica, please come and sort this out for me.' There is security in knowing that she is there if I need guidance and that there is someone whose job it is to look after me and answer my questions. (fieldnote on conversation with student, Endsleigh)

Similarly, at Bigtown, the mentor's presence could create what one PGCE student later referred to as 'a false sense of security', though it was a valuable support at the time.

> Belinda would always ask if I wanted her there, or if we wanted her to look after one group, or she would be there to give a nudge or a wink, or perhaps set things in the right direction. (interview, student, Bigtown)

One means used to inhibit dependence, by widening students' experience, particularly within the Articled Teacher Scheme, was to negotiate access to other classes within the mentor's school. Although such opportunities were useful for gaining insights into other age groups, they had limited educative possibilities.

First, lack of a mentor's timely intervention could restrict the learning that was likely:

> It's different, observing in someone else's classroom, to going into the mentor's, who wants you to ask questions about things and tells you everything as they go on. (interview, student, Endsleigh)

Second, experience of working in other classrooms in the school was still within a single school's professional culture. Even where staff cultures tolerated some variety in pedagogic practice, the values, beliefs and principles, from which it was derived were often widely shared in any school which was performing effectively. Where unified and supportive staff cultures were a strong cohesive influence on members, observing and participating in other classrooms could reinforce acculturation and student dependence. Moreover, since shared staff values and attitudes were most clearly expressed through behaviour, uniformity in teaching approaches might also be part of the staff culture. Articulating the nature of the shared view might only reinforce student dependence by appearing to give independent confirmation:

> I think there are fundamentals of the school. Everyone has ideas about what teaching is and how it should be brought about — they talk about these — and that brings them together as a team . . . because everyone has such a belief. (fieldnote of conversation with student, Endsleigh)

As 'culture bearers' (Nias, Southworth and Yeomans, 1989), staff members tended to confirm their shared set of values, and the teaching strategies consistent with them, subject to the demands of a specific school context, rather than facilitate the growth of objectivity and independence in students.

Consequently, there was a tendency, particularly within the Articled Teacher Scheme, for the school which was 'home' to remain the yardstick for other school placements:

> It's like coming home. We're part of the furniture here and in another school it's like being a fish out of water . . .
> When in the other school we had the 'When can we go back to Endsleigh?' attitude all the time. (interview, student, Endsleigh)

Third year BEd students also were influenced in behaviour in their current school by their current class teacher model:

> I have watched my class teacher to see how much he talks to them or says to them or does he just use a head movement. When they line up now I know that I can just nod at each table and they will go, because that's what they've been used to. (interview, student, June Lane)

However, they were less susceptible to acculturation than articled teachers, since they had already taught in three other schools during their course, with considerable time for analysis and reflection back in college, were taking full class responsibility for 80 per cent of the time, and had begun to develop an eclectically constructed personal pedagogy:

> I think over the three experiences we've had we have pulled out bits from everywhere. Just walking into different classes. I think wherever you are and whoever you are with you are going to think, 'Oh yes I like that, that's quite nice, that would probably work for me'. Or there are bound to be things as well that you think 'No. I wouldn't do that'. (interview, student, June Lane)

To summarize so far, close attachment to one school could produce circumstances in which appropriate induction became acculturation to the professional and personal values, attitudes, beliefs and norms of one school. Acculturation could then lead to dependence, when students used that school's model as the yardstick for measuring their performance, rather than being encouraged to develop a personal pedagogy, increasingly refined through self-analysis and critical analysis of a range of other models whose qualities were not taken for granted or considered unproblematic. The longer the time with that school, and the earlier it was in a student's course, the greater the likelihood of dependence and acculturation. Joining a supportive school might have considerable benefit in giving students a positive model of staff relationships. But the more supportive the school (particularly the mentor and teachers whose classes students shared), and the greater a student's sense of belonging, the greater the chance of acculturation.

Learning to See: Independence

A fundamental part of the mentor's role, then, was to help students achieve a transformation from dependent apprentice-novice to a learner-practitioner stance of critical analysis and supported self-development. The change involved students replacing the yardstick of their mentor and host school's model of professional effectiveness with one influenced by, but independent, of a range of models observed, critically analyzed, and synthesized with their own model-in-action. In making the transition students relied heavily on mentors' capacity and willingness to help and encourage them to analyze their own work and that of their mentor and colleagues. In explaining why they made particular teaching decisions, mentors needed to avoid becoming merely self-justificatory. Otherwise, students' capacity to be self-analytic could be limited to comparison with a mentor's and host school's model of an effective professional rather than with an ideal which was uniquely the students. Self-analysis might amount to nothing more than a judgment of how effectively a student had adopted the attitudes, beliefs practices of the host professional culture. Students could be restricted to knowing what their base school already knew. When they moved to other placements, alternatives which did not conform to the yardstick of a supportive and self-assured host mentor and school might be discarded as inadequate, or flawed, and students might experience culture shock because:

> On our course you get so ingrained into one way of thinking that it's a real jolt to go into another school. It really was a shock to the system. (interview, student, Hillyway)

Equilibrium might only be restored by return to a familiar system:

> I lost confidence while I was on practice (in another school). As soon as I walked back into the mentor's classroom I was all right again. I ought to have found the block experience school an easier class. (interview, student, Bigtown)

Learning to 'see' worked at two levels for students. The first was learning to perceive what was significant and informative within the everyday life of classroom and school — making visible the invisible, because 'It's difficult to know the questions to ask. Sometimes things are so obvious you don't notice them' (interview, student, Endsleigh). The second was being able to separate what was unique to one school from what was relevant to primary teaching in general. Left to their own devices, students might believe that a committed and skilful staff's solutions to the learning and teaching problems of one situation constituted a universal set of answers to teaching needs. As one student commented:

> At the moment I feel as if I am some type of sponge . . . just absorbing everything that is going on and unless I can get an objective opinion about things I don't really know whether everything I am absorbing is doing me good or not. (interview, student, Endsleigh)

To some extent the capacity to evaluate teaching methods was helped by informal encounters with other students, who had experienced other schools, and who described subtly different sets of practices and assumptions about teaching. There were also planned parts of the course programme when professional tutors were catalysts for discussion of experiences in schools.

However, mentors were physically well-placed to help students acquire the perceptual skills needed to make sense of their school's and their own professional practices — since they had regular access to the students' teaching and were familiar with the context in which it happened.

There is evidence that some mentors sought to develop students' perceptual and analytical capacities. For example, the Hillyway mentor was concerned about the perceptiveness of one of her students:

I think that she does a lot of good things but on occasions she appears a little bit distant, not picking up on everything she could do . . . I don't think that she gains from visits to other classes unless she's got somebody with her saying 'Now look, this is what's happening as far as the reading is concerned.' (interview, mentor, Hillyway)

As chapter 6 has suggested, many mentors also used a range of techniques and strategies for encouraging students to become self-aware, with particular emphasis on questioning:

She is trying to get us to think and question for ourselves. She sometimes provides us with some thoughts but says we should make up our own minds about things too. (fieldnote of conversation with student, Endsleigh)

However, when it came to locating current experience within a broad professional framework, mentors themselves could experience the same perceptual problem as their students. Before they could help students to learn to see, mentors themselves needed the perceptual skills with which to build an objective perspective on their own and colleagues' professional practice. Yet familiarity tends to encourage assumptions which make objectivity difficult (Abercrombie, 1969). Mentors were usually both models and products of the very school professional culture they needed to understand and explain. They had been chosen for the role invariably because they were experienced and skilled senior teachers, including deputy heads, and so were important 'culture-bearers'. Indeed, they had often helped build the culture they exemplified. At Bigtown, for example, the deputy head/mentor had a key role in a head's plans to create a particular professional culture within the school. As their heads' close allies, deputy heads were legitimately committed to the development and perpetuation of a preferred culture and its characteristic pedagogy.

Moreover, the possibility existed that because the appropriateness of long-established pedagogic practice, deeply rooted in shared personal values and beliefs, was often largely taken for granted and seen as unproblematic by staff members, mentors might find as much difficulty in 'seeing' the elements of the professional culture of their school as did the students who needed their help and support. Members and exemplars of a particular school culture, mentors might see it reflected back to them by their similarly acculturated colleagues. This could mean that much of their 'taken-for-granted' cultural knowledge was as invisible to them as it was to students, since they 'lived' it as part of their daily lives, and were committed to its perpetuation. The temptation was to justify practice rather than invite critical analysis:

(The student) said, he now sees the value of an integrated day — that you can teach small groups — all that I have been trying to tell him. He now can see the reasons why I do it in the class because he's seen what it's like when he hasn't got groups. (interview, mentor, Carlton)

The paradox was that those coherent, welcoming, supportive staff cultures which students found so appealing might also present them and their mentors with the greatest perceptual problems. The stronger the attractions of membership, the harder it might be for mentors and students to make objective sense of their experiences, unless a self-critical stance was a significant part of the school's professional culture.

Strategies for Learning to See

Some mentors were able to enhance students' perceptual skills, and help them to become self-reliant, so that a student who had felt 'mentor-dependent' could eventually say:

> I feel like I am functioning as myself more than I did. I used to function from asking Erica things all the time . . . but I am not now. I am more me dependent. (interview, student, Endsleigh)

These mentors offered their students significantly more than an unanalyzed passive model. Their behaviour differed from that of other teachers whose classrooms students shared, yet who were not perceived to be mentor-like because 'Some of the staff don't contribute to their (students') professional development' (interview, mentor, Endsleigh). Such staff:

> are not providing any kinds of real means of reflection, it really is a case of modelling and just getting experience of different age groups. (interview, link tutor, Bigtown)

By exposing their own self-questioning and the thinking behind their own actions, mentors encouraged the development of student's self-analytic capacities, and so helped students subject their own actions to rational scrutiny. For example:

> Through discussion I would give as many ideas as I can, always telling them why I have done it. (interview, mentor, Bigtown)

and:

> I have spent a lot of time telling them why I did things, even what might seem the most obvious little things about management. (interview, mentor, Endsleigh)

Mentors also gained in self-awareness by articulating their practice for students, because:

> It made me think — why am I presenting this activity in this way, how else could I have done it?... And I shared my thoughts with them. (interview, mentor, Endsleigh)

Working with other staff in the school was not inevitably acculturating, provided that mentors had a perceptive understanding of their colleagues' strengths and weaknesses, and were able to influence the location of student placements in other classes. When mentors recognized the danger of dependence they encouraged their students to look beyond their mentor for models of effectiveness, recognizing that access to other practices could be a valuable step towards developing an independent perspective and a personal pedagogic model:

> They get to know one person so very well in half a term, they become a bit inflexible — they think that way is the best way. It's not, it's one way. I think it's something they have to come to terms with. When they are with me, it's all very well for me to say there are other ways of doing it than this, mine's not the only way. But until they actually experience other ways, they have nothing to build on. (interview, mentor, Endsleigh)

Articled teachers and PGCE students regularly had periods with classes other than the mentors'. Such placements had some effect in making students less mentor-dependent. For example, one mentor deliberately placed a student in a situation where she knew the student would need to draw on her own strengths and skills.

> I threw her into a class where I knew the teacher could not communicate with adults, which also was an awkward class; and I saw her absolutely 'go'. (interview, mentor, Flenley)

Many mentors went beyond a training role. They actively contributed to students' educational development by helping them acquire and refine their analytical skills, and by encouraging them to progress from emulating others' skills to critically examining their own teaching. However, it could be difficult for mentors to find sufficient time. There were often problems arising from the competing demands on mentors from their other roles within school:

> There are a lot of occasions where she will sit down during lunch-time when there is about 10–15 minutes to go, and say, 'Is there anything you want to ask or talk about?' If there is something that is really bugging me, but I know it is going to take more than ten minutes, there is no point in really bringing it up until you know that you have more time. (interview, student, Endsleigh)

So that:

Questions seem to fade away and you reach a point where if you haven't
known the answers up to now, it won't make much difference if you
don't know them tomorrow. (interview, student, Endsleigh)

Within limitations of time often snatched from lunchtimes and after school,
mentors sought to move students progressively towards self-analysis, variously
described by mentors as 'a chance to learn from themselves' . . . (Bigtown), 'getting the student to actually build on what they've got and what they need to get'
(June Lane), and 'encouraging them to think more for themselves and take some
responsibility for their own learning' (Endsleigh).

The goal was that a student like Beryl, who had hesitantly said of her mentor
'I think she would try to get me to analyze the lesson' (Bigtown) was able to
contribute as full partner in the constructively critical analysis of her own teaching, exemplified at the beginning of chapter 5.

Mentors were flexible in the pace at which they encouraged students to
become self-reliant, and as chapter 10 shows, attempted to respond to students
individually wherever possible. However, in one respect mentors were not flexible nor encouraged students to depart from their mentors' model. They presented students with a consistent model of values and attitudes, often dominated
by a love of teaching and concern for the interests of the children. For a student
such a model might mean being aware that

She (mentor) likes the children, she has a respect for the children, she
is enthusiastic about education. (interview, student, Bigtown)

But for the mentor it meant that:

If I got really cross, because the control was hopeless and the children
were suffering, I would interrupt. (interview, mentor, Bigtown)

Broadening the range of students' experiences, partly within the school, but more
crucially in other schools, seemed to have been decisive in helping students
become self-reliant, so that having spent a school experience away from her
articled teacher mentor, a student was able to say:

It's almost like being weaned off something. If we hadn't had the cut off
period from Erica [mentor], I think I would be less independent than I
am now. I suppose it's like having children really, saying 'Just get on and
do it, you will be all right. You can go home on the bus alone, nothing
will happen to you.' (interview, student, Endsleigh)

Course structures also contributed to the growth of students' perceptual skills,
objective capacities and growing independence, by giving access to several schools.
Articled teachers worked in three schools, and PGCE students worked in four
schools in all. BEd students had already worked in three schools by the time they

reached their third year, and would work in five schools, in all, during their degree. They too valued the support of their mentors and schools, and, typically, felt 'as though we have belonged' (interview, student, Kenleigh). But by this stage they were already developing a personal teaching model, and saw their mentor as critic of and contributor to that, rather than as a model to be followed:

> I like the way John teaches and I do value what he says and I do reflect on it and alter my next lesson maybe. . . . I might agree with it but then again, once you come to do the lesson again, I would probably still stick to my own methods. I think as I go through the course I am getting my own ideas and sometimes it's harder to fit in with a school or with the teachers, because I have started to build my own ways of teaching. Which I suppose is good. (interview, student, June Lane)

Summary

We have suggested that it is an appropriate part of the mentor's role to induct students into the routines and norms of their host schools. However, because induction is partly a process of acculturation, students' wish to 'fit in', coupled with schools' encouragement for them to do so, can mean that acculturation becomes the outcome as well as a means. Acculturation presents dangers of students becoming dependent on a restricted professional model, particularly where schools are welcoming and act as long-term hosts.

Whilst mentors have an important role in ensuring students' experience is educative, and that they 'learn to see', as prominent exponents of their schools' professional culture, mentors too may share students' perceptual difficulties. If students are to be educated rather than acculturated, mentors themselves need to have an independent educated perspective.

Ultimately the most powerful educative influence on students in their school-based work was the opportunity to experience a wide range of classroom and schools, supported by mentors who were themselves self-questioning, and who were able to give time to encourage in students an analytical and self-aware stance. Under such conditions, students might develop the capacity to make their own objective judgments, and so build a personal model of effective professional practice, firmly grounded in personal beliefs capable of being articulated:

> Over a period of time everyone formulates their own philosophy and way of doing things. We at least get into different classrooms, so it's not as though we were just with the one person all the way through. Even if I hated the way Dennis taught, even by not liking what he's doing, it's enabling me to firm my own views. (interview, student, Deepvale)

Research in California into what mentor teachers do when they work with beginning teachers 'makes us question whether it is appropriate to regard these mentor teachers as field-based teacher educators and their work as a form of "clinical teacher education" ' (Feiman-Nemser *et al.*, 1993, p. 165). Our evidence is that mentors can be, and sometimes are, educators, but that they are not inevitably so. First it may be necessary to educate these potential educators. This raises major issues about the nature of processes hitherto described as mentor training. — some of which will be considered in chapter 13.

Chapter 10

Being an Effective Mentor

Robin Yeomans

This chapter builds on earlier ones to consider the features characteristic of effective mentoring in primary school initial teacher education. Since we recognize that successful mentoring outcomes are affected by favourable conditions, chapter 11 will consider those conditions which help mentors to perform effectively.

The Meaning of Effectiveness

To define the mentor's role is to begin to define effectiveness, since clarification of the role helps to identify relevant skills and strategies, and so provides criteria by which effectiveness can be evaluated.

HMI comments on mentors have highlighted the importance of an objective perspective, a sophisticated view of students' role in school and of mentors' contributions, and a carefully planned programme of experience and support:

> Well-trained confident mentors are clearly beneficial to the students. When, on the other hand, they display a narrowness of view arising from experience mainly in one school, a view of the student as the teacher's helper rather than as a trainee professional, or inconsistency in the amount of practical support they offer, the quality of the students' experience is sharply reduced. (HMI, 1991, p. 28)

The students and mentors in our case studies confirm the view that mentors can make a valuable contribution to students' development, although 'there are lots of variables in between the best and somebody just doing it in name only' (interview, partnership class teacher, Aimshigh). Chapter 5 has suggested that the mentors' role needs to be considered in terms of structural, supportive and professional dimensions, and that in professional terms, mentoring involves training, education and assessment. That analysis is derived from observation of mentoring practice and mentors' descriptions of their role, partly influenced by their training and by the College view of their role expressed in course documentation, including feedback forms. The latter encouraged mentors to see themselves as educators, and emphasized skills of reflection and self-evaluation as part of the competence of a beginning teacher.

We recognize that effective mentors are also initially context-oriented. Their first concerns are with responding to the particular teaching context of their own school and preparing students to work within it. Then mentors begin to react to, reflect on and analyze their own and students' behaviour in dealing with specific situations, in order to enhance and consolidate students' skills, provide them with the means of self-development, and so help prepare them for other teaching contexts. We share the view that 'a reflective orientation to teaching should stress the giving of good reasons for educational actions' (Liston and Zeichner, 1989, p. 1), and that encouraging a reflective stance in students means that any definition of effective mentoring should encompass

> developing teachers who are able to identify and articulate their purposes, who can choose the appropriate means, who know and understand the content to be taught, who know and understand the world views and cognitive orientations of their (pupils), and who can be counted on for giving good reasons for their actions. (*ibid.*, p. 2)

A further yardstick for the effectiveness of primary initial teacher education mentors is their contribution to achieving DFE criteria for initial training of primary school teachers. In terms of classroom skills these emphasize:

> equipping teachers to use a range of teaching methods and organise their classrooms in a variety of ways, so that they can offer whole-class teaching, as well as individual and group work, so as to respond effectively to the different needs of their pupils;
>   Ensuring all teachers are able to maintain order and discipline in their classrooms. (DFE, 1993, p. 6)

We note that the Criteria suggest that the outcomes of initial teacher training should also be 'the foundation for further professional development' (p. 5), and that competencies also define '... personal qualities which all newly-qualified teachers will be expected to have developed' (p. 8). As far as school-based teacher education is concerned, we suggest that competencies which assume that learner teachers should acquire the 'necessary foundation' to develop 'vision, imagination and critical awareness in educating their pupils' (DFE, *op. cit.*, Annex A, p. 17), depend on mentors whose professional concerns embrace an educative as well as a training element. This view of the mentoring role is consistent with that characterized by McIntyre, Hagger and Wilkin (1993) as 'developed mentoring' — being concerned with:

> — helping learner-teachers to become aware of, and to question their preconceptions, in offering them new ideas from their own experience

and practices, and in guiding the learner-teachers in the use and development of ideas acquired from various sources. (p. 94)

Similarly, we share the view that

The promise of mentoring is not only in helping beginning teachers learn how to teach, but also in helping them learn how to reason about and learn from their teaching. (Feiman-Nemser, 1991, p. 2)

because

Learning to teach involves more than learning to act like a teacher. It also entails learning to think like a teacher. (*ibid.*, p. 19)

Such descriptions run counter to assumptions that primary teaching is a relatively simple job, requiring limited pedagogic skills which can be learnt in a relatively short time simply by copying a skilled teacher (for example, Hillgate Group — see Furlong in this volume).

In short, HMI, mentoring practice and theory, and Criteria for primary initial teacher education provide adequate justification for the view that criteria for evaluating mentors' effectiveness should be grounded in the expectation that effective mentors will be educators as well as trainers and assessors. With this assumption in mind, we now consider the essential nature of effective mentoring.

The Essentials of Effectiveness

Chapters 5 and 6 have explored in detail the complexity of the mentor role and the range of the skills and strategies used by mentors. There are dangers in attempting to construct a model of effective mentorship by appearing to present an exhaustive taxonomy of desirable skills and appropriate strategies, and we do not suggest that the tables in chapter 6 do so (see tables 6.1 and 6.2). They reflect the range of skills and strategies mentors used rather than provide a catalogue of essential requirements, and so represent an empirically-derived ideal model rather than a description of an effective mentor.

However, effective mentors were multifaceted performers, although it was possible for mentors to perform successfully in a single dimension of their role. They used strategies and skills which were appropriate for structural, supportive and professional dimensions of their role. Further, because effective mentoring within structural and supportive dimensions was the means to achieving the end of professional effectiveness, rather than an end in itself, particular significance needs to be given to those mentor skills and strategies which helped them work across the professional dimension as trainers, educators and assessors. Nevertheless, mentors could work effectively with students without the full range of skills

identified in chapter 6 — either because they substituted appropriate alternatives, could draw on colleagues' skills (especially in curriculum expertise), or did
not find themselves in circumstances where a particular skill was needed.

The tables also suggest particular relationships of role dimensions and
elements with specific skills and strategies. This relationship leads to a further
feature of effectiveness — namely that mentors needed to be able to identify the
element of their role which was appropriate at a particular time, and then select
those skills and strategies which were relevant to particular circumstances and
were likely to achieve the purposes of that element.

The suggestion that being effective needed a wide range of skills and strategies, and the ability to make effective judgments about which to use and when
and how to use them, implies that effective mentors are special people. This
raises the issue of mentors' personal qualities.

In an article which warns against an over-emphasis on competencies, Smith
and Aldred (1993) use the term 'wisdom' to describe the qualities of 'non-
instrumental understanding, contemplation and self-knowledge', suggesting that
'the qualities that the mentor needs are distinct and unusual, complex and rooted
in the kind of person he or she is, not simply in the abilities they have' (p. 112).
They point out that the model mentors give students is as much concerned with
their 'ways of thinking' as with pedagogic skills, that 'he or she knows well enough
about means . . . But the mentor has also some understanding of needs: of what
education is for' (p. 110). Mentors' personal qualities have been discussed already
in terms of their relevance to the skills of particular role dimensions (chapter 6),
and their contribution to effective relationships (chapter 7). Without seeking to
revisit these issues, redefine the nature of wisdom, or construct an ideal portrait,
we suggest that some qualities are of particular importance for the role taken as
a whole. The key qualities are a sense of purpose and direction, sensitivity and
perceptiveness, self-awareness, openness and open-mindedness, and flexibility.
Indeed, the list offers a possible agenda for mentor training. A sense of direction
and purpose was concerned with 'trying to see a road through to a competent
teacher' (mentor, Endsleigh), and informed all decisions mentors made, taking
into account both the mentor's 'map' and 'the need to say different things to the
students because they would have different needs' (mentor, Bigtown). The need
to identify and respond to individual circumstances, and to discriminate between
alternative courses of action, rather than apply blanket solutions, was the main
source of the demands on mentors' sensitivity and perceptiveness, and affected
their judgments about students' learning and colleagues' capacity to help. Chapter
9 discussed the significance of perceptiveness in 'seeing' situations and teaching
performances objectively, as well as addressing their context-bound implications.
Self-awareness is an important form of 'seeing', since sufficient understanding
of the nature of mentors' own craft knowledge to enable it to be articulated, a
realistic view of their own skills, and a clear understanding of the relationship
between a mentor's selection of skills and strategies and their own motivating
values, attitudes, and beliefs, was the basis from which mentors made rational
judgments about students and facilitated students own self-knowledge.

Where openness is concerned, McIntyre, Hagger and Wilkin (1993) have suggested that for learner-teachers to understand that

> the order, attention, interest and comprehension which experienced teachers generally achieve in their classrooms are the consequence not so much of their charismatic personalities, their general teaching styles, or the authority of their positions, but rather of the particular actions they take in the classroom and of the considerations which lead them to take these actions.

requires that

> their mentors consistently discuss their own teaching, as well as that of the learner-teachers, in an analytical way which draws attention to the actions and considerations underlying their successes (and no doubt their occasional failure). (p. 96)

The development of such understanding relies on the openness and open-mindedness noted earlier in some mentor-student relationships (chapter 7), and which encourages trust in students by affirming that 'the mentor too is a learner' (Smith and Aldred, 1993).

Finally, flexibility has been mentioned in terms of the day-to-day conduct of the structural role dimension (chapter 6). However, it was also needed more widely; first, in coping with conflicts within the role such as that implicit in the transition from supporting to training, educating, and then assessing students; second, in being prepared to deviate readily from a notional ideal pattern of development, part of the framework within which effective mentors often worked.

Concern with personal qualities is consistent with belief in the value of mentor training, since qualities emerge in behaviour, and behaviour which contributes to mentoring effectiveness can partly be learnt by using mentor training programmes to develop latent personal qualities (Yeomans, 1993a).

We now consider the patterns of proceeding which underpinned the choices mentors made about particular aspects of the role and the strategies and skills relevant to them.

Patterns of Proceeding

Chapters 6 and 7 have discussed the link between specific aspects of the mentor's role and the skills and strategies on which they relied. This relationship is one part of an 'ideal' pattern of proceeding which informed each aspect of the mentor's role, and indicated skills and strategies most likely to be relevant to each phase of students' development. Many mentors also worked within patterns of development related to the needs of the specific teacher education programme they contributed to. These were notional frameworks which informed decisions about the nature, phasing and pace of the planned student experience. However, mentors used such frameworks flexibly in responding to individual circumstances and particular students. Consequently, 'contingent patterns' of proceeding sometimes emerged as learnt responses to specific features of a mentoring context, derived from experience. We now consider ideal and contingent patterns, and examine the factors which encouraged 'ideal patterns' to be modified. Finally, we shall examine the concept of an 'optimum fit'. This was the means by which effective mentors ensured that, within a consistent broad framework, students experienced a pattern of mentoring which best matched their short and long-term individual needs and circumstances.

Ideal Patterns

There tended to be an underlying long-term cycle within a mentor's work with one student. This was largely governed by time, was the outcome of experience, and became modified by the needs of the particular scheme. In the initial stages of a school-based phase, the emphasis was on the structural dimension of the role. This phase was dominated by the need to create the conditions in which a student could perform well. It included planning and organizing the student's programme, negotiating its details with other staff who were affected, and ensuring the induction of the student into the school and classroom cultures. Supportiveness tended to be particularly important once the student had begun to familiarize themselves with their class and the school, and were experiencing the detailed realities of the school and classroom life. Where students' early teaching performance was concerned, mentors work as trainers tended to precede that as educators in order and importance, partly because, in the interests of students, teacher and children, context-specific training was a necessary part of the induction process, and partly because, both mentor and students first concern was with students' classroom survival.

> The first thing was to give them a taste of what it is like to teach . . . the real life of teaching — so that they could be sure that they had made the right decision about wanting to teach. I concentrated a lot on classroom control and discipline in the first two or three weeks and stressed how important it is to get that right to begin with. The skills of teaching, basic organization, planning and evaluation of a lesson and resources, needs to be covered before going on to the detailed planning and progression side of things. (interview, mentor, Endsleigh)

As students became familiar with their school context, developed a clearer understanding of the detail of their role within it, and gained in confidence, they became less dependent on short-term advice and support. This change was reflected in an increased emphasis on mentors working educatively, as they sought to encourage student independence. Finally assessment tended to dominate the mentor's agenda towards the end of a school experience, when its emphasis was summative.

Embedded within that long-term cycle was a recurring short-term one which governed the structure of day-to-day mentor-student contact and discussions. Ideally mentor-student contact followed mentor observation of the student at work, which led to formative and summative assessment of the students' performance (see chapter 4). Subsequent meetings tended to mix training and educative agendas initially, the mentor also seeking to be supportive. Then discussion about planning and organizing students' subsequent work usually followed in the light of discussion of previous performance.

The third component of ideal patterns was sequences of student activity which individual mentors had themselves developed as a response to their experiences as teachers and mentors. To some extent, these were influenced by the nature, stages and requirements of students' particular courses. Effective mentors tended to have their own clear and often detailed overall plan for the development of student activity. This is evident in the work of three of the mentors who were supporting students in their first formal contact with school in partnership phases. The Hillyway mentor described as 'a bit of a vague timetable' for her articled teachers' first weeks in school, a programme which reflected thoughtful anticipation of what might best promote their growing confidence:

I am aiming at her being able to do her observational tasks wherever (the relevant activities) happen to be taking place in the school, spend a large amount of time with year 1 class building up gradually, when the class teacher feels confident and the student feels confident, to actually take a teaching session, and also doing a little bit in year 2. (interview)

In a different course, a PGCE mentor described a pattern with broadly similar intentions, which he used to carefully nurture two students through their first formal contacts with groups of pupils:

It was mostly observation at first. They started to take groups then. I gave them an outline of the type of thing I wanted them to do. They found the ideas, we discussed it, and planned the group together. Then they started to take registration and followed the procedure that I use in the morning, copying exactly what I'd done. And they took stories. Then we developed into them taking a group activity they had planned entirely themselves. (interview, mentor, Greenvale)

The planned pattern of development constructed by the Bigtown mentor for the same course is significant because in addition to its detail and careful development, it illustrates how ideal patterns were modified in the light of individual circumstances. Although her plans for the two students are initially the same (steps 1 to 4, and 9), and she seeks to capitalize on the benefits of collaboration (steps 7 and 8) nevertheless, she also decides to treat them individually in the light of their unique strengths and needs (steps 5, 6 and 10).

(Step 1)
The progression tended to be, they would observe me and would help around the classroom.

(Step 2)
I have always found that anybody I have had has just naturally gone to groups and helped. From there the next stage was for me to come out of the classroom situation, but still in the classroom, talk to one of the students — I would then talk with one student through what I had done, Why I was doing that, where I hoped to go, what went before and where I hope to go in the future with them, and meanwhile the other student had control of the class almost but I was still there, so I would still really have the main bits of control.

(Step 3)
From there it was, them telling a story, so I was in the class, but popping out.

(Step 4)
From there the students did some group work.

(Step 5)
. . . but one of the students wasn't happy with the class so I made myself available within the class but suggested that they take control, so I would say, do the register, so they got used to bringing the children in, as it was in the beginning, now they come in themselves; bringing the children in, calling the register, then introducing something, or maybe not introducing something, just doing the register.

(Step 6)
The student who wanted the whole class, he took it, I then worked with groups. At times I would have a specific group, other times I would wander round with the other student, helping. Sometimes coming back to talk to the whole class and other times not, depending again on the student and their confidence.

(Step 7)
I did feel it was important for them to plan together an activity and teach it in a given time, So I gave them a task, told them what I wanted them to achieve. So they went away to the staff room, planned it, came back to me, talked me through it. I then let them do it.

(Step 8)

I then got the students to comment on each other in a positive way; which didn't always happen.

(Step 9)

From that stage I then gave the students a chance to teach by themselves and said I would be in and out.

(Step 10) Formality

She has known that she has had a couple of weeks planning for this, we have talked through her notes, and that was formal. We went to the staff room, I also said I will watch and make notes for you, but then this has come at the end, I wouldn't have done it at the beginning. I suppose I have had to build up to it. (interview, Belinda, April)

Belinda's overall strategy is an example of how a mentor's ideal pattern becomes modified by emerging needs, and begins to develop some of the characteristics of 'contingent patterns'.

Contingent Patterns

Contingent patterns affected mentors' performances of their role in two ways. First, there were the preferred sequences which were triggered by anticipating or responding to particular circumstances. Second, there were changing patterns of response which were the outcome of 'reflection-in-action' on the immediate dialogue between a mentor and student.

As mentors grew in experience, they developed their own systematic patterns of proceeding contingent on particular circumstances. Having worked with several students, they discovered sequences of response which seemed appropriate for particular kinds of students, phases or sets of conditions. These preferred patterns were the outcome of considered analysis of an individual student's needs. In time mentors learnt to interpret the significance of a set of circumstances, and then might draw on a bank of responses. It is beyond the scope of our current work to be able to identify these patterns in detail. But feedback conversations between mentors and students show some evidence that mentors used recurring patterns of strategies which were triggered as a rule-like response to specific conditions. The order, balance and frequency of these sequences of strategies were determined by monitoring immediate cues from students, and in the light of judgments already made about their progress. For example, productive feedback conversations tended to approximate to the following pattern:

Student encouraged to comment early — to give cues on insight.

Monitoring student confidence and self-awareness enables mentor to decide timing, frequency and form of praise.

or reflecting back to help student 'see' themselves.

There was some reference to general principles illuminated by student activity.

Telling, suggesting, questioning strategies used, their balance depending on students' stage of development.

In some circumstances the mentor had already decided that a situation urgently demanded a particular emphasis whatever the students' likely response. For example, although a yardstick of success for a mentor was that, as a consequence of developing insight into learning and teaching processes, students' progress was reflected in growing independence and an ability to construct their own solutions, time was not always on the mentor's side. The short-term needs of a tentative student nearing a critical assessed experience might prompt more 'telling' than 'questioning'. Or a student showing few signs of taking responsibility might gain more from confrontation than from encouragement.

A further consequence of the classroom teaching skills of effective mentors was that they had developed the generic skills characterized by Schon (1983 and 1987) as 'reflection-in-action', and by a mentor as 'having to think on your feet because situations arise as you are doing it (mentoring)' (interview, Belinda). The ability to rapidly reevaluate teaching situations and change direction during the act of teaching could transfer from teacher to mentor role. Skilled mentors were able to monitor newly-perceived needs and draw selectively from their repertoire of strategies and skills. Within the course of a single teaching episode or feedback conversation, the impression of random responses, might mask a complex rational pattern which was a response to constantly changing needs. The feedback dialogues between a skilful mentor and a student resembled closely Schon's description of reflection in action as 'a reflective conversation with the materials of a situation' in which 'each person carries out his own evolving role in the collective performance' (p. 31).

Responding to Differences

The most significant of the circumstances which determined mentors' decisions about how to proceed were differences in the structure and stage of a teacher education scheme, mentors' own level of skill, the students themselves, and the context of the school and class.

Different schemes carried different expectations of mentors' contributions to student development. The school-based emphasis of articled teacher and PGCE schemes involved mentors from the beginning to the end of a student's course, so that these mentors were engaged with the full range of a student's development from novice to beginning teacher. Consequently the mentors' role and the related skills and strategies needed to be wide-ranging. Further, they dealt with different students at different stages in their courses, ranging from partnership to assessed final school experience. For articled teacher mentors, sustained if intermittent contact over two years made demands on their capacity to retain an objective perspective on the performance of students with whom they had well-established personal relationships. On the other hand, BEd mentors' relatively brief contact with their students meant they had to assess individuals' needs rapidly and then respond flexibly. However, they could expect that their students were broadly familiar with the culture of schools, and had developed some teaching skills.

Mentors also needed to be aware of the limitations on what they could hope to achieve imposed by their own circumstances, opportunities, qualities, skills, and experience. It was possible to be effective without being a mentoring paragon, provided that mentors' organization took account of such factors as their own limitations, competing demands on time (especially where deputy heads were concerned), the ways in which their college link tutor and colleagues could constructively contribute to the mentoring process (see chapter 8), and how their personal qualities might affect the relationship with their students (chapter 7).

Effectiveness also relied heavily on mentors' flexibility in responding to students as individuals. Flexibility was especially important where mentors were responsible for two students, and might be tempted to treat them similarly, even though 'some students come back at you with a lot of things, others don't' (mentor, June Lane). Consequently some mentors created an individual programme by first assessing individual needs:

> I just had to find out where they were. I couldn't have written an individual programme. What if I had got one student who has obviously had an awful lot of experience in primary schools — knew how to talk to children — and another who absolutely froze. They couldn't have followed the same plan. (interview, mentor, Flenley)

The Kenleigh mentor's experience illustrates the effect such differences could have on each of the structural, supportive and pedagogic dimensions of a mentor's role.

> The thing I have had to think very carefully about this time is that they are totally different personalities. So one student immediately made the rapport with me. She came more than half way, she was always prepared for what she wanted to know and was very anxious to get things sorted out for herself. She was a very outgoing person, who, even before the start of the practice had got a relationship with me, with parents, with the other staff because of her personality and her desire to get it right and to be prepared. Whereas the other student obviously doesn't have the same ease of interpersonal skills, and so really, on the preliminary visits I didn't feel I'd made a particular relationship with her. So that's something I was endeavouring to do before I actually started any formal observations. I've made as many times as possible to chat to her in the

classroom, in an informal setting, over lunch. So that she knows me. I have probably made more overtures to her than she has to me, because that isn't part of her personality. (interview, mentor, Kenleigh)

Frequently mentors had to allow for differences in students' levels of confidence, dependence, self-awareness, openness, readiness to question and to be self-analytical. Since these differences also were reflected collectively in overall differences in classroom competence, mentors had to consider carefully which aspects of performance they should focus on and how they might do so in ways which would also develop those qualities in students. At Endsleigh, the mentor felt that

> I've learnt more about them and I think I shall be more critical of Emily, be more sure that what I ask is seen to be done and more supportive of Eileen. That sounds a bit strange but I think I have got to be behind Emily and make sure that she's actually coming up with the goods. Eileen wants to run before she can walk, so she needs to be slowed down a little bit and told, 'well you know you have still got time. You are going to make it'. (interview, mentor, Endsleigh)

At Bigtown, the mentor's perception that one student was more confident than the other led her to deal with similar classroom skills in different ways.

> With the display we worked together — with Bill I could say 'I think so and so isn't right'. With Beryl, we talked together, and I started with things I liked. She said it had been done in a rush, and then she commented on what she thought about some aspects, and I then made some suggestions. Part came from her, part from me. (interview, mentor, Bigtown)

Being effective also meant that mentors had to take into account how the nature of the school itself might influence how they mentored. Although concerns with physical and organisational constraints might dominate the structural dimension of the role, the social and psychological climate was more important in making long-term mentoring decisions. Of particular significance were the quality and extent of support from the whole staff, and the need to consider how dominant were a school's assumptions about teaching norms, given that 'the mentor realizes that she is training students within a particular school's culture' (Clarke, 1993b, p. 23).

One further consideration permeated differences in individual sets of circumstances, and so contributed to a mentor's effectiveness. This was how changes over time influenced mentors' decisions.

Changes Over Time

In the instances under discussion, mentoring was spread over four weeks, one year or two years, depending on the scheme. Inevitably student needs changed over time, even within an intensive four-week experience. This meant that no decisions about how to proceed as mentor could ignore where students were in their course or in their development. For example, similar sets of circumstances could prompt different responses at different stages. At Hillyway,

> (the student) 'standing back' in the classroom was considered as being reticence at first and thought to be 'not a bad thing', but as time moved on, it concerned Hazel (mentor) more and more. (Wooldridge, 1993b, p. 56)

Feedback was often informal early in the mentoring process, but the need to ensure that self-awareness developed meant there was a need to make feedback more formal, for example by written confirmation. When summative assessment was imminent, mentors' observations carried a more intimidating implication. It could seem that

> everything gradually got more formal and an atmosphere of assessment was created. (interview, student, Endsleigh)

If the passage of time had not been matched by developing student skill and self-awareness, urgency increased. At Endsleigh

> Once I may have used a joke, or let something ride so that they become self-aware. But by now I'm saying 'Don't do X, don't let them do Y, don't tell them off until they're quiet, which I wouldn't have done to start with. But if they're about to go into school on their own, then they need to know. (interview, mentor, Bigtown)

To summarise, in trying to work with students effectively, mentors constantly needed to select appropriate strategies from a wide range of possible courses of action. Whilst they were guided to some extent by broad 'ideal' patterns of proceeding, they also had to evaluate the effects of a range of interacting circumstances on both short and long-term mentoring decisions. The uniqueness of individual circumstances demanded individual responses. A mentor's paramount skill lay in the capacity to achieve an optimum fit between the needs of an individual student in a unique situation and the selection of the appropriate element of the role and the relevant skills and strategies.

Achieving an Optimum Fit

'Fitness for purpose' has been recommended as the criterion by which to evaluate solutions to problems of match in primary school teaching and learning strategies (Alexander, Rose and Woodhead, 1992). However, 'best fit' solutions have a history in management literature, where they are concerned with ideas about the

ACHIEVING AN OPTIMUM FIT

optimum fit of.......

A

Ideal/preferred pattern

>>> ———————————————time———————————————>>>

Role Strategy Skill

with

B

contingent factors

(negative)		(positive)
initial -------------------------------- **course phase** -------------------------------- final experience		
hostile ------------------------------------ **context** -- supportive		
inexperienced ------------------------------- **student** ------------------------------- experienced		
anxious		confident
unskilled		skilled
closed		open
unaware		aware
inexperienced -------------------------------- **mentor** -------------------------------------		
experienced		
restricted skills		broad
skills		
early -- **time** -- late		

decides

C

optimum

<<< ———————————————————————————>>> Role Strategy Skill

relationship of optimum management styles to the contexts in which management decisions are to be made (for example, Fiedler, 1967; Fiedler *et al.*, 1977, Handy, 1984). They also share some ground with the work of Gray and Gray (1985), who proposed a 'mentor/protégé helping relationship model and major mentor functions/roles' model which indicated 'varied types/levels of help mentor provides to enable protégés to gain competencies' [*sic*], 'confidence, realistic values, experience, and so on needed to function autonomously as a complete professional' (p. 41). Whilst we do not claim to provide a 'ready reckoner' for mentoring practice, it may be helpful to consider diagrammatically the nature of the decisions mentors need to make when they decide how to respond to a student.

Effective mentors met long-term and short-term decisions with a pre-existing strategic pattern of procedure, which gave a framework within which to consider how to proceed (A). The realities of a specific student working with a specific mentor in a specific set of circumstances within a specific course at a specific time caused mentors to modify their ideal way of proceeding (B). The outcome of their complex analysis is that the mentor adopted the strategies and used the skills which were best suited to performing the aspect of the mentoring role which matched that set of circumstances.

Of course, since we have suggested that long and short-term decisions are affected by this sifting process, there may be a hierarchy of levels and meta-levels at which it happens. Momentary adjustments of strategy could be the outcome of implicit 'knowing-in-action' (Schon, 1983) within an existing optimum fit analysis which had already influenced the existing course of mentoring. Further, mentors who were skilled in achieving an optimum fit were not necessarily engaged in a process which they could or needed to articulate.

Chapter 11

Conditions for Effective Mentorship Within the School

Joan Stephenson and John Sampson

In this chapter we shall be considering the broad set of conditions within the school that enable facilitate mentorship. The particularities of different 'sorts' of mentorship and an examination of what effective mentorship might mean are issues for elsewhere in this book. As we have collated and analyzed the data the issues that have arisen most frequently appear to be concerned with the people involved: the mentor, themselves, the headteacher, and the whole staff teams as well as structural and organizational factors. In attempting to identify conditions which appear to have a bearing on successful mentoring we will examine each of these separately and then attempt a synopsis. The order in which the headings are taken does not necessarily imply that we consider any one factor to be of more importance than another at this stage in our research though we believe that a consideration of the people involved from within the school is a natural starting point.

The Mentor

Allemann's view (quoted in Stott, 1992) is that:

> Mentoring relationships can be established or enriched by learning or encouraging mentor-like behaviour rather than by selecting certain types of people. (*ibid.*, p. 331)

Allemann's emphasis is on mentor training and development, an issue that is addressed in chapter 13. Allemann suggests that there is no right type of person to be an effective mentor. Chapters elsewhere in this book have indicated that mentors do need certain key skills and qualities. Rather than take issue here with Allemann we would suggest that there are certain conditions that enable mentors to act effectively. One clear basic condition is for the mentor to be a willing and committed participant. Chapter 4 has explained how mentors were chosen; by the headteacher with the mentor's agreement. It is also apparent that many mentors were actually committed to the whole notion of partnership between school and college:

> (The mentor) believes in mentorship. She recognizes it as a partnership between student, school and mentor. (Clarke, 1993b)

The Mentor's Credibility

> I know from talking to the headmistress that Hazel is thought of extremely highly in the school and she's probably one of the teachers who didn't want to take the headship because she liked and enjoyed working with children. She's the kind of teacher that never has discipline and control problems. (interview, link tutor, Hillyway)

Evidence from case studies suggests that the credibility of the mentor is important. This has to be recognized by staff within the school, particularly the headteacher. Credibility was often apparent to students in the way that mentors were discussed by staff when not present. The student at Hillyway was able to confirm the link tutor's viewpoint when discussing indicators of credibility:

> *Heather:* Usually the way they talk about them [the head and the mentor] when they are not there.
> *Interviewer:* So how do they talk about them when they are not there?
> *Heather:* Well mostly in a very affectionate way really. They talk of how organized they are for one thing. (interview, student, Hillyway)

From the student's perspective it was important to be associated with a mentor who had credibility. The mentor's place within the set of staff relationships seems to influence the set of relationships for the student:

> I think that there are always certain members of staff who always get on much better together and if you are initially part of that then that's really good because if you are part of that set of staff you will always remain part of that because that's how everything works. (interview, student, Endsleigh)

Finally the credibility of the mentor affected how some students responded:

> I have a lot of respect for her experience and I will listen to her. (interview, student, Bigtown)

The importance of the mentor's credibility in facilitating the mentor-student relationship has already been explored in chapter 7. Here it is sufficient to summarize by suggesting that the mentor needs to have credibility with staff in the school.

The Mentor's Status

The mentor's credibility was important. This was often connected to their status within the school. Chapter 4 has shown how a number of mentors in the case studies were deputy headteachers. Deputies were undoubtedly chosen for two main reasons. Headteachers may have identified them as the teacher most likely to have the skills and qualities to ensure an effective mentorship. They may also have selected deputies because of the status that being a deputy would bring to mentorship. The different status of the mentors and the way it relates to their ability to develop and sustain worthwhile relationships with students has been examined in chapter 7. However, the high status of a mentor within a school could also mean that mentors have less time to fulfil their role than others may.

Students recognized that despite the deputy's other commitments they were often getting a good mentorship experience. They recognized that the sort of teacher who was deputy head was also a positive classroom model for them:

> Because she is the deputy head we could use more of her ... but she had got a lot on her plate and she is rushing about and you are left, getting a few flying words at a time — they are valuable. I think what we got from her was very valuable in the end, the quality was high. (interview, student, Bigtown)

However, the balance is a fine one. Deputies have a large degree of other responsibilities within a school and in some cases these seem to have prevented them from effectively carrying out the role:

> For these two students, the mentor as deputy head, was seen as a restriction on the role. There were already many demands on her that took her out of the teaching space. The other mentor was a class teacher with an 'A' allowance. She seemed less pressured and the two students have a more positive outlook. (Frecknall, 1993)

> The deputy head's role is a very full one and it brought with it some difficulties in respect of student expectations, especially with regard to formal or informal feedback. (*ibid.*)

> I would say that it just seemed to me she was overloaded. (interview, student)

This is in keeping with the findings of Corbett and Wright (1993) that:

During the first year of the course (Articled Teacher) it became evident that the role of mentor was proving difficult for deputy headteachers and those with senior management positions. The role was time-consuming and demanding, which meant that either the mentoring or the deputy headship suffered as they tried to juggle two demanding tasks. (pp. 24–5)

Status is important if students are to feel that they are receiving a quality experience but there is a fine line between the mentor who has a high status within the school and the availability of time to mentor effectively. Or to put it another way, deputies made good mentors when they had the time to be a mentor:

Belinda as a mentor — no problem — Belinda as deputy head and mentor, a big problem because there were times when she was only there something like 65 per cent of the time. (interview, student, Bigtown)

Mentor's Self-development

There is little doubt that all the participants taking part in the mentoring process felt they had learnt something from the experience:

It is a two way dialogue, when I have written the observation I do give it to the students to read and I do encourage them to actually reply to me on the observation sheet before any of it is photocopied or typed so that it's not just a one way thing. (interview, mentor, Kenleigh)

It can be seen from interviews with both mentors and students that many of these gains were in the area of professional development where mentoring helped each to add to their range of skills and knowledge.

She (the student) came in an extra time so we could talk, just for one day's worth and about another two hours afterwards to sort of dissect the day as it had gone. But that's fine, And you learn a lot yourself from doing it as well. The things you take for granted like how to dismiss children from the classroom area. They said like go and you think, 'Oh no'. So you remember how you do these things. (interview, mentor, Aimshigh)

Mentors were able to develop analytical skills whose value they could perceive as useful in other contexts.

But I mean do feel free to say if there is anything at all that I haven't covered. You know, letting me know so that I can build that in because, as I have said, it is for your benefit but it's also for my benefit in that I hope I will have staff that I will be doing appraisal with and some of these strategies I would hope to be using as a head later on. So it is helpful to me and the more that we chat about it and get it right the better. OK. (conversation, mentor with students, Kenleigh)

Part of the willingness of mentors to fulfil the role appears to be linked to their perception that the whole process was an educative one for them. It is, therefore, a necessary condition for effectiveness that mentors understand that, in terms of learning, mentoring is a two-edged sword.

The Headteacher

Interest and Involvement of the Headteacher

The headteacher was found to be an ingredient in ensuring the effectiveness of the mentoring experience for the students in several of the case studies. Indeed we would concur with Corbett and Wright's (1993) view that the headteacher's role is crucial. We will describe the behaviour of headteachers from case study material and analyze this in respect of the conditions for effectiveness of mentorship.

The behaviour of headteachers as culture creators (Duigan and Macpherson, 1987; Nias, Southworth and Yeomans, 1989) was important both as an example of 'how things are done here' and as educative leaders. Part of the way in which the headteacher promotes a supportive school culture can be seen in the way that they extended a warm welcome to both the visiting researchers and the students:

I (the researcher) received a friendly welcome from the headteacher and from Gail (the mentor). The head and another member of staff involved me in a discussion about the book sale. (fieldnote, Greenvale)

For many of the students a meeting with the headteacher was the first real contact with the school and its staff. Consequently, the head had a vital role in giving immediate messages to the students about the school and the way people treated each other:

The headteacher came in in the morning, told us quite a lot about the school; dished out all the documents that the booklet required him to provide and made us feel very comfortable. (interview, student, Deepvale)

It was also often the head who was able to excite the students with their own sense of enthusiasm about education and about their school in particular:

The head who took us round, was extremely enthusiastic about the school, which I found very good. (interview, student, Aimshigh)

Where mentoring proved successful the headteacher's interest and commitment to the scheme was not just an initial factor but was continued. This continued involvement was with both the students and the mentors themselves. Esther, the headteacher at Endsleigh, provided a good example of the variety of ways in which a headteacher was able to maintain interest and to support both the students and the mentor. In many ways the headteacher was acting as an additional mentor to both the students and to Eve the mentor:

> The headteacher continues to take an interest in the work and develop-ment of Emily and Eileen, sometimes joining them and Eve in discus-sion. It was significant that the head and deputy head's shared office was often the space that was used for discussion between the mentor and the Articled Teachers. (fieldnote, Endsleigh)

Esther involved herself by taking an interest in the students' files and by being approachable:

> The headteacher also involves herself through reading their files, writing comments in them, and asking them informally how they are getting on. The Articled Teachers seemed to appreciate this interest in them and clearly find her to be approachable if she is around and Eve isn't around to answer queries. It is clear from talking to them informally that they also value her perspective. (fieldnote, Endsleigh)

The mentor considered that this was accomplished in a supportive way in which there is a good deal of mutual trust:

> She (the head) is important because she is there. She leaves it to me. She trusts me to keep her informed of anything that she ought to know, which I do. She sees their files. She sees the comments I have written and she adds her two penn'orth as well. She notices different things which is good. She supports them, talks to them, involves them in the staff. She looks at their personal development profile sheets. She is reading their assignments and she will read the comments I have written about their assignments. She is interested in what's going on but she hasn't got time for the mundane day-to-day running of it. She leaves it to me to judge what she should be involved in and any important decisions obviously I would consult her first. Which year groups to place them in for school experience. I keep her abreast of where they are and what they are doing and why. When they moved from me to year four she was aware of the fact that they were moving. (interview, mentor, Endsleigh)

At times the supportive interest and involvement was concerned with specific problems that arose in the day-to-day role of the mentor:

> Sometimes I go to Esther and say, 'look I've got this problem, what do I say, what do I do?' and we talk things through. (interview, mentor, Endsleigh)

The mentor was able to feel supported but not threatened since the headteacher acknowledged the importance of the mentor:

> Esther has been very supportive. She was making assessments as well. She would show me everything she wrote and talk through everything she wrote and said to Emily and Eileen. (interview, mentor, Endsleigh)

Not surprisingly Wooldridge was able to conclude that:

> Though Eve had the responsibility of mentoring the two Articled Teachers the headteacher, Esther, had a significant role in facilitating her work. (Wooldridge, 1993a)

There was clearly a very positive relationship between headteacher and mentor. Most of the examples from Endsleigh show the headteacher in a supportive role.

Case study material presented so far in this chapter has shown the headteacher taking an active role with the students as well as with the mentor. It may be equally valid to say that this positive relationship might display itself by the headteacher maintaining a more distant watching brief. The headteacher at Hillyway preferred to emphasize her trust in the mentor and her availability if required:

> I would say that I haven't done as much as maybe I would have liked to and there is no doubt that if I had a different mentor maybe I would have to do more, I really can trust Hazel. (interview, headteacher, Hillyway)

Headteachers and Professional Development

A further dimension of the headteacher's role within the school affected the conditions for mentorship. Where headteachers sought to create conditions in which their staff could develop professionally they also provided conditions in which mentors and students could flourish. For example, the headteacher at Deepvale had a quiet but effective role in promoting professional debate and this was noted and appreciated by staff. The headteacher's credibility in the school was also high:

> So, yes, there is professional debate. All credit to David (the headteacher) really, because he is quite relaxed about a lot of things. I have a great

respect for David in his approach to things, detailed thinking and planning going on, he appreciates the pressure of being at the chalk face, so he actually tries to do what he can to remove a lot of the administrative and background pressure at that level, when discussions take place in the staff room they are not starting from nothing — that's what I'm driving at. A fair amount of thinking will have taken place and that something has been put down on paper, and that starts the thinking. (interview, mentor, Deepvale)

To summarize the importance of the headteacher, we would suggest that conditions for effective mentoring are set partly by the involvement and interest of the headteacher in the scheme itself and also by their involvement in the school. Mentors and students benefited from heads who bore the characteristics of effective headteachers portrayed in other studies of headteachers' roles in effective schools. (ILEA, 1985; Mortimore *et al.*, 1988). These heads:

. . . liked to talk but they also knew when to keep quiet and let others have their say. Indeed they had a marked capacity to listen with care. Even though they may be very busy, they seem to have all the time in the world for anyone in difficulty. (ILEA, 1985, 3.260)

The Whole Staff

The Culture of Collaboration

It is a recurring theme of the schools researched that where mentoring was effective, staffing tended to be stable and included experienced teachers. This is not to say that the staffing was static. In every case there were also teachers who had less experience but these were in the minority. The nature of the experience can be illustrated by considering two of the schools, one from each of the schemes using mentorship for long periods in the course:

The school is fortunate in having a good mix of age and gender within the teaching and support staff. The head is now well established within the school and has followed a policy of appointments that have balanced the experience of his staff both in curriculum areas and years of service. Carlton-cum-Chardley is a school with a regular turnover of staff who leave on promotion, most senior staff members stay for three years or more and have a keen interest in staff development which has been warmly nourished within the school. (Stephenson, 1993)

The main body of the staff of 14 teachers, including the headteacher, deputy headteacher and part-time staff, are well established and experienced, i.e. have taught at the school for more than three years. There are two newly-appointed teachers. (Wooldridge, 1993a)

One result of using schools with stable staffing was that there tended to be the feeling of being part of a team. The staff shared similar views and pulled in the same direction. Whilst stability of staffing does not inevitably lead to a sense of being a team it did seem to contribute to a culture of collaboration (Nias, Southworth and Yeomans, 1989). Many of our twelve case study schools had qualities reminiscent of a culture of collaboration. One sure sign of the collaborative approach was the nature of interpersonal relationships between the staff. Relationships have been discussed in chapters 7 and 8. Here it is sufficient to notice that researchers were quick to see the positive ways in which the school staff treated each other in the staff room as an important aspect of the nature of the team:

> All were obviously on friendly terms with first names being used, coffee being made for each other and body language suggesting they were relaxed and yet still attentive to what each other was saying. (fieldnote, Deepvale)

Although chapter 9 has indicated the pitfalls of students identifying too closely with their host school, if the mentorship scheme was to operate successfully the staff team as a whole had to be committed and interested. Headteachers were quick to realize this and in most cases carefully consulted their staff. Students were quick to perceive and value whether or not there was a commitment from the whole school staff to mentorship:

> I think all the teachers have been so friendly and interested. They could have been friendly but not particularly interested but they were interested in what you were doing and were friendly and helpful. I think that's the main thing everybody made you feel welcome. (interview, student, Greenvale)

Gaining the impression that a class teacher was not prepared for them gave the students a different view of the levels of commitment of the whole staff:

> I don't know at what point she knew that she was going to have me in her class but I understood she didn't know at the beginning and that she didn't really know how to handle me or what experience she was expected to give me. (interview, student, Aimshigh)

The high level of commitment of some of the school staffs also showed in the way teachers contributed to the students' development. In one sense the whole staff acted in a mentor-like way at times, in that the whole staff seemed willing to take a measure of responsibility for the development of the student:

> It isn't just me as mentor, we have taken it on as a school thing and not just the class teacher who the students have to be with, but anybody and

everybody gets involved in it so it is a whole school process so that the students always know that there is somebody else that they can turn to if I can't necessarily answer their problem. (interview, mentor, June Lane Junior)

This statement by the mentor at June Lane was verified by the researcher when he noted that:

I sit in the staffroom with the mentor and the two students in the middle of the afternoon. We are discussing teamwork. The deputy head comes in and soon he is joining in the conversation and sharing his own experience. (fieldnote, June Lane Junior)

The contribution from the whole staff then is important. The culture of the school that they help to promote, how welcoming they are, their contribution to corridor displays, the cooperation that exists between them, the behaviour of their children in the shared spaces of the school and their willingness to have students in their classroom, are all features of this. So, too, is the willingness of the staff team to treat the students as another member of the team. One aspect of this is the willingness of the staff to share their expertise.

I think sitting in the staff room at break and them encouraging you to get involved in the conversation and making you feel relaxed has helped. They haven't switched off from us they have tried to involve us as well. (interview, student, June Lane Junior)

Lunch time. The students are involved in staff room talk. Bill asks how the children form the letter S, and several staff offer answers. He also gets help with his College seminar on 'Special Needs', and information about how such children are dealt with in the school. Belinda (mentor) spends some time there planning with Beryl her programme of work for Friday. Beryl has a copy of a new National Curriculum science document, and this starts a discussion with one of the staff, who tells Beryl about a science course she has been on recently. (fieldnote, Bigtown)

This could be a particularly important role when students were having difficulties. We have even been able to report how one school staff tried to support a student after a disastrous art session:

. . . she had had to spend the playtime clearing up. When she went in the staff room at lunch time all the staff knew and shared their horrors — everyone had one. (fieldnote, Deepvale)

On the other hand if students felt that they were being exploited then they would not get the best from the experiences they gained. One way in which the commitment to the scheme and to the students showed itself was in the way individual teachers responded to the students. Some experiences were possibly well intentioned but failed to make the students feel part of the team or even to feel that their needs were of importance. In some cases the students were left to wonder what commitment there was when they found that staff were actually unfriendly and unhelpful, when they felt very much outside the team because of the way they were treated. Fortunately such instances were rare but clearly demonstrate the importance of a whole staff commitment and the need for favourable attitudes towards students in general.

The Culture of Professional Debate and Development Within the School

We have already referred to the headteacher's influence on the nature of professional debate in the schools. Our evidence is that where staff were able to discuss and analyze professional issues among themselves, they created a climate which nurtured discussion and analysis of professional issues with their students. This ability to articulate their own professional practice is a necessary condition for effective mentoring. Typified by the extent to which the staff at Deepvale were involved in broader educational activities beyond their own school.

> Generally the staff were well established and experienced. They had not had much recent experience of students but the school had been recommended by a LEA adviser as a suitable placement in which students would learn and develop. The headteacher had recently been seconded to the National Primary Centre at Oxford, the mentor had completed a secondment at the London Institute some years ago and one of the class teachers was just completing a MA. (Sampson, 1993b)

In other schools teachers were following DPSE courses and similar advanced work at local HE institutions. However, it is not just the pursuit of courses outside the school that contributes to a culture of professional development. Indeed it could be argued that the professional development that occurs within the school is more important to the creation of that culture. This can be reflected in staff room discussion, Sampson (1993b) also noted that at Deepvale:

> The first time I visited there was discussion about the Art Interim Report and on most other occasions some professional matter was discussed.

While a student at Endsleigh commented that:

> Everyone had ideas about what teaching is and how it should be brought about — they talk about these . . . (fieldnote, Endsleigh)

Schools were involved in professional debate in diverse other ways. This included policies for curriculum subjects, involvement in LEA course provision, School Development Plans as well as apparently superficial concerns such as the levels of agreement on domestic issues such as display. These all give a view of the school staff as a group who have clear and shared views on the purposes of schooling and are willing to articulate them. This is often reflected in the way that the schools and the mentors themselves see the role of mentor as being concerned with raising levels of professional debate within the school.

Organizational and Structural Conditions

Time

> I have reorganized myself so that I can be free to observe in detail. (interview, mentor, Carlton)

The mentor here has understood the role in terms of preparation and the time factor involved in this: It is important to find a regular talking time. Dennis, the mentor at Deepvale, meets his students to discuss their work once a week. He felt that planning, in particular, had to be well thought through:

> . . . we would then work out who would be in charge of which group, or who would be in charge of the class at certain times during the day. (interview, mentor, Deepvale)

He also ensured that class teachers had time to discuss plans with students:

> . . . and we arranged the first day next term for their final visit, a supply will do half a day in each of the classes so that the class teacher can actually sit down and go through the folders in detail. (interview, mentor, Deepvale)

The importance of having adequate time is highlighted by the students' perception when they don't meet:

> In patches she was very busy and I think the first week we did have two minutes or so saying how we got on and what we thought but I actually can't remember other than a quick, 'Are you all right?' it actually ever happening after that time. (interview, student, Aimshigh)

Some mentors had strategies for getting round both the lack of time and the way in which the time was used:

> Not surprisingly the Partnership class teacher sometimes does not have time to do written evaluations before debriefing sessions. When this

happens students are encouraged to give their feedback first. (Clarke, 1993a)

> She sees mentoring as similar to supporting other members of staff although, because of time restrictions, goals have to be short term. (*ibid.*)

Though time problems were sometimes seemingly beyond resolution:

> I think she [the mentor] left it up to us pretty much. She wasn't usually around because being deputy head she often has to do extra duties everywhere and I suppose she actually used us in a way so that she could go and do something else. (interview, student, Aimshigh)

Some mentors were able to juggle their commitments so that they could give time to students because the student's presence gave them some relief from normal classroom duties. This would depend on the strength of the student and would need to be balanced carefully so that the student was not merely cut adrift in the classroom:

> I don't mind giving up hours after school if it means that there is time, especially with a strong student like my last final one, I was able to leave the classroom, hand over to him; I popped in at times and at other times I watched — again that was negotiated — and we discussed things at the end of the day. (interview, mentor, Bigtown)

For other mentors the only solution seemed to be to affect their personal lives. Gail, for instance, found the role time consuming and had:

> affected the time I had tea at home. (interview, mentor, Greenvale)

rather than having any affect on her other roles within the school.

Demands on the time of the mentor affect effectiveness, another factor which has a bearing on the time, in hours and minutes, a mentor can spend on the process features elsewhere in this chapter where the issue of deputy head-teachers as mentors is examined.

The number of students

Another way of getting round the time factor was when students used each other as sounding boards, as in these examples from one pair:

> Got feedback from each other as well. (interview, student, Greenvale)

> We did similar things so we could say, 'Well yours seemed to go well', and we could talk about it together like that. (interview, student, Greenvale)

Pairs of students, particularly in longer term school experiences, can give each other some degree of peer mentoring. During the partnership experiences mentors in the affiliated schools scheme had a pair in their own class and a pair elsewhere. In all the block experiences in all the schemes mentors had students in classes other than their own. Mentors with students in classes other than their own express one time drawback as they saw it:

> There isn't the time or the opportunity for you to leave your own class too often, to actually go and watch the students in other classes. (interview, mentor, Deepvale)

Following feedback from mentors they each now have responsibility for only two students, normally placed in their own class, for partnership experiences. Unless a large number of students can be placed in a school so creating a large amount of 'relief from' normal class teaching it would appear that a necessary condition for mentors with their own class responsibilities is that two students is the maximum.

The size of the school
The size of primary schools compared to secondary schools has been used as an argument against making primary teacher training as school based as the recent model for secondary PGCE (Circular 92/00). In the schemes operated by the College, schools had between two and four students. This seems to have put a considerable strain on smaller schools. In a recent report for the National Primary Centre a mentor in one of the researched schools has described the difficulties his school had in acting as an affiliated school to the College because of its size. The six-class urban 8–12 school found it a strain to have student placements for two pairs of students, and a total of four students as individuals. Indeed one class of children had a student presence in one form or other for most of the year (Blackburn, 1992). Clearly schools must not be overwhelmed by the number of students. One student felt particularly strongly about the number of students one school had through partnership experience and other block experiences:

> I mean, I actually questioned the number of students this school had in, full stop! (interview, student)

During 1992/93 the nature of affiliation has changed so that a slightly smaller number of students needs to be accommodated but there is still quite a strain on the school's resources.

Summary

In this chapter we have shown that there is a range of conditions within schools that affect the effectiveness of mentorship. These include the people involved, particularly the mentor and the headteacher but include the other staff as well. The way in which mentorship is organized is important, the number of students a school has is partly determined by factors such as size of school but also by the number of students any one teacher can effectively mentor. This has some impact on the time available for mentoring, as does the other roles a teacher has to perform within the school. The time factor is too important to overlook, mentors will need to be provided with sufficient time, either through funded supply cover or through careful, flexible use of the time when students have responsibility for classes. The following tables may act as a checklist for future discussion about the conditions within a school that will enable mentorship to be carried out effectively though it is recognized that some of these are tentative.

The mentor:
- must have a clear understanding of the role;
- must have credibility and status;
- needs time to discuss practice with students.

The headteacher
- must be interested and involved in the scheme;
- must be an effective leader in terms of professional development and school culture;
- should have some direct involvement with the students.

The staff
- should be established but not static, with a balance of new and more experienced teachers;
- should have a culture of collaboration;
- will have a shared view of effective practice;
- will need to show a friendly and interested attitude to the students;
- should take a measure of responsibility for the development of skills in the student;
- would ideally share their expertise;
- should be prepared to share their weaknesses as well as their strengths;
- should have a culture of professional development.

Organizational and structural factors
- the school should be of a size to accommodate the students without distorting the balance of students/teachers in the school;
- the mentors should have time to fulfil their role;
- students should be placed in pairs when possible to allow peer mentoring.

Chapter 12

Sustaining the Quality of Mentorship

John Sampson

. . . come in to watch them (the students) teach as some kind of quality control. (fieldnote of comment by mentor, Deepvale)

At a mentor support meeting Dennis, the mentor at Deepvale, specifically checked that the link tutor would visit the students at his school. He saw this as a necessary part of the role of the link tutor. Here he was specifically concerned that his judgments of the students were comparable with those of mentors of other students and that it equated with the assessment of the link tutor. He was expressing concern for the quality of his mentorship.

This focus on the quality of mentorship and hence the students' experience was not a central concern of the TEAM research but nevertheless evidence has been gathered that will shed some light on this issue. This evidence indicates that the quality of mentorship was sustained through a variety of factors. Firstly, there was the process of the initial selection of schools and mentors. Secondly, there was the establishment and then the development of shared understandings and expectations. Thirdly, there was the monitoring of mentorship as it happened.

The Initial Selection of Schools and Mentors

A vital factor in controlling the quality of mentorship and the student experience was the selection of suitable mentors and schools. Students would need to be exposed to effective primary practice and they would also need to be well mentored. Chapter 11 examines the conditions which could facilitate effective mentorship and recognizes the importance of careful selection of the school and the mentor. The initial selection process offers one means of sustaining the quality of mentorship. However there is also the implication that ITT institutions will need to know their partners well and that any relationship must be an open and honest one.

In the Articled Teacher Scheme and the PGCE and BEd schemes different means of selecting the schools and mentors were linked to the different background to the courses. The Articled Teacher course was a newly accredited course in which the LEA had considerable input and in which central government clearly expected LEAs to play a large role. Here the selection process was open to schools from the LEA who bid to be part of the scheme. These bids were then compared to criteria as described in chapter 11. This process was carried out jointly by the LEA and the College. In the one-year PGCE and the BEd degree there were established courses with established links, this made the selection of schools less a matter of concern to the LEAs and more a concern for the institution and the schools themselves. For example, the schools that were to have an enhanced role in the one-year PGCE were largely selected by the ITT institution. The course leader and the Head of Department for Teacher Education met with LEA advisers and discussed the possibility of approaching certain schools with this role in mind. As a result of this discussion a number of schools were approached by either the course leader or the Head of Department in person.

In the majority of cases the selected schools were already well known to the college. They were also schools in which students had been successfully placed for other forms of school experience at some time. Carlton-cum-Chardley, chosen to act as Affiliated School within the one-year PGCE, had been involved in the 'Partnership Experience' and the Block Experiences of the PGCE for the last five years and, apart from the newly-appointed staff, most teachers had some experience of supervising students in their career in the school. Similarly Endsleigh, a school chosen for the Articled Teacher Scheme, had been used to place second, third, and fourth year BEd students on 'school experience' for more than ten years. Indeed the single exception among the researched group of schools was Deepvale. This school was strongly recommended by the LEA adviser and had other interesting features in terms of staff development.

The selection of the mentor is a key issue in terms of assuring the quality of mentorship. It is the mentor that the student is most closely going to relate to; it is the mentor who will initially provide the model and will go on to fulfil the multiple dimensions of the role outlined in chapter 5. This chapter showed clearly the key function that the mentor serves in enabling the transition from student to beginning teacher. Consequently the choice of mentor is vital to enable the quality of the course to be sustained.

In the case study schools the selection of the mentor had largely been a responsibility of the headteacher. In cases where the school was well known there have been examples of tutors suggesting possibilities to the head but the main responsibility for choice has lain with the head, who knew the school, the varied workloads of the staff, their different aspirations and how students are likely to be received by them.

In all cases experienced teachers were chosen, some were deputies and others held other posts of responsibility. It is interesting to note that of the six mentors in the Articled Teacher Scheme three had the deputy of the school involved. The proportion in other case studies across a range of courses gives a very similar breakdown. Headteachers and mentors realized that it was an important role that would have possible effects on the mentor's own professional development, the contribution that the mentor would be able to make to the normal operation of the school and their attractiveness to other schools when new appointments were being sought. The last is an interesting issue for headteachers to consider, the mentors at Carlton-cum-Chardley and at Kenleigh were both promoted to posts in other schools. This may mean that teachers with this kind of experience are attractive to other schools?

Mentors need to be effective teachers. Chapters 7 and 8 show the importance of the mentor's ability to establish good relationships and the conditions that will permit effective mentoring. Each of these will contribute to the quality of the student experience. However, careful choice of mentors and their schools in itself does not guarantee that students have similar experiences. It is the development of shared understandings about expectations between mentors and between mentors and tutors that I will now consider.

Establishment of a Shared Understanding

The variety of courses at the College using some form of mentor or mentor-like teacher meant that there were different ways in which the issue of shared understandings was faced. In the Articled Teacher Scheme headteachers, and at a later stage mentors, were party to the planning and the validation process. This was a new experience for all of them. Nevertheless the school partners had an opportunity to participate in the planning and it is reasonable to suppose that they therefore had some grasp of the purpose of the course and the detail in which it was to be organized, undertaken and evaluated. This was not the case in either the one-year PGCE or the BEd third year schemes. In each of these the initial shared understanding came about through the schools being previously associated with the course and through mentor training. The training of mentors for the Articled Teacher Scheme also contained elements in which mentors were given the opportunity to develop a shared understanding of the course and their part in it. The possible content of mentor training will be explored in chapter 13. Here, it is worthwhile to indicate some of the evidence for ways in which the training helped to establish and maintain quality control.

One of the established aims of teacher education at the College is that beginning teachers should be reflective practitioners. Through the mentor training course mentors were made aware of this. Sampson (1993b) noted how a mentor tried to put this into effect by questioning his students rather than continually giving them tips. This is not an uncommon feature of other case studies of mentors in action carried out by TEAM. Wooldridge (1993a), too, notes that some of the procedures undertaken as part of the mentoring the student received had been informed by the mentor training sessions. Essentially it was the mentor training that first brought home to mentors the importance and complexity of their role, the need for positive regular feedback to the students, how, and with what frequency, this should be carried out, the purposes of feedback and the need to articulate practice. It was also mentor training that made mentors aware of the procedure that needed to be carried out if students were to be assessed fairly. By drawing attention to these factors and by offering mentors some of the tools for carrying out their role the training courses attempted to sustain quality. That is, the training attempted firstly to identify those factors thought to affect the quality of mentoring as far as the organizing tutors were concerned and, secondly, the training sought to make mentors aware of their role in sustaining the quality of effective student practice. However, although the training was seen as a means of enabling mentors to be effective the actual issue of quality was never explicitly raised during the training course.

Training was seen as an ongoing need throughout the period of mentorship rather than a once and for all experience. The first training sessions were largely proactive in that the organising tutors largely took the lead in characterizing the mentor's role and describing the necessary skills prior to the mentoring experience. The need for a form of training that could be seen to be both proactive and reactive was recognized by both trainers and mentors. In all the schemes an initial period of mentor training was followed-up by a number of mentor support meetings. In the Articled Teacher Scheme there were at least two such meetings a term, making six in all, and in the one-year PGCE there was one in each section of school experience, making four in all. In the mentoring scheme covering the third year of the BEd there was one meeting part way through the students' four week block experience. Blackburn (1992) has written elsewhere of the usefulness of these meetings from the mentor's perspective. He claimed that they enabled a sharing of experiences. They also gave mentors a degree of confidence that their expectations of students were appropriate for the students' stage of development. This, at least led to an evenness of quality. Mentors were also able to air concerns and to clarify procedures for the forthcoming period of school experience:

> . . . we try to run it so that there is a mentor's meeting which goes over what we intend the students to cover in the next half term. So that every mentor has got a rough idea that the students will be expected, for example, to tell three stories a week or plan 'x' number of sessions showing progression or . . . — there is a clear framework within which they [mentors] can work. (interview, link tutor, Greenvale)

In this example the tutor indicates that mentors' meetings helped ensure shared expectations.

Sampson (1992a) has reported how there was a clear shared view of expectations between the mentor at Greenvale, an Articled Teacher Scheme school, and the course leader who also fulfilled the role of College link tutor. Part of this shared view was partly an outcome of the half-termly mentor support meetings and the initial training period, as well as from supporting documentation.

Students also noted the impact of these meetings. One student at Carlton noted that initially there seemed to be little opportunity to meet the mentor for planning purposes. However there was a perceived improvement which the student attributed to the mentor support meetings:

> I think all the Partnership schools must have got together at one point and discussed what they were doing with various students. After that, that improved a lot. (interview, student, Carlton-cum-Chardley)

It may well be that the support meeting helped the mentor to realize that they were not fulfilling their role in the same way as other mentors and that as a result of the meeting the student's experience was improved. Here there seems to be some evidence that the actual process of the other mentors describing their activity to that point acted as a guide to the mentor at Carlton. The implication here is that the quality of the experience is sustained by meetings which discuss how the mentors have carried out their role, as well as giving greater guidance for the next stage of any experience. These meetings act as an opportunity both to monitor and evaluate quality and react to issues as they emerge. They also provide an opportunity for both mentors and trainers to define standards and so enhance the quality of the next phase of the mentorship scheme. They can, therefore, be both proactive and reactive.

In addition to the mentor training course and the support meetings, mentors were provided with support material. On occasions this was the same material students were given and on others they were provided with specific documentation. Each of the courses involved in the mentoring schemes at the College provide students, mentors and class teachers with a variety of support materials. In addition to the Student Handbook, which in all cases contained general administrative matters, the aims, content and a course programme, and assessment issues, there was a variety of other documents to support mentors and students.

In the Articled Teacher Scheme there was a Mentor Handbook which dealt with general administrative matters, the course aims, content, and programme including the mentor's part in this, and had a section devoted to the mentor's role. There were also a block school experience which gave detailed expectations for both students and mentors. A Professional Competency Profile gave an outline of the expectations at different stages of the course. This covered areas such as; knowledge of schools and schooling, the National Curriculum, curriculum specialization, child development and learning, assessment and evaluation, planning, classroom management and teaching skills, whole curriculum skills and issues, and reflection. This was completed by the student with the mentor.

In the one-year PGCE supporting material included a Partnership Experience Booklet which gave information on the aims and expectations for the period the students are in school, and suggests tasks and activities the students should undertake. There were also block school experience booklets which gave detailed expectations for both students and mentors of the block experiences and included a further section summarizing the roles of the students, the class teacher, the mentor and the link tutor.

Supporting material for the BEd year three school experience was a similar Block School Experience Booklet.

In short, in all the College's mentorship schemes the students and the mentors have clear written guidance as to what each can expect from the other.

The list of competencies in the Articled Teacher Scheme was one further aid to the establishment of the broad framework of agreement. However, even where lists of competencies are used there can still be considerable debate about their exact meaning in action. While a novice bricklayer may be able to produce a wall as evidence to match a competency there are areas of teaching that are not so easily defined as competencies for the student teacher. A simple competency statement concerning the student's ability to control a class for instance would presumably also have to take into account a whole range of circumstances, many of which may be beyond the student's immediate control. Another problem with competencies which Pring (1992) has pointed out is their absoluteness, there being no shades of competence. Nevertheless a competency profile enabled further debate about understandings of purpose between mentors themselves and between mentors and tutors. Some of this debate was conducted as the course proceeded, whilst ongoing training also provided a forum.

However whilst guidance sought to promote and provide parity of experience for all students, mentoring was ultimately redefined and transformed by the way an individual teacher performed the role. Consequently two implications follow. First there is a need to monitor what mentors actually do if the quality of the student experience is to be sustained. Second, an explanation of how quality in mentorship schemes is achieved is inadequate unless it takes account of mentors' and others' contributions to ensuring that students are monitored effectively. I now turn to these aspects of the work of mentors in action.

Monitoring and Further Development

Once the mentorship schemes were operating in schools the main participants were the mentor, the student and the college link tutor. The relationships between these, and between other significant participants, has been explored in chapters 7 and 8. Here I want to consider the way in which these three each contributed to monitoring the quality of the student experience.

The TEAM case studies indicate that these three parties all contributed to sustaining the quality of mentorship and the student experience. It was in effect a triangle of relationships where each party drew upon others to satisfy themselves that quality was sustained and where each contributed to others' experiences to ensure that they were effective. It could best be summarized as a diagram:

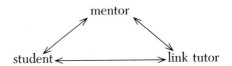

The provision of a college link tutor was initially not explicitly seen in terms of quality control, but that was one aspect of the role that was to emerge. Each cluster of three schools in the Articled Teacher Scheme and the six affiliated schools in the one-year PGCE had a College tutor attached to the school. This link tutor visited the school on a regular basis with the mentor as a focus rather than, as in more traditional forms of supervision, the students. In the Articled Teacher Scheme the role of the link tutor was initially described as: providing continuous regular contact with the student's school, headteacher and mentor; providing the main link between the school and the college; together with the student and the mentor planning, carrying through and monitoring the student's work in the school; supporting the mentor in observing the student's work and in providing feedback to the student; assessing school experience in conjunction with the mentor.

During the partnership period of the PGCE and the Articled Teacher Scheme the link tutor was mainly concerned to ensure that the system functioned smoothly, that the explanations made in the supporting documentation made sense to everyone involved and that the students and the school had a productive shared experience. Much of this support seems to be concerned with reassurance for the mentor. This reassurance should be seen as a form of quality control. Part of this role became concerned with an evaluation of the degree of shared understanding. Early experiences at Bigtown were a focus for discussion between mentor and link tutor. Here the link tutor suggested that part of the early role was the confirmation of expectation.

> Early on it was talking to the Head and Belinda [the mentor] about what was expected, confirming Belinda's approach to the two students, looking at some of the student's work and discussing it with them. (interview, link tutor, Bigtown)

In this case confirming what was expected of the mentor and the students was a way of ensuring that the quality of the course was maintained.

Similarly the link tutor at Greenvale saw that part of her relationship with the mentor was concerned with giving reassurance:

> . . . really with Gail [the mentor] it's reassuring her that what she is doing is right. She wants an overview from me comparing what she's doing with my knowledge of what other mentors are doing and how other students are performing. She wants a sort of bench-mark to make sure that her judgment and the way she is treating the students is acceptable to the college. (interview, link tutor, Greenvale)

The link tutor, then, can be seen as someone who was concerned with sustaining the quality of mentorship. This is not just the link tutor's own perception. The giving of reassurance, and the provision of some sort of bench-mark of quality against which mentors can evaluate their performance is also how Gail (a mentor) perceived the link tutor's role:

> . . . (the link tutor is someone) to say yes you are doing the right thing.
> Really because you are stuck out in a school on your own . . . it is useful
> for the link tutor to discuss what the others [mentors] are doing and to
> say yes you are doing a similar sort of thing. (interview, mentor, Greenvale)

Mentors actively sought 'bench-marks' to help them evaluate that what was happening in their school was effective. This is a clear indication that they were
concerned about sustaining the quality of the experience. They used the link
tutors to keep them informed about the course's expectations, and how other
mentors were meeting them. Mentors also apply their own form of quality control by asking link tutors for their perception of the students. In this respect the
mentors are clear that they are part of a team and look for support from the link
tutor. This provides a useful means of monitoring and sustaining quality at the
same time. In short, an important impetus to the quality of the experience came
from the mentors themselves.

Students also became directly involved in the concern for the quality of their
mentorship. Some difficulties were inevitably concerned with course expectations. In Deepvale there was concern over the students' schemes of work during
a four-week block school experience. The mentor was uncertain about the exact
nature of a scheme of work, particularly its length. The mentor sought advice
from the link tutor. One of the students explained the role the link tutor played
in resolving that particular issue:

> . . . [the link tutor] came and spoke to Dennis [the mentor] first and then
> came and spoke to both Debbie [the other student] and me basically to
> set our minds at rest that we were now doing the right thing . . . (interview,
> student, Deepvale)

One is left to speculate about the conversation between the link tutor and the
mentor but the issue was clearly resolved. To the student this seemed a casual
conversation confirming that schemes of work were acceptable, in fact it was an
interesting example of a link tutor taking responsibility for the quality of the
student experience, first of all by monitoring, and then by supporting the mentor
to ensure that expectations were similar across schools and within the school.

The Deepvale student indicated a further monitoring impetus, namely that
students too liked to have the reassurance that the link tutor brought. Here
Diane a student on serial practice at Deepvale, explained that, despite the apparent assurance from the mentor, she still looked for more from the College:

> I think it's just the reassurance, . . . the teachers will say what they think
> of your lessons when you've done them but I think it's just the reassur-
> ance to double check. (interview, student, Deepvale)

The student clearly perceived that the link tutor could confirm that the quality
of her experience and the quality of the feedback she was receiving from the
school was at the right level.

Summary

This chapter has shown how the quality of the students' experience was sustained. The initial process of selection of both schools and mentors is an important factor. Once the selections were made shared understandings and expectations were established and developed. This was facilitated by training, literature, ongoing support meetings and the presence of the link tutors. Finally, the students' experience was monitored by the students themselves, the mentors and the link tutors.

Sustaining quality in higher education is of considerable concern, not least since the publication of the White Paper on Higher Education and its chapter on 'Quality Assurance in Teaching' (DES, 1991). Whitty (1992) argues that a concern for quality must inform the whole process of teacher education and training. When considering school-based teacher training the essential question must be what are the implications for quality of placing the training and educating of student teachers into the hands of school-based mentors? As this chapter has shown our experience has been that mentorship schemes do not need to shy away from this issue. Quality is sustained and indeed developed rather than controlled as suggested by the Committee of Vice-Chancellors and Principals. It is not merely 'an operational function applied at all levels by an institution' (Elton and Partington, 1991). Instead it can be seen to be actively sought and created by all parties to the mentorship scheme.

Chapter 13

Implications for Primary School-Based Teacher Education

John Sampson and Robin Yeomans

In this final chapter we consider implications for the policy, nature, structure and practice of school-based teacher education arising from issues which have been considered in previous chapters, and in the context of arrangements for primary initial teacher education under Circular 14/93. First, we consider the broad structure of the mentoring process, before looking at issues connected with its organization. Finally we give separate attention to the contributions of schools and HE institutions within a context of partnership.

The Shape and Structure of School-Based Initial Teacher Education

Government requirements for primary initial teacher education in Circular 14/93 (DFE, 1993) adjust the concept of partnership to place an increased emphasis on schools' contribution to initial teacher education. Primary student teachers will spend increased time in school, and schools are invited to consider taking lead responsibility for training. Higher education institutions are also required to ensure that all schools wishing to play a part in initial teacher education are able to do so. Without naming mentors, the Circular ensures that mentors are likely to be a permanent feature of the partnership which supports students in primary initial teacher education.

Our research offers evidence that mentors have the opportunity to make an important positive contribution to primary students' development as teachers, and that, where all dimensions of their role are developed, effective mentors are a significant positive influence on students. We recognize that an increased emphasis on school-based learning within courses can enhance their quality by offering students extended access to the craft knowledge of skilled primary teachers, and an opportunity for induction into the culture of teaching — both of which can be achieved more effectively in school than in college. However, there are dangers in assuming that the quality of initial teacher education is inevitably improved by the act of making it more school-based. The move offers access to enhanced quality rather than being an improvement in quality in itself. Adjusting the balance of time spent in school and HE institutions is intended to achieve a more effective match between students' needs for training and education, in the form of experience, analysis of and reflection on experience, and the acquisition of knowledge, and the locations where these can most effectively be achieved. Any shift which itself fails to reflect an optimum fit between location and need would simply create a new mismatch.

Although there are subtle shifts of emphasis in new criteria for teacher education, its essential purposes have not changed. Self-reliance remains one mark of an effective teacher. Student teachers need to be trained to deal with the complexities of modern primary school classrooms within a National Curriculum context, and educated so that they can develop both their own solutions to current problems and the capacity to respond flexibly to future circumstances. Whilst the former benefits from close contact with positive models, the latter gains by making personal sense of school experiences, and assimilating them into a personal model which, by being concerned with purposes as well as processes, enables individuals to become self-reliant. So, making teacher education more school-based shifts the location of the problem, but does not essentially change it. If the prevailing school/higher education balance is criticized because it makes inadequate use of the range of skills of all parties, then a similar concern exists for the new arrangements. We suggest that both mentors and college tutors need a broad range of training and education skills. Indeed, the model of the mentor's role offered in chapter 5, also provided a helpful starting point for thinking about the contributions of higher education tutors. The difference between mentors' and tutors' roles is likely to be one of emphasis. Mentors (and class teachers) and higher education tutors are each best placed to develop particular aspects of student learning, whilst being able to contribute to and complement the others' areas of strength. Though the case for an adjusted partnership is strong, the case for handing primary initial teacher education to schools lock, stock and barrel is weak.

We have suggested that relationships are at the heart of the mentoring process, and we further suggest that at the heart of effective school-based education is the relationship between the mentor and college tutor. Their roles also embody institutional relationships, are the means by which they are interpreted, and by which a flexible response to the full range of student needs can be achieved. The shift towards school places greater responsibility on the mentor, since time spent in school provides opportunities to work with students in both training and educative modes. But time in school does not inevitably provide the conditions under which both training and education can be achieved. In particular, mentors may not have adequate time released from class responsibility. Nor may they easily achieve psychological distance from and an objective perspective on the subjective experience of teaching within a particular school. Further, there is no inevitable correlation between skill as a primary teacher and mentoring skills, since the latter draws on an overlapping but wider spectrum of skills than the former. In short, we doubt that primary mentors unsupported can achieve all that colleges have achieved and more, and that they need to be able to act in sustained partnership with tutors from HE institutions.

We recognize the unique contribution of teachers' 'craft knowledge'. We also share with Adler and with Frost a concern that students confront taken-for-granted pre-existing beliefs and agree that 'teacher education programme must render problematic the taken-for-granted assumptions and explanations and challenge the student teacher to "examine the moral and professional ambiguities"' (Adler, quoted in Frost, 1993, pp. 137–8). However, we fear a 'division of labour in which the school teacher/mentors are concerned with observable classroom competence while the college tutors are left to deal with questions of theory and values'. We lend our support to the hope that 'mentorship in schools is allowed to develop in a way which goes beyond narrow behaviourist approaches' (*ibid.*, p. 132) and continues to emphasise reflective practice as 'theory arising from and rooted in practice' (*ibid.*).

If the emergence of reflective, analytical, self-aware beginning teachers is to continue to be the goal of initial teacher education (and to seek less would be to acknowledge a decision to lower standards), then higher education must continue to play a major part in teacher education. Effective reflection needs not only an analytical stance (encouraged by mentors who themselves possess that quality), but also time and distance by which it is achieved, since student reflection needs to expose those things which hitherto have been unexamined and taken-for-granted, and may include professional concerns which familiarity has rendered unproblematic for mentors. Whilst mentors may be able to support reflective and reflexive analysis by encouraging student questioning, but time and distance unencumbered by important short-term concerns are more easily achieved in higher education contexts.

We acknowledge the need for schools and higher education partners each to take the lead in particular aspects of student support and development. But we suggest that responsibilities should overlap and are attracted to the concepts of 'redundancy' and 'slack' (Landau, 1969) as a means of ensuring that the work in school and college are complementary. Just as students need to spend time with teacher experts who can also analyze and articulate the nature of their skill, they also need to spend time with those who have expertise in teaching within an inter-adult context, in generalizing from the particular, and helping students distance themselves from the persuasive professional sub-culture of a single school. Both major tasks require more time and different learning contexts than either tutor or mentor can provide alone, but both tutor and mentor can contribute constructively to the other's priorities, provided their relationship enables a clear understanding of the other's contribution, and builds from that. The nature of the overlap and of its key concerns might be as follows:

induction	training	education

H E

how things are done in school | how might you do it? | Why might you do what you might do

how things are done here | these are ways to do it | what might you do?

SCHOOL

Mentors will need to spend time out of their classroom and away from their class of children. This in itself was a concern for some of our mentors. The role conflict for mentors who need time away from their own class to fulfil the role of mentor effectively, yet perceive that they need to spend time with their children if they are to be effective teachers, is a limitation on the expansion of mentorship schemes in primary schools. Effective classroom teaching contributes to effectiveness as a mentor, but there are conflicts of loyalty which underline the continuing value of the tutor's contribution. We continue to hold the view that for tutors to retain ultimate responsibility for the welfare of students helps to ease problems of role-conflict for mentors, and keeps a balance within the legitimate tension between the needs of school students and student teachers.

In chapter 9 it was suggested that student teachers' access to a range of experiences facilitating comparison within and between schools, supported by mentors who were themselves self-questioning, and had time to encourage in students an analytical and self-aware stance, helps them avoid the dangers of acculturation to the ways of working and thinking of one classroom or school. It seems to us that there are considerable dangers in courses which expose student teachers to no more than two schools, and locate their learning predominantly within one school. Students need to be exposed to a variety of schools if they are to be able to develop into autonomous, educated teachers. Exposure to the perspectives of at least three schools will enable students to begin to generalize from the experiences of different contexts in which individual teachers and school staffs find different solutions to the problems of achieving fitness for particular purposes (Alexander, Rose and Woodhead, 1992). There is little point in increasing the time spent in schools without widening the range of experience gained there.

Organizing the Mentoring Process

Choosing Schools

Given that Alexander, Rose and Woodhead, HMI (1991) and Dearing (1993) have recognized the difficulties of many primary schools in coming to terms with the complexity of the National Curriculum, and that engaging in school-based teacher education adds further complexity, we do not believe it is in the interests of all schools or of student teachers that schools should participate in initial teacher education as of right, as Circular 14/93 appears to suggest. Student teachers can benefit from sharing in the enquiry processes of schools seeking to develop their own solutions to 'fitness for purpose' problems, given the 'apprenticeship dimension of school-based work'. However it can be in no one's interests that student teachers should be placed in schools which are not engaging constructively with the complexities of the relationships between curriculum, pedagogy and children's learning in a National Curriculum context. Financial considerations may tempt some schools. But the time, effort and skill needed, and implications for children and the whole staff of school commitment to school-based initial teacher education, mean that participation can be a benefit, or an irksome burden — whose educational cost to the school could outweigh any financial return. Schools may have to consider their own phase of development and learning climate in deciding whether or not they benefit from a major student presence. It is to be hoped that they will also consider the benefits student teachers might gain. A renewed concern with the nature of teaching and learning a natural outcome of working with students, and schools' self-evaluation may gain from articulating skills, practices and policies. However, a head might legitimately ask whether school development will be at the expense of student development, or pupils and staff may suffer from the need to take account of student needs.

It follows that schools which participate in school-based courses should be chosen with care. Selection may need to be on grounds of convenience of access, appropriateness and quality of experience. Practical considerations such as geographical location (Corbett and Wright, 1993) and school size (see chapter 11) may limit choice. The latter may be a limitation if small size leads to a restricted range of student experience. We do not suggest that the quality of teaching and learning for children differs between small and large schools. But given the complexity of small school class groupings and staff cultures, large schools may be able to provide students with a wider range of teaching models, enable them to sample differences between phases and ages without the complexity of vertically grouped classes, and experience the implications of staff membership and school organizations in relatively simple structures. In practical terms, there is a limit to how frequently a given group of children should work with student teachers. This means that small schools may not wish to contemplate having several students in the school for most of a school year, and that rural schools in particular may well find that they are unable to provide enough variety of experience for students.

In large primary schools mentors may more easily be able to find time to be with students, if the schools accept large numbers of students. This would increase the resources paid to the school, would provide more time when students rather than staff were teaching classes, and so would offer greater flexibility for deploying staff, including mentors. However, this implies large schools in which mentors are happy to leave their own classes — acceptable with final school experience, but less so in earlier stages of a student's course. Our experience with the Bedford College Affiliated Schools Scheme was that numbers of students in a school had to reduce from four to two students even in many large primary schools. Small primary schools are likely to continue to have difficulty taking students on long-term placements which carry sustained mentor responsibilities, unless such resources are provided as will ensure that mentors have sufficient non-contact time to adequately support students whilst mentors' own classes are adequately taught.

Corbett and Wright have asked how colleges may gain 'current reliable and valid evidence of a school's performance and management record' (p. 221). Their concern raises issues of the nature of the power relationship between school and HE institutions, and predates the principle of self-selection required in Circular 14/93. Given the complexity of the school effectiveness debate, it is difficult to see how mutually acceptable and public criteria for selection could be established. However, most existing partnership relationships emerge from the belief of school and HE institution that their relationship can be mutually beneficial. Self-selection does require that schools are self-aware, and have a realistic appreciation of the obligations placed on them, as well as of the rewards. Mentoring schools need to be places where the whole staff contribute by being supportive, effective classroom practice predominates, individual teachers willingly welcome students into their classroom for significant periods of time, and, by sharing openly successes and failures, staff talk implies that the relationship between teaching and effective learning is problematic. An assumption that school-based courses are mere extensions of existing traditional supervisory relationships will lead to impoverished outcomes for students and a teaching force of deteriorating quality.

It would be disastrous in practice if a school or HE partner was unwilling, and Circular 14/93 acknowledges that 'schools and higher education institutions entering into partnerships need to do so on the basis of mutual trust and willing cooperation' (p. 12). Hence it is difficult to see how the requirement that 'all primary schools, both maintained and independent, should have an opportunity to contribute to ITT if they wish to do so' (*ibid.*) could work in practice, if it means that one partner has the right to enforce the relationship. Such an arrangement establishes an unreliable basis for a fruitful partnership. Therefore we suggest that the only realistic long-term alternative to partnerships by mutual agreement is independent accreditation of schools as appropriate settings for teacher education, perhaps as an additional outcome of *Ofsted* inspections. The logic of *Ofsted* powers to take on the running of unsatisfactory schools sits uneasily with the implication that any primary school is fertile soil for student-teacher development. However, within traditional supervision systems, HE institutions already report difficulty in finding sufficient primary school partners. Our experience is that schools and mentors need to be confident about their own institutional and individual professional development before partnerships in primary school-based schemes become symbiotic experiences. We anticipate that the major problem of choice will continue to be a shortage of volunteers, and that schools will need to be able to choose their degree of responsibility for students, with some continuation of arrangements in which higher education institutions continue to take major responsibility for student support and supervision.

Choosing the Mentor

Mentors need to be effective teachers because a key dimension of the mentor role is to provide student teachers with a model of effective teaching, including key skills such as curriculum planning, classroom control, organization, and pedagogy, especially in schemes which involve some explicit form of apprentice relationship. However, our evidence is that pedagogic skill alone is an incomplete basis for mentoring. The complexity of the mentor role, and of the skills and strategies needed calls for multi-faceted professionals who have enabling, interpersonal and analytic as well as pedagogic skills (chapter 6). We have acknowledged the sophisticated personal qualities from which such professional skill is derived (*ibid.*). Teachers who have the capacity to take on such a role need to be chosen with as much care as do schools. Whilst willingness to accept the role is a necessary condition, volunteering is not a sufficient qualification for the role.

In practice, choice rests with headteachers, who are well-placed to have a clear view of staff's skills as teachers and colleagues, and of their personal qualities. But headteachers also need a clear understanding of the implications and complexity of mentorship, and of the personal and professional qualities the role demands. It may be relatively straightforward to identify a 'natural' mentor, whose school responsibilities already enable them to demonstrate with colleagues the skills they need as mentors. Heads may find greater difficulty in identifying latent mentor qualities in those colleagues who may become effective mentors, but as yet have restricted opportunities to demonstrate appropriate skills in their existing school roles.

Mentors need status and credibility in the school. We have noted that one way some heads ensure this is to select deputy heads as mentors. Such choices raise two concerns. First, given the fragility of staff cultures in the face of changes in personnel, it would be understandable that heads might choose deputy heads as mentors in order to ensure that students were inducted into ways of working and behaving which were consistent with the professional culture which heads sought to create and sustain in the school. There is no inevitable conflict of purpose between a mentor's need to help students critically examine professional practices, and a deputy head's obligation to sustain the school's dominant professional culture, but such a Janus-like stance requires a head and deputy who feel secure within a staff culture which values openness. Second, we have seen that deputies frequently have an existing high work load with little spare time beyond their role as class teacher and deputy headteacher. One primary head reported that his deputy head mentor spent much less time with the headteacher during mentoring phases (Holt, 1993). Headteachers will want to ensure that the whole school role of mentor/deputy heads will not suffer. Students also have reported that deputy head mentors may have a restricted amount of time to devote to them (chapter 11), and deputies themselves may be concerned about neglecting their role as class teachers. In short, when choosing mentors, headteachers will need to consider carefully how far existing responsibilities allow potential mentors to perform multiple roles effectively, recognizing that being a mentor can be relevant experience for staff hoping to move into primary school management. Experienced teachers moving towards deputy headship may be ideal candidates who can gain professionally from the opportunity to mentor.

Time

Mentors need time to plan the students' programme, negotiate it with colleagues to ensure a variety of experience, to observe and analyze students' performance, and to discuss it with them in a manner which promotes a professional dialogue. Time is spent in discussion with college link tutors and the headteacher when the progress of the student and the effectiveness of the system are analyzed. But how mentors work with students has time implications too. It takes more time to promote a professional dialogue which encourages students to become analytically reflective practitioners, capable of devising their own solutions, than to feed them instant solutions in problematic circumstances. Mentors too may need to spend time developing their own self-awareness, objectivity, and particular skills such as situation analysis, articulation of practice, and questioning. This last point will be developed further when mentor training is discussed.

Commitment to the role means that mentors often give a considerable amount of their own time to the role, in addition to that created by supply teacher cover. Continued enthusiasm and goodwill may depend on being given adequate time for their role, either by providing appropriate cash resources, or by ensuring that HE provides extensive and active support to the mentoring structure.

Unlike secondary school-based schemes, where distinct mentor and teacher-tutor roles are possible, because there are often staff with non-contact time for 'staff development', primary school size and primary/secondary differential funding mean that this division of labour, supported by time, is seldom possible, and that higher education needs to continue to accept a considerable share of responsibility for student education.

Schools' and Mentors' Contribution to Partnership

The School's Contribution to Partnership

We have made clear that we find it difficult to separate the effectiveness of mentors from the school context in which their contribution is located. We have distinguished between mentor as a title and mentoring as an activity to which several parties contribute, with the mentor orchestrating contributions. Other staff welcome students into their classroom for significant periods of school-based work, advice and support, and through example and explanation, share their craft knowledge. Students are influenced by the whole web of relationships and the climate of professional debate which sustain the school's personal and professional cultures. However, given the emphasis in some forms of school-based training on dominant links with one particular school (for example, Articled Teacher Scheme), we emphasize the distinction between induction which can support training and education and acculturation which can have indoctrination as an outcome. The nature of the school's dominant professional culture will have a significant effect on whether student teachers learn to adopt models in an unquestioning way or become independent thinkers able to critically examine their experiences. Staff cultures characterized by openness, acknowledgement of difficulties, and mutual learning within supportive relationships will help student teachers develop an independent professional self.

The head makes an important contribution too, and in different schools this may mean a 'hands on' or a 'hands off' approach, where each is characterized by concerned engagement with the scheme and monitoring of students' progress, within a context of trust in which day-to-day responsibility is devolved to mentors.

Mentors

Being a mentor is a demanding role. Within the schemes we have discussed, there were phases when mentors had students in their classrooms and others where they did not. Elsewhere at least, one scheme advocates that mentor and class teacher responsibilities should be separated (Brown *et al.*, 1993). We have found advantages within both strategies, but in practice, convenience often necessitated that the mentor had to have a student in their class, since this helped to create time for a mentor to observe students with minimum disruption to pupils. The benefits of a close relationship with and knowledge of students, and of the pupils for whom they were responsible, were balanced by the need to retain objectivity and achieve distance.

Given the contribution of credibility as a teacher to credibility as a mentor, mentors need to be positive practitioner models in classrooms and staffrooms, whether or not students teach in the mentor's class. Yet we have already suggested that being an effective teacher of children is a necessary but not sufficient condition for being an effective mentor to student teachers. In earlier chapters we have indicated the skills, strategies and qualities which are relevant to effective mentoring. Some of these, such as analyzing, questioning, assessing, are also necessary for successful primary teaching. Others, such as negotiating, facilitating, articulating, enhance the effectiveness of a primary school teacher without being necessary to success in that role, although they may contribute to those dimensions of a primary teacher's job concerned with colleagues, collaboration, and whole school effectiveness. All the above call for refocusing and adaptation for mentoring purposes of skills found already in some primary teachers.

A problematic aspect of any analysis of mentorship is mentors' personal qualities. Because mentors rely extensively on skills exercised within a context of adult relationships, including those with peers, personal qualities have a considerable influence on a mentor's effectiveness. Hill *et al.* (1992) suggest that mentors need to provide a supportive supervisory relationship which offers help and support without encouraging dependence, and chapters 7 and 8 have emphasized the contribution of relationships to successful mentorship. Mentors need to have particular qualities, however embryonic, if they are to form effective relationships with students, colleagues and tutors. The key qualities appear to be openness, sensitivity and perceptiveness and confidence. Flexibility, valuable for teaching, also becomes obligatory when confronted with the need to change strategies and select appropriate skills in response to time and different rates of student development. The constant move from a supportive relationship to an assessment one can be a particular difficulty, especially when a mentor's assessments carry long-term implications for a student's subsequent career.

The significance of personal qualities in mentors' performance leads us to consider what contribution mentor training programmes can make, given that careful choice should make it possible to assume that mentors will have effective classroom teaching skills. Can mentor training hope to develop qualities not already evident in teaching behaviour?

Can Mentors Benefit from Training?

Our case studies include two mentors (at Bigtown and Kenleigh) who had been inducted into course procedures, but not trained in mentoring processes. Both were considered effective by students and link tutors. We recognize that there are 'natural' mentors, whose personal qualities enhance their teaching skills, enable them to transfer those skills to mentoring, and will ensure that they respond constructively to new challenges within mentoring. Experience of teaching, perhaps accompanied by previous professional development in relevant areas such as assessment or appraisal, has further refined skills which can be applied to mentoring contexts after a period of induction to mentoring procedures and processes. However, the existence of such teachers is not an argument for leaving all mentors to work out their own solutions to the demands of the role, particularly since school-based work is to make a greater contribution to primary initial teacher education. Learning to see, in the form of the capacity to deconstruct and reconstruct practice, can be facilitated by time, and space to achieve objectivity and distance in a training context where mentoring practice and experience are shared with a group of active mentors. We note that a recent HMI report (1993) on German teacher education seems to suggest poor consistency in the quality of a system where there is no mentor training.

We suggest, therefore, that there is a need for training which can build skills knowledge and qualities which are additional to those needed for an effective teacher, but which may enhance teacher effectiveness. Currently the body of training knowledge and experience lies with higher education institutions. Although it is increasingly shared by experienced mentors. Improvement in the quality of training rests on a clear understanding of the nature of the role, and experienced mentors are important in the development of such understanding.

However, these seem typically to be deputies or other teachers actively seeking promotion. This in itself is likely to mean that as teachers are promoted, there will be a need to maintain and train a steady stream of replacement mentors.

Mentor training may not change people by giving them qualities not already evident or latent within their teaching. But it can stimulate latent qualities, make mentors self-aware, and by changing perspectives of the mentoring role, create opportunities for under-used attributes to flourish. Moreover, we argue that for some teachers, learning how to act like a mentor may be a necessary prelude to learning to think like a mentor. In time the fusion of mentor-like thought and action can develop authentic mentoring skills which achieve the same outcomes as apparently effortless mentoring derived from personal qualities. In other words, if mentoring behaviour is authentic in appearance it can be effective in its consequences. We need to consider therefore what might be the nature of mentor training which can achieve effective outcomes for mentors and students, as one aspect of the broader contribution of higher education institutions to school-based teacher education structures.

The HE Contribution to Partnership

We consider that the higher education sector continues to have a major role within primary school-based initial teacher education partnership structures as the source of mentor training, as the agent which ensures the quality of provision, and as a major contributor to the development of students' subject knowledge and wider educational perspective.

Higher Education and the Nature of Mentor Training

For us there are two related issues to address as far as the nature of mentor training is concerned. The first concerns forms of learning, the second concerns its content.

We have suggested that although mentors need some form of support and development different mentors will gain differently from the process, according to the experience, knowledge, skills and qualities they bring to it. New insight and understanding for some will inevitably be confirmation for others. Moreover, there will be varying degrees of engagement within the agenda of courses for mentors. The levels of complexity found in our analysis of the mentoring process should be similarly reflected in courses for mentor development. These too need to involve the following dimensions:

induction: acquiring information about mentoring contexts and processes
training: learning how to mentor
education: internalizing mentor qualities, values, attitudes and beliefs

Acquiring information about mentoring contexts and processes and learning how
to mentor are customary parts of reported primary mentor training courses (for
example Hill *et al.*, 1992; Corbett and Wright, 1993; Brown *et al.*, 1993), and of
our own. Courses deal with contextual and procedural issues. Their purpose is to
ensure that mentors understand the parameters within which initial teacher
education courses function nationally, are familiar with the internal structure and
organization of the course they contribute to and the detail of responsibilities and
the procedures through which they are exercised. Induction also should be concerned with knowing about the complexities of the role, so that mentors are clear
about the extent of their responsibility and students are ensured adequate treat-
ment. This induction dimension is relevant to all mentors, however naturally
skilled. However, courses which are concerned predominantly with procedural/
organizational issues, and do no more than inform mentors about their role offer
limited possibilities of having an impact on the quality of student experience.

The training dimension of mentor preparation programmes should be concerned with identifying, analyzing, practising elements of mentoring skills, and
articulating reactions to the experience of different aspects of mentoring practice.
The extent to which course members confront these experiences and openly
share their reactions with other course members will influence the educative
dimension of the course. This dimension is concerned with the refinement, acknowledgement, analytical reflection on and application of personal qualities. For
example, Watkins' (1992) secondary mentoring scheme focuses on interpersonal
skills, and mentors are encouraged to be open about their own experiences and
to learn how to introduce personal change while acting supportively. The West
Sussex model (Hill *et al.*, 1992) also concerns itself with interpersonal skills. At
Bedford the emphasis has been on interpersonal and analytical dimensions of
mentoring, and on the development of objectivity by addressing experientially
the problematic nature of perceptual skills.

Experiential learning can be a means by which the appropriateness of new
behaviour is acknowledged, and individuals may themselves begin to confront
attitudes which they recognize as unhelpful for mentor and teacher—particularly
some of the pitfalls of being isolated within one school and one way of 'seeing'
teaching, with the implications for becoming a blinkered mentor who seeks to
acculturate students.

We suggest that there are three broad groups of teachers who may become
candidates for mentoring courses. The first are those 'natural' mentors already
mentioned, whose qualities, attitudes values, beliefs, and skills need refocusing to
the implications of acting as mentor, through the induction dimension of mentor
preparation. The second group contains teachers whose qualities and skills are
such that heads have recognized latent capacity to become effective mentors,

although these qualities may not have been fully or formally reflected in their current school role. Such teachers will benefit from induction and training dimensions, and may find that whilst the educative dimensions of the programme expose some implicit assumptions about learning and teaching with children and adult student teachers, the consequence of making values, attitudes, and beliefs explicit is self-confirmation and an enhanced sense of professional worth. There exists a third group who are appointed as mentors and who may not be prepared for the role, for lack of some appropriate qualities, skills, values, attitudes or beliefs. Indeed, there is a possibility that heads might be tempted to send staff on mentor preparation programmes as a way of developing their teacher skills, given that some heads already recognize that the process is one which promotes broad professional development. For these teachers, mentor preparation concerned with self-awareness may lead to personal development and change. Participation of experienced mentors as co-leaders of preparation programmes will be a valuable catalyst for the development of trainee mentors. But since personal change tends to be painful, it may lead to rejection of values and attitudes which are essential to effective mentoring, such as collaboration, openness and supportiveness. Mentor trainers do not decide who joins programmes. Indeed, the possibility that the demand for mentors may be greater than the supply of suitable candidates means there is a danger that some mentors may be unsuited to the role, whatever their preparation programme may contain. The best safeguard that can be achieved may be to ensure that all mentoring preparation programmes are accredited and that all mentors are required to join a programme, so that there exists the minimum guarantees of quality that mentors have been exposed to a programme — though the effect of that exposure will remain largely within the mentor's control.

We recognize that mentor preparation courses will be of limited length unless additional resources are made available. It is realistic to expect that programmes in the order of thirty hours in length are more likely to become the norm in BEd and PGCE courses than the extensive programmes made possible by additional funding for mentor training available for articled teacher courses. At Bedford, as at West Sussex (Hill *et al.*, 1992), preparation programmes have preceded and have been spread throughout the period of mentorship. This has helped mentors to avoid any sense of isolation, share problematic concerns with peers engaged with similar concerns, and heighten their awareness of the importance of their role in the professional development of the students.

However, education involving personal change takes far more time than does induction and skills training. Time pressures may mean that mentor preparation becomes restricted to induction and training in those aspects of the work that can most easily be addressed or are examined superficially. Whilst 'natural' mentors may suffer less than others from such constraints, because being self-educating may be part of their qualities, the majority, who may need time and support to ensure that they encourage student independence, may be tempted to rely on quick-fix solutions which may not lead students beyond narrow applications and short-term dependence.

At best, where effective mentor preparation leads to skilled and sensitive mentoring it has the possibility of changing teacher behaviour. Mentors may appear to acquire new personal/professional qualities, the quality of their teaching may be enhanced, and positive models for professional collaboration provided by mentor-mentee relationships. In looking at others, mentors may begin to understand themselves more clearly. In articulating ideas and explaining practices they may become clearer about what they think and do professionally. At worst inadequate mentor preparation could mean that school-based initial teacher education becomes a mechanism for recycling narrow professional prejudices.

Higher Education Institutions and Sustaining Quality

We believe that there must be systems in place that ensure the quality of the student experience. As chapter 12 shows, sustaining quality is achieved through genuine partnership between students, mentors and the college tutors. At Bedford the college-based link tutor has had a vital role in supporting students' concern that they have positive school experiences and mentors' concern to provide such experiences. The link tutor ensures that mentors do not work in isolation and provide a broadly equivalent quality of support.

Higher Education Institutions and the Wider Education of Students

A key role of the college course has been to set specific experiences in a broader perspective. We have noted examples of mentors sharing this wider educative role, but they do so largely within the day to day context of enabling students to be successful in a particular class and school at a particular time. As courses progressed students developing skill and understanding have been challenged by time spent in other schools which may have different dominant professional cultures. But it has already been suggested that it is largely within a college context that students have been helped to make sense of the range of experiences. They need to meet, to share experiences, engage in guided discussion which decontextualizes experiences and considers their wider educational implications. They may then formulate their own theory derived from practice, yet informed by research findings.

Thus we suggest that primary school mentors and students are each likely to continue to gain from the educative support of higher education in primary initial teacher education.

Conclusion

There is a great danger that the implications of this research could be misunderstood. To articulate the successes of twelve innovative, committed mentors who are part of schools with similar qualities is one thing. To suggest that their qualities mean that all mentors are likely to behave similarly would be a grave distortion and misunderstanding. We take a different view of our research implications. Our major conclusion is that committed, sensitive, perceptive, supportive, analytical and articulate mentors, whose qualities reflect the professional and personal dimensions of the school cultures they belong to, make a very good job of mentoring. However, we have tried to show that the commitment of time and energy required to be an effective mentor demands mentor qualities and conditions which will not be achievable in all primary schools. Having seen such commitment in action, we are concerned that increasing the school-based element of initial teacher education will be ineffective unless resources are available which create the time for mentors' commitment to be focused and their energy released. Even then, it will not be sufficient to divert resources into schools whose staffs (mentors included) lack the personal and professional qualities shown by these twelve mentors and their schools. They too had difficulties at times, often a consequence of overload from other demands placed upon them. In short, it could be a disaster to simply transfer responsibility to schools and let them get on with mentoring. The price could be newly-qualified teachers with a narrow view of teaching skills, derived from a limited number of inadequately analyzed experiences, set in primary schools whose professional practices government has frequently vilified within the recent past. Yet the extension of school-based initial teacher education comes at a time when government policy presents teachers with conditions in which they need to be even more flexible, skilful and inventive.

However, appropriately funded school-based arrangements which recognize the complexity of the process, provide for adequate mentor training, and create a form of school-higher education partnership which acknowledges the strength of each, could make a major contribution to the development of the education of student teachers, teachers and school pupils. The extended presence of students in school may itself become a catalyst which causes staffs to ask fundamental questions about professional practice, stimulated by the presence in classrooms of beginning student teachers who watch and seek explanations for every teacher action. The outcome could be an enhanced capacity to analyze and articulate the nature of teaching and learning. There could develop a virtuous circle of enhanced effectiveness of schools as loci of initial teacher education, of teachers as mentors, and of mentors as teachers who are self-analytical practitioners able to deconstruct and articulate practice and finally reconstruct more effective classroom performance.

References

ABERCROMBIE, M.L.J. (1969) *The Anatomy of Judgment: An Investigation into the Processes of Perception and Reason*, Harmondsworth Penguin.

ADELMAN, C., JENKINS, D. and KEMMIS, S. (1976) 'Rethinking case study: Notes from the second Cambridge conference' in SIMONS, H. (Ed.) *Towards a Science of the Singular*, Norwich, CARE, University of East Anglia.

ADLER, S. (1991) 'The reflective practitioner and the curriculum of teacher education', *Journal of Education for Teaching*, **17**, 2.

ALEXANDER, R., ROSE, J. and WOODHEAD, C. (1992) 'Curriculum organisation and classroom practice in primary schools', a Discussion Paper, London, Department of Education and Science.

ALLEMAN, E., COCKRANE, J., DOVERSPIKE, J. and NEWMAN, I. (1984) 'Enriching mentoring relationships', *Personnel and Guidance Journal*, **62**, 6, pp. 329–335.

ARMITAGE, S. and BURNARD, P. (1991) 'Mentor or preceptor?', *Nurse Education Today*, **11**, 3, pp. 226–30.

ARMSTRONG, M. (1980) *Closely Observed Children: The Diary of a Primary Classroom*, London, Writers and Readers.

ASHTON, P.M.E., HENDERSON, E.S. and PEACOCK, A. (1989) *Teacher Education Through Classroom Evaluation: The Principles and Practice of IT-INSET*, London, Routledge.

BALL, S. (1983) 'Case study research in education: Some notes and problems' in HAMMERSLEY, M. (1983) *The Ethnography of Schooling: Methodological Issues*, Driffield, Nafferton.

BARBER, M. (1993) *Report of a Contribution to the Joint NUT/Oxford University Conference on Initial Teacher Education*.

BARRETT, E. and GALVIN, C. (1993) *The Licensed Teacher Scheme: A MOTE Report*, University of London, Institute of Education.

BARRETT, E., BARTON, L., FURLONG, J., GALVIN, C., MILES, S. and WHITTY, G. (1992a) *Initial Teacher Training in England and Wales: A Topography Modes of Teacher Education Project*, University of London, Goldsmiths College.

BARRETT, E., BARTON, L., FURLONG, J., GALVIN, C., MILES, S. and WHITTY, G. (1992b) 'New routes to qualified teacher status', *Cambridge Journal of Education*, **22**, 3, pp. 323–326.

BEDFORD COLLEGE OF HIGHER EDUCATION (1989) *Proposals for Third Year Student School Experience*.

References

BEDFORD COLLEGE OF HIGHER EDUCATION (1990) *Third Year School Experience Booklet.*

BEDFORD COLLEGE OF HIGHER EDUCATION (1992) *Primary BEd Year Three: School Experience Programme Handbook*, mimeo, Bedford.

BEDFORD COLLEGE OF HIGHER EDUCATION (1993) *Primary PGCE School Experience Handbook.*

BELL, A. (1981) 'Struggle, knowledge and relationships in teacher education', *British Journal of Sociology of Education*, **2**, 1, pp. 3–23.

BENTON, P. *et al.* (Eds) (1990) *The Oxford Internship Scheme*, London, Gulbenkian Foundation.

BLACKBURN, R. (1992) 'On being a mentor', *Search*, **5**, 1, p. 17.

BOOTH, M. and KINLOCH, N. (1990) 'A training course for school supervisors: Two perspectives' in BOOTH, M., FURLONG, J. and WILKIN, M. (Eds) *Partnership in Initial Teacher Education*, London, Cassell.

BURGESS, R.G. (Ed.) (1982) *Field Research: A Source Book and Field Manual*, London, Allen & Unwin.

CLARKE, H. (1993a) *Mentorship at Flenley. Studies of Mentorship in Action*, mimeo, Bedford College of Higher Education.

CLARKE, H. (1993b) *Kenleigh School. Studies of Mentorship in Action*, mimeo, Bedford College of Higher Education.

CLARKE, K. (1992) Keynote speech at the North of England Education Conference, Southport, 4 January 1992.

CORBETT, P. and WRIGHT, D. (1993) 'Issues in the selection and training of mentors for school-based primary initial teacher training' in MCINTYRE, D., HAGGER, H. and WILKIN, M. (Eds) *Mentoring — Perspectives on School-Based Teacher Education*, London, Kogan Page.

COUNCIL FOR THE ACCREDITATION OF TEACHER EDUCATION (1986) *Catenote 4: Links between Initial Teacher Training and Schools*, London, CATE.

DAY, C. (1993) 'Reflection: A necessary but not sufficient condition for professional development', *British Educational Research Journal*, **19**, 1.

DEARING, R. (1993) *The National Curriculum and its Assessment: An Interim Report*, London, NCC/SEAC.

DELAMONT, S. (1992) *Fieldwork in Educational Settings: Methods, Pitfalls and Perspectives*, London, Falmer Press.

DES (1972) *Teacher Education and Training* ('The James Report') London, HMSO.

DES (1983) *Teaching Quality*, London, DES.

DES (1988) *Qualified Teacher Status, Consultation Document*, London, DES.

DES (1984) *Initial Teacher Training: Approval of Courses* (Circular 3/84), London, DES.

DES (1988) *Qualified Teacher Status, Consultation Document*, London, DES.

DES (1989a) *Initial Teacher Training: Approval of Courses* (Circular 24/89), London, DES.

DES (1989b) *Articled Teacher Pilot Scheme: Invitation to Bid for Funding* (memo 276/89), London, DES.

DES (1991) *Higher Education: A New Framework*, London, HMSO.

DES (1991b) *School-based Initial Teacher Training in England and Wales: A Report by HM Inspectorate*. London, HMSO.

DES (1993) *Report on German Education*, London, DES.

DEWEY, J. (1974) *John Dewey on Education: Selected Writings* (ed. R.D. ARCHAMBAULT), Chicago, IL, University of Chicago Press.

DFE (1992) *Initial Teacher Training (Secondary Phase)*: (Circular 9/92), London, DES.

DFE (1993) *The Initial Training of Primary School Teachers: New Criteria for Courses* (Circular 14/93), London, DFE.

DULGAN, P. and MACPHERSON, I. (1987) 'The educative leadership project', *Educational Management and Administration*, **15**, pp. 49–62.

ELLIOTT, J. *et al.* (1981) *School Accountability*, Oxford, Blackwell.

ELTON, L. and PARTINGTON, P. (1991) *Teaching Standards and Excellence in Higher Education: Developing a Culture for Quality*, Sheffield, Committee of Vice-Chancellors and Principals.

FEIMAN-NEMSER, S. (1991) 'Helping novices learn to teach', paper presented for the International Study Association on Teacher Thinking, Surrey.

FEIMAN-NEMSER, S., PARKER, M. and ZEICHNER, K. (1993) 'Are mentor teachers teacher educators?' in McINTYRE, D., HAGGER, H. and WILKIN, M. (Eds) *Mentoring: Perspectives on School-Based Teacher Education*, London, Kogan Page.

FIEDLER, F. (1967) *A Theory of Effective Leadership*, New York, McGraw-Hill.

FIEDLER, F., CHEMERS, M. and MAKER, L. (1977). *Improving Leadership Effectiveness: The Leader Match Concept*, New York, Wiley.

FOREMAN, P.B. (1948) 'The theory of case studies', *Social Forces*, **26**, 4, pp. 408–19.

FRECKNALL, P. (1993) *Aimshigh Junior School. Studies of Mentorship in Action*, mimeo, Bedford College of Higher Education.

FROST, D. (1993) 'Reflective mentoring and the new partnership', in McINTYRE, D., HAGGER, H., and WILKIN, M. (Eds) *Mentoring: Perspectives on School-based Teacher Education*, London, Kogan Page.

FURLONG, J. (1992) 'Reconstructing professionalism: Ideological struggle in initial teacher education', in ARNOT, M. and BARTON, L. (Eds) *Voicing Concerns: Sociological Perspectives on Contemporary Education Reforms*, Wallingford, Triangle Books.

FURLONG, V.J., HIRST, P., POCKLINGTON, K. and MILES, S. (1988) *Initial Teacher Training and the Role of the School*, Milton Keynes, Open University Press.

GARDNER, P. (1993) 'The early history of school-based teacher training', in McINTYRE, D., HAGGER, H. and WILKIN, M. (Eds) *Mentoring: Perspectives on School-Based Teacher Education*, London, Kogan Page.

GLASER, B.G. (1978) *Theoretical Sensitivity*. Mill Valley, CA, Sociology Press.

GLASER, B.G. and STRAUSS, A.L. (1967) *The Discovery of Grounded Theory*, Chicago, IL, Aldine.

GRACE, G. (1987) 'Teachers and the state in Britain: A changing relation', in

LAWN, M. and GRACE, G. (Eds) *Teachers: The Culture and Politics of Work*, London, Falmer Press.

GRAY, W.A. and GRAY, M.M. (1985) 'Synthesis of research on mentoring beginning teachers', *Educational Leadership*, **43**, 3, pp. 37–43.

HANDAL, G. (1990) 'Promoting the articulation of tacit knowledge through the counselling of practitioners', keynote paper at the Amsterdam Pedalogisch Centum Conference, Amsterdam, Holland, 6–8 April 1990.

HAMMERSLEY, M. and ATKINSON, P. (1983) *Ethnography: Principles in Practice*, London, Methuen.

HANDY, C. (1981) *Understanding Organisations*, Harmondsworth, Penguin.

HILL, A., JENNINGS, M. and MADGEWICK, B. (1992) 'Initiating a mentorship training programme' in WILKIN, M. (Ed.) *Mentoring in Schools*, London, Kogan Page.

HILL, D. (1991) 'What's left in teacher education, the radical left and policy proposals', Hillcole Group Paper 6, London, Tufnell Press.

HILLGATE GROUP (1989) *Learning to Teach*, London, The Claridge Press.

HIRST, P. (1990) 'The theory practice relationship in teacher training' in BOOTH, M., FURLONG, J. and WILKIN, M. (1990) *Partnership in Initial Teacher Training*, London, Cassell.

HMI (1982) *The New Teacher in School*, London, HMSO.

HMI (1983) *Teaching in Schools: The Content of Initial Teacher Training*, London, DES.

HMI (1987) *Quality in Schools: The Initial Training of Teachers*, London, DES.

HMI (1988a) *The New Teacher in School*, London, HMSO.

HMI (1988b) *Initial Teacher Training in Universities in England, Northern Ireland and Wales*, London, HMSO.

HMI (1991) *School-based Initial Teacher Training in England and Wales: A Report by HM Inspectorate*, London, HMSO.

HMI (1993) *Aspects of Vocational Education Training in the Federal Republic of Germany*, London, HMSO.

ILEA (1985) *Improving Primary Schools*, London, ILEA.

LANDAU, M. (1969) 'Redundancy, rationality and the problem of duplication and overlap', *Public Administration Review*, **29**, pp. 346–58.

LIGHTFOOT, S.L. (1983) *The Good High School*, New York, Basic Books.

LINCOLN, Y.S. and GUBA, E.G. (1985) *Naturalistic Inquiry*, Newbury Park, CA, Sage.

LISTON, D. and ZEICHNER, K. (1989) 'Action research and reflective teaching in preservice teacher education', paper presented at the annual meeting of the American Education Research Association, San Francisco, March.

McINTYRE, D. (1991) 'The Oxford internship scheme and the Cambridge analytical framework: Models of partnership in initial teacher education', in BOOTH, M., FURLONG, J. and WILKIN, M. (Eds) *Partnership in Initial Teacher Training*, London, Cassell.

McINTYRE, D. and HAGGER, H. (1993) 'Teachers' expertise and models of mentoring' in McINTYRE, D., HAGGER, H. and WILKIN, M. (Eds) *Mentoring: Perspectives on School-Based Teacher Education*, London, Kogan Page.

MCINTYRE, D., HAGGER, H. and WILKIN, M. (Eds) (1993) *Mentoring: Perspectives on School-Based Teacher Education*. London, Kogan Page.

MCNAIR, A. (1944) *Teachers and Youth Leaders (the McNair Report)*, London, HMSO.

MAYNARD, T. and FURLONG, J. (1993) 'Learning to teach and models of mentoring' in MCINTYRE, D., HAGGER, H. and WILKIN, M. (Eds) *Mentoring: Perspectives on School-Based Teacher Education*, London, Kogan Page.

MERRIAM, S.B. (1988) *Case Study Research in Education: A Qualitative Approach*, San Francisco, CA, Jossey-Bass.

MILES, M.B. and HUBERMAN, A.M. (1984) *Qualitative Data Analysis: A Source Book of New Methods*, Newbury Park, CA, Sage.

MONAGHAN, J. and LUNT, N. (1992) 'Mentoring: Person, process, practice and problems', *British Journal of Educational Studies*, **XXXX**, 3, August.

MORTIMORE, P., SAMMONS, P., STOLL, L., LEWIS, D. and ECOB, R. (1988) *School Matters: The Junior Years*, Wells, Open Books.

NIAS, J. (1987) *Seeing Anew: Teachers' Theories of Action*, Deakin, Deakin University Press.

NIAS, J., SOUTHWORTH, G.W. and CAMPBELL, P. (1991) *Whole School Curriculum Development in the Primary School*, London, Falmer Press.

NIAS, J., SOUTHWORTH, G. and YEOMANS, R. (1989) *Staff Relationships in the Primary School*, London, Cassell.

O'HEAR, A. (1988a) *The Daily Telegraph*, 12 December 1988, p. 8.

O'HEAR, A. (1988b) *Who Teaches the Teachers?*, London, Social Affairs Unit.

PARLETT, M. and HAMILTON, D. (1977) 'Evaluation as illumination: A new approach and the study of innovatory programmes' in HAMILTON, D. (Ed.) *Beyond the Numbers Game*. London, Macmillan.

PATRICK, H., BERNBAUM, G. and REID, K. (1982) *The Structure and Process of Initial Teacher Education within Universities in England and Wales*, Leicester School of Education.

PATTON, M.Q. (1980) 'Qualitative evaluation methods' cited in MERRIAM, S.B. (1988) *Case Study Research in Education: A Qualitative Approach*, San Francisco, CA, Jossey-Bass.

PRING, R. (1992) 'Standards and quality in education', *British Journal of Educational Studies*, **40**, 1, pp. 4–22.

ROGERS, C. (1983) *Freedom to Learn for the 80's*, Columbus, OH, Merrill.

ROWLAND, S. (1984) *The Enquiring Classroom*, London, Falmer Press.

SAMPSON, J. (1993a) *Apprenticeship in Action: A Study of Mentorship at Greenvale, Studies of Mentorship in Action*, mimeo, Bedford College of Higher Education.

SAMPSON, J. (1993b) *Mentoring at Deepvale. Studies of Mentorship in Action*. mimeo, Bedford College of Higher Education.

SCHON, D.A. (1983) *The Reflective Practitioner*, New York, Basic Books.

SCHON, D.A. (1987) *Educating the Reflective Practitioner*, San Francisco, CA, Jossey-Bass.

SMITH, R. and ALDRED, G. (1993) 'The impersonation of wisdom,' in MCINTYRE,

D., HAGGER, H. and WILKIN, M. (Eds) *Mentoring: Perspectives on School-Based Teacher Education*, London, Kogan Page.

STENHOUSE, L. (1978) 'Case study and case records: Towards a contemporary history of education', *British Educational Research Journal*, **4**, 2, pp. 21–39.

STEPHENSON, H.J. (1993) *The Faces of Janus? A Study of Mentorship at Carlton-cum-Chardley. Studies of Mentorship in Action*, mimeo, Bedford College of Higher Education.

STRAUSS, A. and CORBIN, J. (1990) *Basics of Qualitative Research: Grounded Theory Procedures and Techniques*, London, Sage.

SYMTH, J. (1991) *Teachers as Collaborative Learners*, Milton Keynes, Open University Press.

SZANTON, P. (1981) *Not Well Advised*, New York, Russell Sage Foundation and The Ford Foundation.

WATKINS, C. (1992) 'An experiment in mentor training' in WILKIN, M. (Ed.) *Mentoring in Schools*, London, Kogan Page.

WHITTY, G. (1992) 'Quality control in teacher education', *British Journal of Educational Studies*, **40**, 1, pp. 38–50.

WHITTY, G., BARRETT, E., BARTON, L., FURLONG, J., GALVIN, C. and MILES, S. (1992) 'Initial teacher training in England and Wales: A survey of current practices and concerns', *Journal of Education*, **22**, 3, pp. 293–306.

WILKIN, M. (1991) 'The development of partnership in the United Kingdom', in BOOTH, M., FURLONG, J. and WILKIN, M. (Eds) *Partnership in Initial Teacher Training*, London, Cassell.

WILKIN, M. (1992a) 'The challenge of diversity', *Cambridge Journal of Education*, **22**, 3, pp. 307–322.

WILKIN, M. (Ed.) (1992) *Mentoring in Schools*, London, Kogan Page.

WILKIN, M. (1993) 'Initial training as a case of post modern development: Some implications for mentoring', in McINTYRE, D., HAGGER, H. and WILKIN, M. (Eds) *Mentoring: Perspectives on School-Based Teacher Education*, London, Kogan Page.

WOOLDRIDGE, I. (1993a) *Endsleigh Lower School. Studies of Mentorship in Action*, mimeo, Bedford College of Higher Education.

WOOLDRIDGE, I. (1993b) *Mentoring at Hillyway. Studies of Mentorship in Action*, mimeo, Bedford College of Higher Education.

WYNFORD-JONES, D. (1989) 'An evaluation of the introduction of a new primary PGCE course, and its effect on a partnership school', unpublished MEd thesis, Cambridge Institute.

YEOMANS, R.M. (1986) 'Hearing secret harmonies: Induction to primary school staff membership', Paper presented at the annual meeting of the British Educational Research Association, Bristol.

YEOMANS, R.M. (1993a) *Partnership at Bigtown: A Study of Support. Studies of Mentorship in Action*, mimeo, Bedford College of Higher Education.

YEOMANS, R.M. (1993b) *Joining the Team. BEd Mentorship at June Lane Junior, Studies of Mentorship in Action*, mimeo, Bedford College of Higher Education.

YEOMANS, R.M. (1993c) *Mentoring at Intake. Studies of Mentorship in Action*, mimeo, Bedford College of Higher Education.

YEOMANS, R.M. (1993d) *Mentoring at Lonetree. Studies of Mentorship in Action*, mimeo, Bedford College of Higher Education.

YEOMANS, R.M. (1993e) 'Are primary school mentors selected or trained?' paper presented at the annual meeting of the British Education Research Association, Liverpool.

YIN, R.K. (1984) *Case Study Research: Design and Methods*, Sage.

List of Contributors

Paul Frecknall is Senior Lecturer in Primary Arts Education, Bedford College of Higher Education.

John Furlong is Professor of Education, Swansea University.

John Sampson is Senior Lecturer in Primary Education, Bedford College of Higher Education, and was Course Leader of the Primary PGCE.

Joan Stephenson is Head of the Department of Education, Bedford College of Higher Education.

Irene Wooldridge is Senior Lecturer in Primary Education and Mathematics Education, Bedford College of Higher Education.

Robin Yeomans is Senior Lecturer in Primary Education, Bedford College of Higher Education, and was Leader of the Teacher Education and Mentorship Research Project.

Index